WOMEN'S EMPLOYMENT AND
MULTINATIONALS IN EUROPE

Women's Employment and Multinationals in Europe

Edited by

Diane Elson

Lecturer in Economics
University of Manchester

and

Ruth Pearson

Research Fellow
School of Development Studies, University of East Anglia

MACMILLAN
PRESS

First published 1989

Published by
THE MACMILLAN PRESS LTD
Houndmills, Basingstoke, Hampshire RG21 2XS
and London
Companies and representatives
throughout the world
Printed in Hong Kong

British Library Cataloguing in Publication Data

Women's employment and multinationals in Europe.
. 1. Western Europe. Multinational companies. Women personnel
I. Elson, Diane, *1946–* II. Pearson, Ruth–*1945*
331.4'813388884
ISBN 0–333–43877–9
ISBN 0–333–46706–X Pbk

Contents

List of Tables

Preface

Notes on the Contributors   xiii

1   Introduction: Nimble Fingers and Foreign
Investments
Diane Elson and Ruth Pearson   1

2   Women's Employment and Multinationals in the
UK: Restructuring and Flexibility
Ruth Pearson   12

3   Women's Employment and Multinationals in the
Republic of Ireland: The Creation of a New
Female Labour Force
Pauline Jackson and Ursula Barry   38

4   Women's Employment and Multinationals in the
Federal Republic of Germany: The Job-Export
Question
Sabine Gensior and Bärbel Schöler   60

5   The Cutting Edge: Multinationals in the EEC
Textiles and Clothing Industry
Diane Elson   80

6   Silicon Glen: Women and Semiconductor
Multinationals
Nance Goldstein   111

7   Production Relocation: An Electronics
Multinational in France and Brazil
Helena Hirata   129

8   Women's Response to Multinationals in County
Mayo
Lorelei Harris   144

9 Fighting Plant Closure: Women in the Strike at Videocolor
Shahizer Aydin and Ilse Lenz 165

10 Fighting Plant Closure: Women in the Plessey Occupation
Patricia Findlay 183

11 Restructuring Women's Employment in British Petroleum
Marilyn Davidson 206

Index 222

List of Tables

2.1   Changes in UK sectoral distribution of labour,
1951–81   13

2.2   Changes in UK manufacturing employment,
1971–81   14

2.3   Women's total employment and share of
employment in UK manufacturing, 1971–81   15

2.4   Women's part-time employment as a proportion
of total women's employment in UK
manufacturing, 1971–81   17

2.5   Analysis of changes in women's employment in
UK manufacturing, 1971–81   18

2.6   Foreign-owned establishments' share of UK
manufacturing employment   22

2.7   Women's share of employment in a sample of UK-
and foreign-owned enterprises in UK
manufacturing, 1980   24

2.8   Manual workers' share of employment in a
sample of UK- and foreign-owned enterprises
in UK manufacturing, 1980   26

3.1   Multinational companies in the Republic of
Ireland by country of origin, 1983   40

3.2   Average rate of profit on US capital investment
in Europe and Japan   43

3.3   Irish labour force participation rates by age and
sex, 1981   44

3.4   Job creation and job loss in Irish
manufacturing   46

3.5   Employment in multinational companies by
industrial sector, Republic of Ireland, 1982   47

3.6   Composition of labour force in textiles and
clothing, Republic of Ireland   52

3.7   Women as a percentage of the labour force in
the electronics and electrical industry,
Republic of Ireland, 1973–83   52

3.8   Distribution of Irish women electronics workers
by country of origin of employer   54

3.9	Occupational segregation in the Irish electronics industry, 1981	55
4.1	Share of developing countries in West German direct foreign investment	64
4.2	Overseas employment of West German multinationals, 1982	65
4.3	Employment of foreign multinationals in West Germany, 1982	67
4.4	Sectoral distribution of women's employment in West Germany	68
4.5	Women's employment in manufacturing, West Germany, 1980	69
4.6	Employment trends in selected industries, West Germany, 1976–82	71
4.7	Employment trends of foreign multinationals, West Germany, 1976–82	72
4.8	Employment trends of selected West German multinationals, 1974–82	72
4.9	Overseas employment of West German multinationals selected manufacturing industries, 1976–82	74
5.1	Average annual growth rates of output and employment, textile and clothing industries, 1973–80	82
5.2	Labour costs in the textile industry, 1980	83
5.3	Average hourly earnings in the clothing industry	84
5.4	Employment in artificial fibre production in selected EEC countries	88
5.5	Concentration characteristics of selected European textile industries	89
5.6	Distribution of textile and clothing employment by type of firm, UK 1975	89
5.7	Major textile and clothing multinationals in the EEC	90
5.8	Tootal's employment, 1973–84	97
6.1	Leading firms in the semiconductor industry	114
6.2	Overseas locations of fabrication and assembly of some major semiconductor producers, 1980	115
6.3	Leading semiconductor multinationals in Scotland	116

6.4 Employment in the Scottish electrical and
electronics industry 117

6.5 Women's wages in selected industries in Scotland
and Great Britain, early 1980s 122

6.6 Ratio of operators and assemblers to technicians
and engineers in semiconductor production in
Scotland 123

6.7 Women in technician level employment,
1984 125

7.1 Distribution of production workers by gender and
skill classification, 1981 136

7.2 Percentage of men and women in each grade,
1981 137

7.3 Average monthly wages in the two plants, 1981
(in French Francs) 138

7.4 Wages in the Brazilian plant as a percentage of
wages in the French plant 138

9.1 Structure of Videocolor workforce in Ulm,
November 1981 168

11.1 Women's share of employment in the UK oil
industry 207

11.2 OTS graduate intake, 1976–83 216

Preface

This book grew out of a Workshop on Women's Employment and Multinationals in Europe held at the University of East Anglia in September 1984. The contributors to this book, together with Stephen Wood of the London School of Economics and Sally Wyatt of the Science Policy Research Unit, University of Sussex, generously applied their energies to a subject which had previously received no coherent attention. While considerable research had been carried out on the implications of multinationals for women's employment in the Third World, and some attention had been paid to the implication for women's employment in the USA, nothing had been done on Europe.

Our appreciation is due to the conference participants who agreed that this lack should be remedied; to Valerie Striker of the University of East Anglia who organised the workshop; and to Jean Ashton, Linda Cooper and Charmaine Arnold-Reed who produced the final typescript.

Diane Elson
Ruth Pearson

Notes on the Contributors

Shahizer Aydin was formerly at the Institute of Sociology, University of Münster. Her research interests are women and industrial relations, and she is currently living and working in Turkey.

Ursula Barry is Lecturer in Sociology and Economics at Dublin College of Technology. She has written a number of papers on women and the Irish economy, and is co-editor of *Information Technology — Impact on the Way of Life* and the author of *Lifting the Lid — Facts and Information on Ireland*.

Marilyn Davidson is Lecturer in Organisational Psychology in the Department of Management Science, University of Manchester Institute of Science and Technology. She has written extensively on the problems faced by women at work. The most recent of her five books is *Reach for the Top — A Women's Guide to Success in Business and Management*.

Diane Elson is Lecturer in Development Economics in the Department of Economics, University of Manchester. She has written widely on women, multinationals and development and is editor of *Male Bias in the Development Process*.

Patricia Findlay is researching industrial relations in the Scottish electronics industry at Nuffield College, University of Oxford.

Sabine Gensior is a Lecturer at the Free University of Berlin and a member of the executive committee of the Berlin Institute for Social Research and Sociological Practice. She has published widely on women in the labour market and is co-author of *Arbeitsmarkt und Frauenerwerbsarbeit*.

Nance Goldstein is an industry analyst for the Commonwealth of Massachusetts and was formerly a Lecturer in economics at Thames Polytechnic, London.

Lorelei Harris is an anthropologist living in Dublin. She has published articles on women and industrialisation in the west of Ireland and has taught Women's Studies and Sociology. She is currently a Researcher for Radio Telefis Eireann.

Helena Hirata is *chargée de recherche* at the Centre National de la Recherche Scientifique, Paris and member of Groupe d'Etude sur la Division Sociale et Sexuelle du Travail. She has written extensively on the international and sexual division of labour and published articles in French, English, Spanish, Portuguese and Japanese.

Pauline Jackson is researching sex segregation in the Irish workforce at Trinity College, Dublin. She has previously worked for the Women's Bureau of the European Commission. She has published several papers on women workers in Ireland and is co-editor of *Gender in Irish Society*.

Ilse Lenz teaches at the Institute of Sociology, University of Münster. She has written widely on women's employment and the new international division of labour, with a particular focus on Japan and Southeast Asia.

Ruth Pearson is an economist who has written widely on women's employment issues in the Third World and the UK. She is currently a Research Fellow at the School of Development Studies, University of East Anglia, where she teaches on gender and development.

Bärbel Schöler has carried out research on the impact of technological change on women's work at the Berlin Institute for Social Research and Sociological Practice. She is currently working on a project on women and politics.

1 Introduction: Nimble Fingers and Foreign Investments

Diane Elson and Ruth Pearson

This book is about the interaction between multinational companies and working women in the UK, Ireland, France and the Federal Republic of Germany. It does not seek to establish whether multinationals are better, or worse, employers of women than firms which confine their operations to one national economy (so-called 'uninationals'). Rather, it examines the contrast between the internationalisation of the activities of multinationals and the localisation of women's lives; and between the changing international division of labour and the persisting sexual division of labour in manufacturing industry. It is concerned with the ways in which multinationals create and destroy female labour forces; and with the clash between global logic and community values.

Multinationals are singled out for specific attention because of their 'global reach' and transformative capacity, not because they are suspected of being worse employers, more likely to discriminate against women than uninationals. No detailed research comparing the equal opportunities performance of multinationals and uninationals is available, but various International Labour Office studies of the employment impact of multinationals suggest that they are likely to be no worse than uninational firms, and probably in many cases significantly better (ILO, 1981; ILO, 1985). This is only to be expected. Multinationals generally have greater capacity to be 'good employers' in terms of wages and conditions of work, because of higher productivity and more sophisticated forms of organisation. Indeed, we should expect multinationals to be in the forefront of improving women's work opportunities. But most multinationals have devoted much more effort to restructuring the international organisation of their activities than to restructuring the sexual division of labour in manufacturing so as to improve women's opportunities.

Though multinationals may tend to offer women better pay and conditions than uninationals, there seems to be little difference in the

1

sexual division of labour utilised. Both types of firm tend to concentrate women employees in a limited range of occupations, and in positions in the bottom half of the jobs hierarchy. 'White collar' women employees are overwhelmingly in secretarial and clerical jobs; 'blue collar' women employees are overwhelmingly in jobs that require 'nimble fingers', such as sewing, food preparation and assembly work. These jobs are generally classified as 'semi-skilled' or 'unskilled' but this is more a reflection of the fact that employers have to provide little training for these jobs, than an accurate description of the job content. A recent report on manufacturing automation highlights the fact that

> assembly uses more sensing (sight, touch) and more mental/ physical dexterity and judgement than most factory tasks. It therefore calls for aptitude and alertness but is at the same time repetitive and boring. Without full concentration by the operator, the product can suffer. (*Financial Times*, 5 February 1985, p. 22)

Nimble minds, as well as nimble fingers, and a capacity for endurance and concentration are required. These attributes are often regarded as 'natural' in women, ignoring the fact that women tend to have already been trained in such skills through their experience in the home and at school (Elson and Pearson, 1981). The fact that these skills are devalued and not given full recognition in job grading is a reflection of the subordinate status of women (Phillips and Taylor, 1980).

Where multinationals do differ from uninationals is in their capacity for international relocation of activities. Multinationals have no specific commitment to any location, even in their 'home' country. A uninational firm is much more embedded in a particular locality whereas a multinational engages in frequent comparisons of the profitability of different locations across national boundaries. Multinational activities are in a continuous state of flux — closing plant at some locations; opening plant at other locations; buying up other firms; selling off divisions that no longer fit its corporate strategy (Dicken, 1986).

Over the last two decades multinationals have been one of the key agents (though not the only agent) in creating a new international division of labour, in which some labour-intensive manufacturing operations have been transferred from some higher cost developed countries to some lower cost developing countries (Fröbel, Heinrichs, Kreye, 1981; Grunwald and Flamm, 1985; Dicken, 1986). This tendency has been reported to be particularly strong in those operations where women are employed. A report for the United Nations Industrial Development Organisation concluded that 'female intensity of employment in an industry in the developed country is usually a strong predictor of this industry's propensity to redeployment. In the USA, for example, women form over 90 per cent of all production workers and operators in the two industries which have been most heavily redeployed to developing countries — electronics assembly and wearing apparel' (UNIDO, 1980, p. 5).

Redeployment from the USA in electronics has generally taken the form of 'offshore assembly' or 'outward processing' in which an American firm ships pieces or components to a subsidiary in a low labour cost country to be assembled and then re-imported into the USA. This procedure is also used in the clothing industry, though here there is also international subcontracting in which formally independent firms in developing countries make up garments to the specification of an American firm which then markets the garments in the USA (Grunwald and Flamm, 1985).

Concern has been expressed that multinational companies in female-labour intensive industries are now involved in a global search for cheap female labour (Safa, 1981; Hancock, 1983). But this needs qualifying: access to internal markets remains an important motivation for foreign investment in developing countries; and much of the offshore processing is carried out in a narrow range of countries such as Mexico, Singapore, Taiwan, Hong Kong and Malaysia, where female labour is more expensive than in many other developing countries.

The vast majority of women employed by multinationals in developing countries are young and unmarried. Multinationals prefer young women with few domestic commitments because they are more 'flexible' — that is, they can more easily do overtime and shiftwork; and they are more 'efficient' — that is, they have better health, eyesight and physical reflexes than older women and are less likely to be tired out by the strains of a 'double day', that is, combining factory work and unpaid domestic work at home (ILO, 1985). Multinationals are not so concerned about wage costs *per se* but about flexibility and productivity. The female labour force they have targetted for employment in the Third World are daughters rather than wives (Pearson, 1986).

This labour force had to be created: it was not already there, just waiting for employment in electronics factories and garment factories. Young women had to be detached from their families, from village life, from aspirations to clerical and secretarial work, before they could participate in factory production. A variety of techniques were used: special accommodation was provided for young women near their place of work by some firms; others sent recruitment agents into the villages to reassure parents about the respectability of work in their factories; some emphasised that they were offering not just a job but a whole new 'modern' lifestyle with 'fringe benefits' like beauty care courses and sports activities; electronics firms in particular often presented an image of work in their factories as being much more like 'white collar' than 'blue collar' work — clean, 'hi-tech', and with opportunities for further training (Nash and Fernandez-Kelly, 1983; Grossman, 1979). The result has been rapid increases in female participation rates at locations to which multinationals have redeployed female-labour intensive operations. Much of the discussion has centred on the implications of the new job opportunities for young women — do they gain greater independence; are they exploited; are patriarchal structures of women's subordination weakened (Elson and Pearson, 1981; Lim, 1983; ILO, 1985)?

Relatively little has been written about the position of EEC countries in the new international division of labour. The major exception is Fröbel, Heinrichs and Kreye, 1981, which claims that relocation of textiles and garment production to 'cheap labour' sites of production in Southeast Asia by German firms is a significant factor in the loss of employment in this industry within Germany. Robert, 1983, generalises this argument and claims that 'female unemployment in Western Europe results principally from the exploitation of female labour in developing countries'. Certainly, in the EEC as a whole, women's employment declined between 1975 and 1983 by 19 per cent in footwear and clothing, and by 33 per cent in textiles. There was also a 22 per cent decline in such employment in electrical engineering (including electronics) in the same period.

But one should beware of jumping to conclusions too quickly. There are other, possibly more significant, reasons for the decline in women's employment, such as productivity changes, industrial restructuring and changes in the balance of skills required in particular industries (Guy, 1984). Moreover, a more recent study has suggested that European firms do not show as high a propensity to relocate female-labour intensive operations in low wage countries as do American firms (Grunwald and Flamm, 1985).

In addition, there has been *inward* investment into Europe by American and Japanese multinationals in electronics and, though to a lesser extent, textiles and garments. Between 1978–81 more than 50 major greenfield investments were made in Europe by American electronics firms; and there were ten major greenfield Japanese electronics investments. In 1983 the UK was the most preferred location outside the USA for American electronics firms, with the Republic of Ireland in third place. Multinationals are creating new jobs for women in Western Europe, as well as destroying old jobs through plant closure. It is necessary to investigate the specific circumstances of particular European countries to reveal the net effect of inward and outward investment, the impact of both domestic and foreign multinationals on women's employment. Government policies and labour market structures and wage costs differ between different locations within developed countries in a way which a simple North/South, centre/periphery model cannot capture.

Men, as well as women, lose and gain jobs as a result of the flux of investment by multinationals. But men and women occupy different positions in the labour market and the production process which means that the impact of multinationals' changing strategies is differentiated. One argument sometimes put forward for a specific focus on women is that women are a 'weak' segment of the labour force (for instance, Enderwick, 1985, p. 100) and therefore deserve special concern. This notion of women's 'weakness' should not, however, be accepted at face value. One dimension of 'weakness' often mentioned is organisational weakness. Women workers in general may not be as strongly unionised as men, and may not resort to industrial action to get higher wages so readily. But there is evidence that this is an effect of where women work, not some intrinsic feminine characteristic. Women are disproportionately concentrated in the services sector and in small firms. Men in the service sector, and in small firms, are also less unionised, and take less industrial action (Purcell, 1979).

The idea of the passivity and quiescence of women workers is thus open to question (Elson and Pearson, 1981). Governments in Southeast Asia have enticed foreign investment with hints about the docility of the 'oriental female', but nevertheless there have been general strikes in the Bataan Free Trade Zone in the Philippines; and protests in support of unionisation in the Free Trade Zones in Malaysia. The possibility of European women resisting the results of multinationals' decisions must be allowed. A focus on women does not mean treating women as passive victims.

Women's employment is, however, generally more sensitive than men's employment to labour demand in the immediate vicinity of the household. Because of the unequal division of domestic responsibilities and greater restrictions on women's freedom of movement, women are generally much more confined than are men to job opportunities very close to home. Women do migrate towards jobs in some cases — but having migrated, the same point applies — they tend to take jobs only a short distance from where they have settled. In Britain, evidence from the National Travel Survey shows that women of all ages travel far less to work than men. For women between the ages of 30 and 64 the distance travelled is only about half that travelled by men (Greater London Council, 1986, p. 522). Locational variations in female participation rates in Britain have historically reflected differences in *demand* for women's labour (Women and Geography Study Group, 1984; Hatton, 1986).

When a multinational sets up a plant in a location with a relatively low female participation rate, it does not so much draw on an existing female labour force: rather it *creates* a new female labour force; and if it closes a plant, and there are no nearby employment alternatives, women may be forced from the labour force, in the sense of no longer being able to combine paid work with their domestic responsibilities (Coyle, 1984, p. 126).

Whereas in the case of men, the changing pattern of investment changes the level of employment; in the case of women, the changing pattern of investment tends to change not only the level of employment but also the size of the labour force, bringing women into the labour force at one time; dismissing them from it at another.

There is thus an even greater contrast in the case of women than in the case of men between the localisation of workers and the internationalisation of capital. The differentiation is deepened by the fact that the community, the network of mutuality outside the factory and the office, is to a large extent the creation of women. It is sustained by their neighbourliness; their attention to kin relations; their voluntary work. The clash between the global logic of profitability and community values of continuity and caring thus has a particular resonance for women; and it is women's unpaid labour in the household that has to sustain communities left devastated by the outward movement of multinationals. So the major concern of this book is not whether multinationals are better employers than uninational firms in equal opportunity terms, but the contrast between the global strategies of multinationals and the circumscribed situation of women workers.

The next three chapters establish the context by giving overviews of the impact of multinationals on women's employment in the UK, Ireland and the Federal Republic of Germany. The UK is the 'home base' of many multinationals, but also host to many American, Japanese and European multinationals. It is also a relatively low-wage area of northern Europe. Ireland shares the low-wage characteristics of the UK, but has no multinationals of its own. It has pursued a policy of encouraging inward investment by foreign multinationals for much of the post-war period. The Federal Republic of Germany, like the UK, is the site of operations of both domestic and foreign multinationals, but has considerably higher wage costs. These chapters present quantitative evidence on the employment of women by multinationals and examine some areas of debate, such as the extent to which multinationals have 'exported' women's jobs from the UK and the Federal Republic of Germany; and the quality and stability of the employment they provide for women — a particular area of concern in Ireland, and in some regions of the UK.

Chapters 5, 6 and 7 present case studies of the strategies of selected multinationals in sectors important to women. Chapter 5 examines the operations of multinationals, both European and non-European, in the EEC textiles and garments industry, still the major source of manufacturing employment for women. It discusses whether the operations of these firms have been dominated by a move abroad for cheap foreign labour, or whether a more complex set of factors is at work, including the introduction of new technology and the use of sources of cheap female labour within Europe itself.

Chapter 6 analyses women's employment in semi-conductor production in Scotland's 'silicon glen' generated by inward investment from American and Japanese multinationals. This is often held to be a great success story, providing thousands of new jobs for women. A more sceptical view is taken here, especially about the future prospects for women's employment in the context of automation and re-integration of different stages of production.

Chapter 7 discusses a classic case of international redeployment, detailing the operations of a French electronics multinational in France and Brazil and the characteristics of the workforce in the two countries. Particular attention is paid to the determinants of the sexual division of labour: the reasons why women, but not men, are thought especially suited for some kinds of work; and how women's and men's work differs in the two countries.

In the subsequent three chapters, the focus shifts from the strategies

of multinationals to the consciousness and struggles of women themselves. Chapter 8 explores the reactions of women in the rural West
of Ireland to the arrival of foreign multinationals, situating this in the
context of women's historical experience. The importance is stressed
of a realistic assessment of the alternatives open to women, in
understanding their reactions.

In Chapter 9 the focus switches to West Germany and the resistance of both German and Turkish women workers to proposals for
plant closure in the context of a complex international restructuring
of corporate activities. In this case a further dimension of the new
international division of labour is present: the migration of workers
from lower labour cost countries to Northern Europe. Resistance to
plant closure is also the theme of Chapter 10, which assesses the
losses and gains of a group of women workers in Scotland. The close
interaction between the women's actions and the life of the community outside the factory is documented, and the possibilities and
problems of solidarity action by other groups of workers employed by
the same firm is assessed. Chapters 8, 9 and 10 show women as being
far from passive victims; and show the vital importance that community values play in their actions.

The final chapter presents an assessment of how a multinational
might go about restructuring its internal sexual division of labour so
as to begin to break down the occupational segregation of women
into 'women's jobs'. To do this, it is essential that the firm recognises
the demands of women's lives outside the factory, particularly the
demands of child care. It is shortsighted for firms to attempt to
organise production without taking account of the organisation of the
reproduction of human resources — without which production is, in
the long run, impossible. The creation of a labour force of young
unmarried women who leave employment when they marry and/or
have children only has advantages when firms have not invested
resources in training them; or when there are few firm-specific skills
involved. In the case of more highly trained and experienced workers, there are costs to the firm, as well as to women, of failing to
modify the organisation of employment.

What general conclusions may be drawn from the cases presented
in this book? The first is that there is no generalised tendency for
multinationals to relocate *all* female-labour intensive operations
away from the EEC countries. Important examples can be found of
such relocation, in which the lower wage costs and higher productivity or flexibility of women in some Third World countries is an

important factor — such as the case described in Chapter 7. On the other hand, the European market remains a vital attraction, not only encouraging European multinationals to keep much female-labour intensive production at home, but also encouraging American and Japanese multinationals to set up new plant in Europe.

However, the second conclusion is that there is cause for concern about the quantity, quality and stability of employment that multinationals are generating for women. In electrical goods and electronics, generally thought of as an expanding industry generating many new employment opportunities for women, the proportion of women in the labour force is tending to fall. The move from electro-mechanical to electronic production in the early 1970s displaced many women assembling electrical goods. The automation of the production of components and the introduction of robots for assembly is now reducing the proportion of women still further. Computer integrated manufacturing is on the way to displacing nimble fingers in an increasing number of processes. In clothing new technology does not seem to be having the same female labour-displacing effect, but homeworking and out-working in small workshops seems to be on the increase.

It is apparent that attracting multinationals to locate in a particular area is one thing; retaining their presence is another. Changing structures of incentives and changing multinational strategies can threaten the operations of factories which are both productive and profitable.

The third conclusion is that in situations of limited alternatives, women tend to respond positively to the opening of plants by multinationals, and are reluctant to take action which may result in the multinationals moving out. However, when multinationals have announced closures that women considered unjustified and threats to the well-being of the whole community, they have been swift to take militant direct action, such as occupations. But it is an unequal contest, with a huge imbalance in the resources available to the corporation and the resources available to the local community.

From women's point of view, the most important point is that the vision and accountability of multinationals must be widened. The multinationals must move, or be moved, from a narrow concern with what goes on at the workplace, with profits and corporate strategy, with takeover bids and shareholders, to a broader concern for the communities in which they operate, and for the interaction between the process of production of goods and services and the process of the reproduction of human resources. This requires changes not just within the multinationals, but in the interaction between multinationals and the financial markets, and between multinationals and government. It requires new forms of accountability and new criteria of success. Positive action programmes such as that discussed in Chapter 11 can bring gains, especially for women in technical and professional jobs. But women who work on the production line also have an interest in understanding the international scope of multinationals, and in organising to subject them to community control. Exchange of information between women working for the same multinational in different countries is an essential part of developing this understanding (Chapkis and Enloe, 1983). Devising strategies for negotiation and intervention is another (Women Working Worldwide, 1983). It is necessary to match the international scope of the multinationals with internationally devised programmes for community control of industry — a difficult task, but one which is now part of the agenda for the future.

REFERENCES

W. Chapkis and C. Enloe (eds) *Of Common Cloth: Women in the Global Textile Industry* (Washington D.C.: Transnational Institute, 1983).

A. Coyle, *Redundant Women* (London: The Women's Press, 1984).

P. Dicken, *Global Shift* (London: Harper & Row, 1986).

D. Elson and R. Pearson, 'Nimble Fingers Make Cheap Workers — An Analysis of Women's Employment in Third World Export Manufacturing', *Feminist Review*, no. 7, 1981.

P. Enderwick, *Multinational Business and Labour* (Beckenham: Croom Helm, 1985).

Financial Times, London, 1985.

F. Fröbel, J. Heinrichs and O. Kreye, *The New International Division of Labour* (Cambridge University Press, 1981).

Greater London Council, *The London Labour Plan* (London: Greater London Council, 1986).

R. Grossman, 'Women's Place in the Integrated Circuit', *Southeast Asia Chronicle*, no. 66, 1979.

J. Grunwald and K. Flamm, *The Global Factory* (Washington D.C.: Brookings Institution, 1985).

K. Guy (ed.) *Technological Trends and Employment — 1. Basic Consumer Goods* (Aldershot: Gower, 1984).

M. Hancock, 'Transnational Production and Women Workers', in A. Phizacklea (ed.) *One Way Ticket: Migration and Female Labour* (London: Routledge & Kegan Paul, 1983).

T. Hatton, 'Female Labour Force Participation: The Enigma of the Interwar Period', Centre for Economic Policy Research, Discussion Paper no. 113, 1986.

ILO, *Employment Effects of Multinational Enterprises in Industrialised Countries* (Geneva: International Labour Office, 1981).

ILO, *Women Workers in Multinational Enterprises in Developing Countries* (Geneva: International Labour Office, 1985).

L. Lim, 'Capitalism, Imperialism and Patriarchy: The Dilemma of Third World Women Workers in Multinational Factories', in J. Nash and M. P. Fernandez-Kelly (eds) *Women, Men and the International Division of Labour* (Albany: State University of New York Press, 1983).

J. Nash and M. P. Fernandez-Kelly (eds), *Women, Men and the International Division of Labour* (Albany: State University of New York Press, 1983).

R. Pearson, 'Female Workers in the First and Third World: The "Greening" of Women's Labour', in K. Purcell *et al.* (eds) *The Changing Experience of Employment: Restructuring and Recession* (London: Macmillan, 1986).

A. Phillips and B. Taylor, 'Sex and Skill: Notes Towards a Feminist Economics', *Feminist Review*, no. 6, 1980.

K. Purcell, 'Militancy and Acquiescence Among Women Workers', in S. Burman (ed.) *Fit Work for Women* (Beckenham: Croom Helm, 1979).

A. Robert, 'The Effects of the International Division of Labour on Female Workers in the Textile and Clothing Industries', *Development and Change*, vol. 14, no.1, 1983.

H. Safa, 'Runaway Shops and Female Employment: The Search for Cheap Labor', *Signs*, vol. 7(1981) no. 2.

UNIDO, 'Women in the Redeployment of Manufacturing Industry to Developing Countries', Working Paper on Structural Change (1980) no. 18.

Women and Geography Study Group, *Geography and Gender* (London: Hutchinson, 1984).

Women Working Worldwide, *The International Division of Labour in the Electronics, Clothing and Textile Industries* (London: War on Want, 1983).

2 Women's Employment and Multinationals in the UK: Restructuring and Flexibility

Ruth Pearson

Since World War II the UK has been both a major importer and a major exporter of capital. Multinational companies, both British-owned and foreign-owned, play a major role in the manufacturing sector. Foreign multinationals account for an increasing proportion of manufacturing employment. Between 1971 and 1981 employment in foreign-owned enterprises in the UK rose by 50 per cent, to reach 15 per cent of total manufacturing employment. A recent estimate suggests that employment in UK-owned manufacturing multinationals accounted for about 24 per cent, so that the total share of multinationals in UK manufacturing employment in the early 1980s was about 39 per cent (Stopford and Turner, 1985, pp. 12, 187).

However, while the employment share of foreign multinationals has been rising, that of UK multinationals has probably been falling, for it is widely believed that the strategies of many UK multinationals have resulted in a contraction of their UK employment and an expansion of their overseas employment. Between 1972–83 a sample of 58 leading UK multinationals increased their overseas labour force by 200 000, while reducing their British labour force by over 600 000. These 58 firms accounted for nearly one-third of all manufacturing jobs lost in the period (Stopford and Turner, 1985, p. 12).

The impact of multinationals on women's employment in the UK needs to be situated in the context of two major trends: the overall decline in employment in the UK manufacturing sector; and the rising participation of women in paid employment, from 38 per cent of the total female population of working age in 1951 to 65 per cent in 1980 (Martin and Roberts, 1984, p. 9).

DECLINE IN EMPLOYMENT IN THE UK MANUFACTURING SECTOR

The sectoral composition of employment has changed substantially, with a decline in the proportion of the workforce employed in manufacturing, and a rise in service sector employment (as is shown in Table 2.1). In addition to this relative decline, employment in manufacturing has also contracted sharply in absolute terms, especially in the 1970s. By 1981, as is evident from Table 2.1, there were over two million fewer jobs in manufacturing than in 1951. The shrinkage in total manufacturing employment reflects both the contraction in Britain's industrial base in absolute terms, and changes in technology and the organisation of production.

However, not all manufacturing sectors have experienced the same rate of decline in employment. Table 2.2 shows the sectoral breakdown of employment in manufacturing between 1971 and 1981. While all sectors reduced their labour force over this period, some sectors experienced reduction above the average for the total manufacturing sector of 26.4 per cent — particularly textiles; metal manufacturing; shipbuilding; clothing and footwear. Others, notably chemicals; paper, printing and publishing; food, drink and tobacco; and instrument and electrical engineering, suffered a smaller than average reduction in employment.

TABLE 2.1 *Changes in UK sectoral distribution of labour, 1951–81*

Sector	1951 Employment		1981 Employment	
	(000)	(%)	(000)	(%)
Primary	1 632	7.8	705	3.3
Manufacturing	8 746	41.7	5 928	28.1
Construction, Gas, Water, Electricity	1 700	8.1	1 427	6.7
Services	8 892	42.4	13 094	61.9
Total	20 970	100	21 154	100

NOTE The classification of sectors changed in 1968, adding more sectors to manufacturing.

SOURCE British Labour Statistics, Historical Abstract; Annual Census of Employment.

TABLE 2.2　*Changes in UK manufacturing employment, 1971–81*

Sector	1971 (000)	1981 (000)	1971–81 Change (000)	1971–81 Change %
Food, drink and tobacco	770	630	–140	–18.2
Coal and petroleum	41	28	–13	–31.7
Chemicals	438	402	–36	–8.2
Metal manufacture	558	314	–244	–43.7
Mechanical engineering	1 051	766	–285	–27.1
Instrument engineering	166	134	–32	–19.3
Electrical engineering	811	673	–138	–17.0
Shipbuilding	193	145	–48	–24.9
Vehicles	815	591	–224	–27.5
Other metal goods	576	445	–131	–22.7
Textiles	622	315	–307	–49.4
Leather and fur	47	30	–77	–36.2
Clothing and footwear	455	266	–189	–41.5
Bricks, glass, cement	306	214	–92	–30.1
Timber and furniture	270	216	–54	–20.0
Paper, printing, publishing	596	508	–88	–14.8
Other manufacturing	339	251	–88	–25.9
Total manufacturing	8 054	5 928	–2 126	–26.95

SOURCE　Annual Census of Employment, 1971 and 1981

WOMEN'S EMPLOYMENT IN THE UK MANUFACTURING SECTOR

The difference in employment contraction between manufacturing sectors has important consequences for women's share of manufacturing employment. Table 2.3 shows the sectoral breakdown of women's manufacturing employment for the period 1971 to 1981. From this table we can identify those sectors in which women's employment has been important in terms of absolute numbers and how women's employment has fared in the context of the decline in employment in the manufacturing sector as a whole.

In 1971 the manufacturing sectors which employed over 100 000 women were food, drink and tobacco; chemicals; mechanical engineering; electrical engineering; vehicles; metal goods; textiles, clothing and footwear; and printing, paper and publishing. Clothing and footwear, which was the largest employer of women in UK manufacturing in 1971, suffered a severe reduction in women's employment.

TABLE 2.3   *Women's total employment and share of employment in UK manufacturing, 1971–81*

| Sector | 1971 | | 1981 | | 1971–81 | |
	Total (000)	Share (%)	Total (000)	Share (%)	Change (000)	(%)
Food, drink and tobacco	305	39.6	255	40.5	–50	–16.4
Coal and petroleum	5	12.2	3	10.7	–2	–40.0
Chemicals	124	28.3	113	28.1	–11	–8.9
Metal manufacture	65	11.6	36	11.5	–29	–44.6
Mechanical engineering	165	15.7	119	15.5	–46	–27.9
Instrument engineering	59	35.5	45	33.6	–14	–23.7
Electrical engineering	310	38.2	222	33.0	–88	–28.4
Shipbuilding	12	6.2	12	8.3	0	0.0
Vehicles	106	13.0	70	11.8	–36	–34.0
Other metal goods	169	29.3	113	25.4	–56	–33.1
Textiles	289	46.5	145	46.0	–144	–49.8
Leather and fur	20	42.6	13	43.3	–7	–35.0
Clothing and footwear	343	75.4	201	75.6	–142	–41.4
Bricks, glass, cement	65	21.2	47	22.0	–18	–27.7
Timber and furniture	50	18.5	44	20.4	–6	–12.0
Paper, printing, publishing	194	32.6	164	32.3	–30	–15.5
Other manufacturing	125	36.9	88	35.1	–37	–29.6
Total manufacturing	2 406	29.6	1 690	29.0	–716	–27.52

SOURCE   Annual Census of Employment, 1971 and 1981.

Whilst total employment fell by 206 000 between 1971 and 1981, some 142 000 of the jobs lost were women's jobs, reflecting the very high proportion of the workforce in this sector which is female. In textiles, too, women's employment fell by 144 000, a reduction of nearly 50 per cent. In the food, drink and tobacco sector, however, the number of women employed was reduced by only 16.4 per cent resulting in a slightly higher percentage of female to total employ-ment in 1981 than in 1971. This was also the case in mechanical engineering, where the 23.7 per cent fall in female employment was lower than that for the sector over all. In metal goods, which includes small tool manufacture, cutlery, nuts, bolts and metal cans and boxes, women's employment fell by 33 per cent compared to 22.7 per cent for the sector as a whole. Overall, women's employment fell by nearly 30 per cent, somewhat more than the fall of just over 26 per cent in total employment in manufacturing. In both textiles and clothing and footwear the fall in women's employment did not change the female intensity of employment (that is, the number of women employed as a proportion of total employment) in the sector; in electrical engineering, however, where women's jobs contracted by 28.4 per cent between 1971 and 1981, female employment contracted more severely than employment for the sector as a whole, leading to a reduction in the female intensity of employment in the sector.

Some trends can be deduced from the above analysis. Food, drink and tobacco, textiles and clothing and footwear are the industries which have traditionally utilised women's labour, particularly in the lower-skilled grades of manual employment. In 1971 they accounted for some 39 per cent of total female employment in manufacturing; by 1981 this was reduced to 35.6 per cent. In the so-called 'New Technology' industries — specifically instruments and electrical engineering — women's employment also fell despite the fact that in many parts of the world there has been an expansion in the number of women employed in certain parts of these industries and a very high female intensity of employment. In the UK these two sectors barely maintained their share of total female employment, which changed from 15.3 per cent in 1971 to 15.8 per cent in 1981. In fact, the proportion of women in the labour force fell by 5 per cent in the larger of these sectors, electrical engineering. By 1981 no industrial sector in the UK employed over 300 000 women, whereas in 1971 three sectors had employed more than 300 000; of nine sectors which still employed over 100 000 women in 1981, six of them had reduced the proportion of women in their labour forces.

The employment position of women in the manufacturing sector is, however, distorted by the fact that the aggregate figures do not differentiate between full-time and part-time employment. Table 2.4 indicates that in some sectors part-time employment of women makes up a substantial proportion of the female labour force. In food, drink and tobacco, which was one of the sectors where women's share of the labour force was maintained over the 1971–81 period, part-time employment accounted for over 30 per cent of total female employment. In clothing and footwear, the proportion of women part-time employees rose from 13.1 per cent to 16.9 per cent in the 1971 to 1981 period according to the census figures, which tend to under-report women's part-time work in this sector (Mitter, 1985). Overall, about 20 per cent of all women employed in the UK manufacturing sector were in part-time jobs, while only 1 per cent of men were employed part-time. This means that the figures in Table

TABLE 2.4 *Women's part-time employment as a proportion of total women's employment in UK manufacturing, 1971–81*

Sector	1971 (%)	1981 (%)
Food, drink and tobacco	31.5	34.1
Coal and petroleum	20.0	0.0
Chemicals	19.4	17.7
Metal manufacture	18.5	19.1
Mechanical engineering	18.2	20.2
Instrument engineering	6.1	20.0
Electrical engineering	20.3	17.6
Shipbuilding	16.7	25.0
Vehicles	12.3	11.4
Other metal goods	23.7	24.8
Textiles	16.6	18.6
Leather and fur	20.0	30.8
Clothing and footwear	13.1	16.9
Bricks, glass, cement	15.4	17.0
Timber and furniture	20.0	28.6
Paper, printing, publishing	18.6	23.2
Other manufacturing	24.8	23.9
Total manufacturing	18.54	20.52

SOURCE Annual Census of Employment, 1971 and 1981.

2.3 overestimate women's share of employment in manufacturing by failing to distinguish between full-time and part-time employment; the figures in Table 2.4 indicate that about 20 per cent of the female labour force is employed part-time and that this proportion has increased slightly between 1971 and 1981.

The employment position of women in the manufacturing sector is affected by overall changes in the level of employment and by changes in the technology and organisation of production which affect the skills composition of the labour force. Elias (1980) breaks down the change in female employment into two components: the sectoral component and the sex ratio component. The first measures what the change in female employment would have been if women's share of sectoral employment had remained unchanged; the second measures the difference between the actual change and what the change would have been with an unchanged women's share of employment. The first component is an indicator of the extent to which the change in women's employment is due to overall changes in the

TABLE 2.5   *Analysis of changes in women's employment in UK manufacturing 1971–81*

Sector	Components of Change in Women's Employment	
	Sectoral Component (000)	Sex Ratio Component (000)
Food, drink and tobacco	−55.5	+5.5
Coal and petroleum	−1.6	−0.4
Chemicals	−10.2	−0.8
Metal manufacturing	−28.4	−0.6
Mechanical engineering	−44.7	−1.3
Instrument engineering	−11.4	−2.6
Electrical engineering	−52.7	−35.3
Shipbuilding	−3.0	+3.0
Vehicles	−29.1	−6.8
Other metal goods	−38.4	−17.6
Textiles	−142.8	−1.2
Leather and fur	−7.2	+0.2
Clothing and footwear	−142.3	+0.3
Bricks, glass, cement	−19.6	+1.6
Timber and furniture	−10.0	+4.0
Paper, printing, publishing	−28.7	−1.3
Other manufacturing	−32.4	−4.6
Total manufacturing	−658.0	−57.9

SOURCE   Calculated from data in Annual Census of Employment, 1971 and 1981, following method used in Elias, 1980, Table 6.16, pp. 214–5.

level of employment in the sector; the second component is an indicator of the extent to which the change in women's employment is due to changes in the sexual composition of the labour force (Elias, 1980, p. 213). Elias' calculations cover the period 1971 to 1978; we have recalculated them for the period 1971 to 1981 using the same method. The sectoral component is obtained by applying the 1971 sex ratios to the change in employment by industry between 1971 and 1981. The sex ratio component is the difference between the sectoral component and the actual change in employment between 1971 and 1981. The results, presented in Table 2.5, suggest that the decline in women's employment has been accentuated by a substitution of male for female labour in many industries.

For the manufacturing sector as a whole, the sex ratio component shows that 57 700 women's jobs were lost as a result of a decline in women's share of manufacturing employment; while 658 300 were lost as a result of the overall decline of the manufacturing sector. However, this sectoral total masks the differences between industries. In six industries there were increases in the female intensity of employment, accounting for over 14 000 jobs more than would have been the case without any change in female intensity. In the other 11 industries there were declines in the female intensity of employment accounting for the disappearance of 72 000 women's jobs over and above those disappearing as the result of sectoral decline. The largest sex ratio component of job decline was in the electrical engineering industry, which reduced female employment by over 35 000 more than would have been the case if the female intensity of employment had not fallen.

Though the massive contraction in female employment in UK manufacturing is largely attributable to the overall shrinkage of UK manufacturing employment, women have suffered disproportionately from the reduction in manufacturing employment during the 1970s. As yet we cannot tell whether the extra job losses were the result of technical and organisational change which reduced demand for low-skilled female manual labour, or for clerical staff in manufacturing industry; or whether women were discriminated against in the process of shedding labour as aggregate demand for the output of British industry declined. Overall, the proportion of women to men employed in manufacturing fell from 37.8 per cent to 33.8 per cent in the period 1978–81, with the major part of that change occurring in the latter half of the decade.

TRENDS IN THE INTERNATIONALISATION OF UK MANUFACTURING

The UK has long been a major exporter of capital. In the interwar years investment was concentrated mainly in colonial countries, including transport and utilities, agriculture, mining and some manufacturing. Manufacturing sectors began to dominate in the 1960s and 1970s, though in recent years service companies like banks, other financial institutions, hotels and advertising agencies, have increased the volume of their outward investments. In the last two decades Western Europe and the USA have become increasingly important as the sites of British outward investment (Stopford and Turner, 1985, pp. 8–9).

The strategy of 'job-export' — or contracting home-based employment and shifting production to wholly- or partly-owned subsidiaries overseas — has been followed by a number of British multinationals in various industrial sectors (see chapter 5 for a study of multinationals in textiles and clothing). Stopford (1979) estimated that the domestic employment of British multinational companies in 1975 was two and a half million, compared to under one million employees of foreign multinationals operating in the UK, and the million plus overseas employees of British multinationals. A more recent estimate for 1983 indicates that the 58 British multinationals accounted for 1 336 000 jobs, compared with 860 000 jobs in foreign-controlled firms in the UK (Stopford and Turner, 1985, p. 183). Between 1972 and 1983 these UK-owned multinationals reduced their home employment by 623 000, a fall of 32 per cent, which corresponds exactly to the rate of job loss by UK uninational firms. During the same period, they increased their overseas employment by 200 000, though most of this overseas employment growth was the result of acquisitions rather than expansion of existing productive capacity. Over the same period foreign-owned enterprises in Britain increased their employment by 10 per cent, a total of 80 000 jobs (Stopford and Turner, 1985, p. 184).

This tendency for British multinationals to expand overseas employment while contracting the number of home-based jobs is also reported in other studies. An ILO study concluded: 'In the period 1965–1980 employment in foreign operations of multinationals has tended to grow more rapidly than in their home country operations' (Gaffkin and Nickson, 1983, p. 40). The 50 largest British manufacturing companies, almost all of which are multinationals, reduced their employment in the UK between 1978 and 1983 by more than 470 000 while expanding overseas employment by 40 000. In the West Midlands the share of overseas employment in total employment of the ten major companies rose from 25 per cent in 1978 to 33 per cent in 1982; their employment in the UK fell by nearly 160 000 (33 per cent of their UK employment in 1979), while their overseas employment rose by over 3500 (Gaffkin and Nickson, 1983, p. 40).

A West Midlands County Council study reported that 'UK company profits on foreign production almost quadrupled in the decade 1963–1973, compared with a two-and-a-half-fold increase in profits on UK operations' (Gaffkin and Nickson, 1983, p. 71). This would suggest that the strategy of many British multinationals was to export jobs to more profitable, and possibly lower wage, countries, a trend which appears to have accelerated in the late 1970s and early 1980s (Stopford and Turner, 1985, p. 183, table 7.4).

A survey carried out by Labour Research at the end of 1979 indicated that in the top 50 UK companies, employment fell by 6.4 per cent between 1973/74 and 1978/79 (*Labour Research Bulletin*, January 1980), a marginally lower fall than the 6.7 per cent in manufacturing employment overall — whilst overseas employment (of the 20 of the 50 companies revealing this) rose by 5.5 per cent over the same period. A survey of employment change in the same companies between 1979 and 1982 indicated that UK employment had fallen by 307 200, some 24 per cent, while overseas employment of the same firms had risen by 38 000, or just under 5 per cent.

However, these studies provide no more than an aggregate overview of the pattern of employment change of British multinational manufacturing companies. Given the importance of such firms in the manufacturing sector as a whole, undoubtedly the tendency to reduce domestic employment and at the same time increase overseas employment will have had a major impact on manufacturing employment in the UK. Unfortunately, the only *comprehensive* statistics available on the changing role of multinationals in the UK manufacturing sector are those from the Census of Production which provides figures separately for foreign-owned enterprises, but not for British multinationals. The remaining discussion in this section will, therefore, focus on this subset of international firms operating in the UK manufacturing sector.

Table 2.6 shows that foreign-owned enterprises, defined as enterprises with 50 per cent or more of their share capital owned by a company registered abroad, have increased their share of employment against the background of decline in the manufacturing sector. From a base of 7 per cent in 1963, employment in foreign-owned manufacturing has risen steadily and by 1981 accounted for 15 per cent of total employment. While total employment in manufacturing began to decline in absolute terms after 1971, employment in foreign-owned firms continued to rise until 1977–78. Since that time the decline in total employment in foreign-owned enterprises has been relatively slower than that in the manufacturing sector as a whole, resulting in a continuing increase in the foreign-owned share of total manufacturing.

The employment share of foreign-owned enterprises has not been uniform over all sectors. While the percentage of total employment in foreign-owned firms increased in every sector between 1971 and

TABLE 2.6   *Foreign-owned establishments' share of UK manufacturing employment*

Sector	1971 (%)	1975 (%)	1981 (%)
Food, drink and tobacco	7	10	11
Chemicals	22	22	31
Mechanical engineering	12	16	24
Instrument engineering	21	26	31
Electrical engineering	16	20	21
Shipbuilding and vehicles	16	19	26
Other metal goods	4	8	8
Textiles	3	4	4
Leather, clothing and footwear	1	2	3
Paper, printing, publishing	2	8	13
Total manufacturing	10.4	13.5	17.2

SOURCE   Stopford, 1979 for 1971 and 1975. 1981 figures calculated from data in Business Monitor PA 1002, 1981.

1981, in some cases foreign-owned firms have consolidated their participation in the UK manufacturing sector to a level well above the average 15 per cent share for manufacturing as a whole. In instrument engineering over 30 per cent of total employment in 1981 was in foreign-owned firms, while in shipbuilding and vehicles, mechanical engineering and electrical engineering the share was over 20 per cent.

FOREIGN INVESTMENT IN THE UK AND THE FEMALE-INTENSITY OF EMPLOYMENT

It would be logical now to go on to consider how the increasing share of foreign-owned firms in total employment in the UK manufacturing sector has affected women's employment. Unfortunately there is no simple way of doing this on the basis of the available statistics. The Census of Employment from which we obtained figures on the sex ratio of employment in manufacturing industry does not cover ownership. The Census of Production from which we obtained the figures on foreign ownership and employment include no data at all on the sex composition of the labour force.

However, it is possible to examine the trends in the sex ratio of employment in those sectors where foreign-owned enterprises have substantially increased their share of total employment. From the figures in Tables 2.3 and 2.6 it can be seen that the 50 per cent increase in foreign ownership in the manufacturing sector took place against a slight fall in the proportion of women in the manufacturing labour force. The traditional and declining sectors which employed large numbers of women — leather, clothing and footwear — showed a very small increase in women's share of the labour force, while foreign-owned firms increased their (minimal) share of employment from 1 per cent to 3 per cent. The major areas of expansion of foreign control were the engineering sectors; in instrument engineering, however, a nearly 50 per cent increase in foreign ownership was accompanied by a slight decline in the percentage of women employed; in electronic and electrical engineering a similar rise in foreign ownership was accompanied by a 9 per cent fall in women's share of employment and in mechanical engineering a doubling of foreign control saw very little change in the sex ratio of employment. This analysis would tend to support the hypothesis that it is the sectoral focus of foreign investment rather than the nationality of ownership which is dominant in determining the sex composition of the manufacturing labour force.

One way of testing this hypothesis would be to compare the sex composition of the workforce in foreign-owned firms with that in UK-owned firms in the same sector. Again, there is not entirely satisfactory data, but one can use the Work Place Industrial Relations Survey (Daniel and Milward, 1983) which included questions on ownership of establishments and the sexual and occupational compositions of the workforce, though its main objective was to discover how industrial relations in Britain had changed over the last 15 years. Tables 2.7 and 2.8 are based on data provided by that survey. However it should be noted that the data is for a single year based on a structured sample rather than providing statistical information on the whole population of manufacturing establishments in Britain. The sample comprised 2000 establishments with 25 or more employees and the data has been weighted to compensate for the over-representation of large firms in the sample.

Table 2.7 shows the mean sex composition of employment in the sample of domestic and foreign-owned manufacturing enterprises in the UK in 1980. In manufacturing as a whole, foreign firms appear to have a lower proportion of women workers than UK firms: 28.7 per cent of the labour force of UK-owned firms were women compared

TABLE 2.7   *Women's share of employment in a sample of UK- and foreign-owned enterprises in UK manufacturing, 1980*

Sector	Total employment		Full-time employment	
	UK-owned	Foreign-owned	UK-owned	Foreign-owned
	(%)	(%)	(%)	(%)
Food	46.0	37.0	34.2	30.6
Drink	28.5	46.6	23.8	45.7
Chemicals	25.0	34.0	21.2	30.9
Metal manufacture	19.9	9.0	10.6	8.6
Mechanical engineering	16.9	11.6	13.0	11.2
Instrument engineering	30.5	41.7	28.3	40.5
Electrical engineering	26.2	42.0	23.7	37.5
Other electrical	38.5	43.0	34.4	34.7
Shipbuilding	37.5	11.2	6.3	9.9
Motor vehicles	9.8	7.4	18.0	7.5
Other vehicles	11.8	16.1	13.6	15.5
Other metal goods	14.2	28.0	22.8	24.3
Man-made textiles	28.2	31.2	32.8	30.4
Other textiles	38.2	20.1	39.2	19.7
Clothing	76.9	98.7	76.1	98.7
Bricks	22.4	37.0	20.7	27.6
Timber	35.0	14.0	17.3	9.2
Paper	36.5	24.0	19.7	22.4
Printing	36.5	32.0	32.8	29.1
Plastic and Rubber	28.4	19.2	30.9	17.0
Total manufacturing	30.34	30.19	25.97	27.55

NOTE   The figures show the mean share of female employment for UK-owned and foreign-owned enterprises in the WIRS weighted sample of 2000 enterprises. The standard deviations are very large, so the figures must be treated with some caution.

SOURCE   Calculated from data supplied by the Workplace Industrial Relations Survey (see Daniel and Milward, 1983).

to 25.5 per cent of foreign-owned firms. When part-time employment is excluded, the ratios converge; 24.4 per cent of UK-owned firms' workforce were female, compared to 25.4 per cent for foreign-owned firms, indicating a greater propensity for UK-owned firms to use part-time female labour. If only full-time employment is taken into account, foreign-owned firms employed a slightly higher percentage of women workers.

In the sectors which we identified previously as having a high penetration of foreign firms, there are some significant differences between the sex composition of employment in foreign-owned and UK-owned firms. In instrument engineering, which is the sector with the highest level of foreign ownership and also a high proportion of women workers, the labour force employed by foreign firms was 41.7 per cent female compared with 30.5 per cent for UK-owned firms. In electrical engineering, it was 42.0 per cent compared with 26.2 per cent. However, in mechanical engineering, the difference was smaller and in the reverse direction; UK-owned firms' labour force was 16.9 per cent female, compared to 11.6 per cent female in the foreign-owned firms in the sector. In the clothing sector foreign-owned firms appeared to employ a larger percentage of women workers than their UK counterparts.

These figures would suggest that there is a tendency for foreign firms in the sectors with a high level of foreign ownership to employ a higher proportion of women than UK-owned firms in the same sector. Such a tendency might be the result of foreign-owned firms making a wider range of job opportunities open to women than do domestically-owned firms. However, although this may possibly be true for managerial and non-traditional occupations in foreign-owned firms, there is no evidence that this is so for unskilled and semi-skilled manual occupations. Another possibility is that foreign multinationals' investment in the UK may be concentrated in assembly type operations, utilising mainly unskilled labour for routine tasks. This has been the pattern of women's employment in multinationals in newly industrialising countries. Multinationals tend to retain a high proportion of technical and professional 'men's' jobs in their country of origin.

There is some evidence from the Workplace Industrial Relations Survey that foreign-owned firms in the electrical and electronics sector have a higher proportion of manual workers than UK-owned firms — 70.9 per cent as compared to 62.7 per cent (see Table 2.8). However, this is not the case for instrument engineering and clothing, where a higher female-intensity of the labour force in foreign-owned firms is accompanied by a lower manual-intensity. Only detailed case studies, which are outside the scope of this present study, can finally answer this question.

These figures can only be taken as a preliminary indication of the interaction between women's employment and foreign investment in UK manufacturing because of the limitations of the Workplace

TABLE 2.8 *Manual workers' share of employment in a sample of UK- and foreign-owned enterprises in UK manufacturing, 1980*

Sector	Manual workers' share of employment		Female manual workers' share of employment	
	UK-owned (%)	Foreign-owned (%)	UK-owned (%)	Foreign-owned (%)
Food	76.4	60.7	42.0	35.8
Drink	68.5	82.9	24.8	49.8
Chemicals	61.5	39.2	21.9	37.6
Metal manufacture	71.8	78.8	7.9	6.9
Mechanical engineering	53.4	56.2	7.1	1.8
Instrument engineering	65.3	58.0	36.3	50.0
Electrical engineering	62.7	70.9	24.9	43.3
Other electrical	55.7	63.7	50.5	50.8
Shipbuilding	75.0	58.5	12.0	1.7
Motor vehicles	78.7	76.8	2.7	4.4
Other vehicles	56.7	66.9	9.0	15.2
Other metal goods	74.1	70.8	27.0	23.8
Man-made textiles	71.3	72.0	38.2	30.6
Other textiles	77.0	86.4	48.4	21.3
Clothing	87.5	84.1	81.7	78.5
Bricks	80.1	73.9	20.6	35.8
Timber	73.3	82.4	14.4	11.8
Paper	75.1	85.2	21.2	9.2
Printing	59.2	38.2	28.9	8.0
Plastic and rubber	70.9	71.2	35.0	21.3
Total manufacturing	63.3	61.2	28.2	28.4

SOURCE Calculated from data supplied by the Workplace Industrial Relations Survey (see Daniel and Milward, 1983).

Industrial Relations Survey. The data base is too aggregated and does not indicate whether foreign firms are engaged in similar or different kinds of production, within a given industry, compared with UK firms. It tells us nothing about the size distribution of firms and the relationship between scale of production, employment of manual labour and its sex composition. Also, because it is only available for a single year, it tells us nothing about the changing pattern of the sexual composition of labour in foreign-owned firms compared with UK-owned firms.

CASE STUDIES OF FOREIGN INVESTMENT IN THE UK:
WHAT DO THEY SAY ABOUT WOMEN?

Over recent years there have been a number of studies of foreign investment in the UK. A paper by Stopford (1979), commissioned as part of an ILO Project on Multinationals and Employment, is the only major study to concentrate specifically on the employment impact of multinationals in the UK. However, it is based on data up to 1977 and is principally concerned to test the validity of the charge that multinationals fail to provide stable employment. No data is given on the sexual composition of the labour force in this study, nor in Stopford's more recent work on Britain and the multinationals (Stopford and Turner, 1985), which adds very little to the data on employment.

A more detailed study by Hood and Young (1983) was sponsored by the Department of Trade and Industry, the Scottish Office, the Welsh Office and the Department of Commerce, Northern Ireland. It focuses on the 'regional dimensions of multinational enterprise policies' (ibid., p. x) and reflects the desire of government to assess the ability of the UK to attract direct foreign investment in competition with other European countries. The study covers the Republic of Ireland as well as the UK, because of 'concern [about] the flow of foreign direct investment within this country as a result of an aggressive neighbour entering the market' (p. 323). It suggests that the marketing strategies of the Irish Development Agency 'point to some of the ways in which promotional policy would be adapted to highlight the advantage of a UK *vis-a-vis* an Irish location' (ibid., p. 325).

In UK government circles foreign investment is seen as a provider of jobs as well as contributing to the balance of payments, and to the modernisation of British industry: 'Foreign-owned companies. . . . bring new technologies, new management styles and attitudes, the injection of capital investment, the generation of exports and new jobs' (Invest in Britain Bureau, 1983). The employment impact of foreign investment is constantly emphasised in the Department of Trade and Industry weekly publication *British Business*: for instance, *British Business*, 18 March 1983 — 'Overseas investors created 60 000 jobs'. Announcements of planned new investment by foreign companies are generally presented to the press and public in terms of their employment generating effect: for example, 'Chips boost creates 1000 jobs' (*Guardian*, 6 March 1984).

Townsend and Peck's study of foreign manufacturing companies i Britain, 1977–81, shows how employment in foreign-owned com panies declined relatively faster in the peripheral areas of the countr towards which government agencies intend to attract foreign invest ment to counteract high unemployment rates. At the same time, i supports Stopford's argument that for the UK as a whole, net jo losses in foreign-owned manufacturing companies stood at a lowe level than in locally-owned firms (Townsend and Peck, 1986).

This study, however, also demonstrates the importance of sub regional analysis to understand how the investment, expansion an retrenchment decisions of foreign firms affect employment in an particular area. In Scotland, for example, foreign job losses wer highly localised in Strathclyde which has lost 23 100 jobs in th four-year period — and in Wales, where the county of Glamorga lost 4500.

In view of this high level of public interest and concern about th desirability of attracting new foreign investment, and the employ ment benefits to the economy, it is somewhat disconcerting to dis cover that no official attention has been paid to the kind of job foreign investment is providing or who will do them. The Hood an Young survey did include one question on gender (cf. Hood an Young, 1983, p. 366, Q. 9: How many women are employed at th plant?) in the section on workforce characteristics. This data i utilised in the main body of the report in a single paragraph repro duced below:

On a proportional basis the breakdown of male/female employ ment is as follows:

	Total	Wales	Scotland	North West	North	N. Irelanc
Percent Male Employment (1980)	68.5	69.4	55.9	85.2	67.4	69.6

Only two regions differ at all from the average, Scotland with a very high proportion of female employees (46 per cent) and the North West with an extremely low female employment ratio (15 per cent); the latter, of course, ties in with the concentration o craft workers among establishments in the North West region.

(Hood and Young, 1983, p. 220)

Studies of the regional impact of foreign investment in the UK reveal a curious ignorance of the sexual composition of the labour force of major sectors involved, reminiscent of the myopia of Third World governments seeking foreign investment in labour intensive manufacturing industries in the 1960s. Hudson (1980), reporting on the impact of regional development policies in Washington New Town, comments:

The outcome of the particular combination of state interventions which is encapsulated in the development of Washington New Town was contrary to this intention [of attracting male-employing manufacturing industry, primarily to absorb the surplus labour force from coal mining, produced as a consequence of National Coal Board policies]. Male unemployment in and around Washington New Town has continued to rise. . . . while many of the manufacturing and service sector activities attracted to the town employ large numbers and/or proportions of women; furthermore the sharp decline in female employment on Washington New Town's industrial estates between 1973 and 1974 has demonstrated that these new jobs are not necessarily permanent. At one level the discrepancy between policy intention and outcome can be accounted for in terms of changing intentions, an abandonment of the goal of attracting male employing activities and a passive acceptance that 'if we didn't take the female employing jobs they would go elsewhere.'

Hudson goes on to comment that once it was realised that a large number of the new jobs were for women 'a rather more active policy was pursued, for a number or workshops were set up by the local Deparment of Employment to show women what sort of work they might do'. This tardy recognition by government agencies, that new investment in Assisted Areas (much of which is foreign — see Killick, 1982) primarily increases female employment, is reminiscent of the attitude of the Mexican Government which promoted foreign investment in the Border Areas in order to solve high male unemployment only to discover that the demand for women workers increased the economic activity rates of women to such an extent that unemployment rates actually rose (Pearson, forthcoming).

This raises a series of crucial questions which any research on the impact of multinationals on women's employment must seek to address. The international character of multinational firms gives them a degree of autonomy from the instruments of control and policy exercised by nation states within national economies. Hudson argues that the impact of regional policy in the North East has had the unforeseen effect of attracting female-employing manufacturing industry to Washington New Town. He also implies that this is in contradiction with other aspects of regional policy which is normally directed towards reducing male unemployment on the grounds of both efficiency and social need.

FOREIGN INVESTMENT AND WOMEN'S EMPLOYMENT IN THE UK ELECTRONICS INDUSTRY

None of the studies quoted above give any further information about the sexual composition of the labour force in foreign-owned manufacturing companies. Townsend and Peck do, however, highlight the active inward investment in the electronics sector, which we established earlier is a sector where there is a relatively high proportion of women workers and one in which, on the evidence available, it would appear that foreign firms tend to employ more women than their UK-owned counterparts.

One of the reasons that the UK has become one of the most favoured locations for international electronics capital is that it provides a low-wage platform from which to penetrate the EEC market (Morgan, 1986, p. 335). However, such investment is not uniformly distributed throughout the country. The electronics sector in the UK shows a highly concentrated regional distribution, partially the result of regional policy which has sought to attract foreign investment to areas of high unemployment, principally to absorb labour surpluses created by the contraction of employment in traditional – and male-intensive – sectors of industry (Hood and Young, 1983; Blackburn, 1982). However, as in the case of Washington New Town discussed above, the outcome has been different; jobs created have either been routine assembly jobs for women (Wong, 1983), or they have been technical jobs requiring specific technical training and external qualifications which have largely been filled by younger male entrants with few opportunities available to unemployed steel workers, coalminers and so forth (Morgan and Sayer, 1983; Massey, 1983).

The electronics sector in Scotland is discussed in detail in chapter 6. Here we discuss the sector in South Wales, which has grown from its immediate post-war base of mostly British firms to include a considerable number of foreign-owned firms operating some of the most advanced electronics factories in the UK. Earlier foreign investors mainly American, but Japanese investment has increased in this sector in recent years, which now accounts for the majority of the 11 Japanese firms in Wales (*British Business*, 26 November 1986).

The Welsh electronics sector has the highest degree of external control for any UK region in this industry and represents the sector with the highest domination by foreign companies in Wales. It has also accounted for the largest proportion of employment created by new investment, rather than by acquisition, though Morgan and Sayer (1984) argue that competition from foreign investment was indirectly responsible for job losses in older indigenous firms which were displaced by foreign direct investment in this sector.

In 1981 some 14 000 people were employed in the electronics industry in Wales (Morgan, 1986); 45 per cent of this workforce is female, accounting for a significant proportion of the 30 per cent of all employees in foreign-owned firms in Wales who are women (Hood and Young, 1983). Apart from the traditional female intensive sectors, clothing and food, drink and tobacco, this is the highest concentration of women workers in South Wales manufacturing.

In the electronics industry, the job of assembler is a virtually all female occupation. Hakim (1979) showed that 84 per cent of all electronics assemblers in the UK were female, and this degree of feminisation has been recorded by a number of studies of the electronics industry in the 1970s in the USA, Mexico and Southeast Asia (Wong, 1983; Cardoso and Khoo, 1978; Grossman, 1979; Pearson, forthcoming). However, female employment in the electronics sector in the UK fell by 40 100 between 1970 and 1981, an average rate of decline of 3.2 per cent per annum, compared to the 0.09 per cent for male employment. During the 1975–81 period female employment in the sector fell by 31 700 while male employment rose by 3500. The percentage of women workers in the electronics labour force fell from 42 per cent in 1970 to 34 per cent in 1981 (Soete and Dosi, 1983).

This fall can be explained partly in terms of the contraction of overall employment, but the differential experience of male and female workers is related to changes in the occupational structure. Morgan and Sayer (1984) report that 'the proportion of assembler or operator grades in the total electronics workforce fluctuated in the 1960s and 1970s as firms met the consumer boom by hiring more operators, only to fall when foreign competition increased and jobs were displaced by automated assembly and integration of circuitry'. This confirms the picture given by Soete and Dosi (1983) which shows that overall the category of operator fell by 28 873 between 1978 and 1981, while other skilled categories — managerial staff, scientists, technologists, technicians, draftsmen, administrative and clerical staff — grew. Soete and Dosi projected that between 1980 and 1985 a further 35 800 operator jobs would be lost in the electronics industry, which would recruit large numbers of the professional and technical categories listed above.

This projection is confirmed by Morgan (1986): employment in the electronics sector declined by 19 per cent between 1975 and 1984 (from 414 000 to 334 000) as the result of a profound recomposition of the structure of employment.

> The most dramatic occupational change has been the 'collapse of work' in the semi-skilled operator category. . . . Since the operator grade is a well-known ghetto of female labour a 'defeminisation' of the electronics industry has been underway in Britain. Females accounted for over 80 per cent of total job-loss between 1974 and 1981 in this sector, and the 'collapse' of the operator grade, largely induced through the automation of assembly work, is the major reason for this gender-specific form of displacement.
>
> (Morgan, 1986, pp. 335–7)

The experience of women hired by electronics companies in South Wales has been contradictory. South Wales has a history of domination by two sectors of heavy industry — mining and steel — with virtually no light industry or service employment until after 1960. While women did enter paid employment in increasing numbers after World War II, South Wales continued to have one of the lowest female activity rates in the UK, as low as 20–25 per cent in some towns in the mid-1960s. The advent of electronic and electrical engineering, and other female-employing sectors, over the last 20 years has presented women with job opportunities previously unavailable; and the increasing level of male unemployment caused by the closure of coal mines, shipyards and steel mills provides additional push factors leading to an overall increase in economic activity rates for women.

The jobs in this sector have been described as un- or semi-skilled, routine, low-paid, requiring no technical training and (fortuitously) no previous industrial experience. Into these jobs were recruited what is described by various authors as 'green labour' — that is, women with no previous industrial work history, many of whom we can assume were not economically active prior to their employment in the foreign dominated electrical and electronics sector (Morgan and Sayer, 1983; Massey, 1983).

These employment opportunities have proved to be limited, and in many cases short-lived for individual women hired by multinational companies. In a letter to all employees at their South Wales factory at Hirwaun in December 1984, the Japanese electronics firm of Hitachi invited all workers aged 35 or over to take voluntary retirement; arguing that older workers are more prone to sickness, are slower, have poorer eyesight and are more resistant to change. They argued that the effect of redundancies earlier in the year which were carried out on a 'last in/first out' basis meant 'we lost most of our younger people *particularly in production areas*' (*Financial Times*, 11 December 1984; emphasis added). Production areas are where women workers are concentrated. Hitachi added, rather inconsistently, that they needed to achieve a 'balance of the over thirty-fives, despite their physical and mental shortcomings, the young despite their being more difficult to control and less mature, and those in between despite their increasing domestic problems.'

The impact on women workers in the South Wales electronics industry illustrates in a number of ways how foreign investment, spearheading new methods of production in new areas, can interact with existing gender divisions in a given locality (for a fuller discussion of this point, see Pearson, 1986). The multinationals recruited a well-defined female cohort into the industrial labour force, many of whom were entering the paid labour force for the first time. This created the circumstances for firms to adopt new forms of labour management and recruitment practices. From the detailed data in Morgan and Sayer (1984) and Maguire (1986) it is clear that the differentiation of the new labour force, including technical and scientific staff as well as women manual workers, from the traditional organised male working class, was the basis of management's ability to negotiate a new style of corporatist collective agreements with unions. Forms of management discouraging active shop floor union participation and militancy were introduced *with* the cooperation of unions, rather than without them, contrary to what has often been the case where a largely female workforce and foreign companies are involved.

The creation of new 'women's' jobs had the effect of reasserting traditional sexual divisions within the workforce rather than transcending them. Morgan and Sayer (1984) refer to the self-assessment of what is a suitable or appropriate job for women which reflects community cultural values, as well as the clearly defined sex-typing of occupations by management. Rather than liberating women from a secondary status, this employment enshrines this secondary status in the workplace itself (see Pearson, 1986). From being dependent non-earners, women are socially reconstructed not as independent earners, but as 'cheap', 'disposable' labour for multinational firms.

MULTINATIONALS IN THE UK — A WOMEN'S ISSUE

The role of women's industrial employment in the electronics sector in South Wales demonstrates the way that foreign investment and control of a fast growing and changing industrial sector can alter the gender composition of the workforce in a given region at a given moment in industrial history. Foreign-owned multinational companies have achieved a vanguard role in the dynamic restructuring of British manufacturing industry and it is for this reason, rather than just on grounds of sexual equity, that the gender and occupational structure of their labour force, together with their recruitment and labour management practices, should command our attention. At the same time, it should be remembered that the global strategies of British multinationals also affect the employment opportunities for women workers; many of the thousands of jobs lost in the UK as the result of rationalisation by British multinationals were in the textiles and clothing sectors, which employ large numbers of women workers.

Because of their international arena of operation, multinational companies have the potential to alter fundamentally the industrial landscape of the UK. The restructuring of individual corporations and industrial sectors involves a reorganisation of jobs, both in spatial terms and occupational terms. Women still make up nearly one-third of the manufacturing labour force in the UK and are thus directly affected by the various forms of restructuring undertaken by multinational companies. The evidence in this paper suggests that because of their concentration in specific industrial sectors, and in specific occupations, certain contemporary trends in international restructuring by multinational firms will have a pronounced local effect on the demand for women's labour in British manufacturing industry.

This is especially true in an industry like electronics where geographical patterns of investment and technology and organisation of production are undergoing rapid change. While a substantial input of so-called semi-skilled labour continues to be required, electronics firms also require a highly trained and flexible input of scientific and technical skills, creating the types of jobs traditionally occupied by men rather than women.

There is some evidence for the UK that foreign firms employ a higher percentage of women in 'manual' grades. Women are employed by multinational companies which may themselves operate at the frontiers of technological advance in a given sector. But the nature of women's employment in such companies generally bears little relationship to this modern technology; women are employed in low grade assembly jobs, and in service occupations in secretarial and administrative positions within such enterprises — the same pattern of sexual and occupational segregation which is familiar throughout British industry.

Foreign-owned multinational companies have demonstrated their ability to use their geographic flexibility to construct new labour practices and negotiating procedures which break with previous traditions in the UK; in some instances, like that of Hitachi in South Wales, the fact that a large part of the labour force is female may make it easier to develop company-specific labour relations, particularly in areas of established male union militancy based on highly organised male-intensive industries.

The statistical analysis in this paper suggests that the form that internationalisation of capital has taken in the UK does indeed provide employment for women; but at the same time, neither the strategies of foreign-owned nor of British multinationals guarantee stability of employment, either for individual women or the female labour force as a whole. What, however, does seem of significance is that multinationals have a capacity to reconstruct labour practices and negotiating procedures while for most women workers in low skill grades of employment, they fail to offer any deconstruction of the sexual division of labour in industry which has always operated to the disadvantage of women. Like women employed by multinationals in export platforms in the Third World, women in the UK are a 'cheap' and 'disposable' labour force, whose employment prospects can be rapidly enlarged by international capital looking for flexible and low paid labour. But such employment can just as easily be reduced when changes in technology and organisation of production lessen the demand for untrained and low-paid labour, as women in the peripheral regions of the UK have discovered over the last decade.

REFERENCES

P. Blackburn, 'The Impact of Multinational Companies on the Spatial Organisation of Developed Nations', in M. Taylor and N. Thrift (eds) *The Geography of Multinationals* (Beckenham: Croom helm, 1982).

J. Cardoso and K. J. Khoo, 'Workers in Electronics Runaways: The Case of Malaysia', Paper presented to Conference on Subordination of Women, Institute of Development Studies, University of Sussex, 1978.

W. Daniel and N. Milward, *Work Place Industrial Relations in Britain* (London: Heinemann, 1983).

P. Elias, 'Labour Supply and Employment Opportunities for Women', in R. Lindley (ed.) *Economic Change and Employment Policy* (London: Macmillan, 1980).

F. Gaffkin and A. Nickson, *Job Crisis and the Multinationals: Deindustrialisation in the West Midlands* (Birmingham: Trade Union Resource Centre, 1983).

R. Grossman, 'Women's Place in the Integrated Circuit', *South East Asia Chronicle* (joint issue with Pacific Research), vol. 19 (1979) no. 5.

C. Hakim, *Occupational Segregation*, Department of Employment Research Paper no. 9 (London: HMSO, 1979).

N. Hood and S. Young, *Multinational Investment Strategies in the British Isles* (London: HMSO, 1983).

R. Hudson, 'Regional Development Policies and Female Employment', *Area*, vol. 12 (1980) no. 3.

T. Killick, 'Employment in Foreign-owned Manufacturing Plants', *British Business*, 26 November 1982.

Labour Research, January 1980.

M. Maguire, 'Recruitment as a Means of Control', in K. Purcell, S. Wood, A. Waton and S. Allen (eds) *The Changing Experience of Employment: Restructuring and Recession* (London: Macmillan, 1986).

J. Martin and C. Roberts, *Women and Employment: A Lifetime Perspective* (London: HMSO, 1984).

D. Massey, 'Industrial Restructuring and Class Restructuring', *Regional Studies*, vol. 13 (1983) pp. 223–43.

K. Morgan, 'Reindustrialisation in Peripheral Britain: State Policy, the Space Economy and Industrial Innovation', in R. Martin and B. Rowthorn (eds) *The Geography of Deindustrialisation* (London: Macmillan, 1986).

K. Morgan and A. Sayer, 'The International Electronics Industry and Regional Development in Britain', University of Sussex Urban and Regional Studies Working Paper no. 34, 1983.

K. Morgan and A. Sayer, 'A Modern Industry in a Mature Region: The Remaking of Management and Labour Relations', University of Sussex, *mimeo*, 1984.

R. Pearson, 'Female Workers in First and Third Worlds: The "Greening" of Women's Labour', in K. Purcell, S. Woods, A. Waton and S. Allen (eds) *The Changing Experience of Employment: Restructuring and Recession* (London: Macmillan, 1986).

R. Pearson, 'Women Workers in Mexico's Border Industries', in D. Elson (ed.) *Male Bias in the Development Process* (Manchester University Press, forthcoming).

L. Soete and G. Dosi, *Technology and Employment in the Electronics Industry* (London: Frances Pinter, 1983).

J. M. Stopford, *Employment Effects of Multinational Enterprises in the United Kingdom*, Multinational Enterprises Working Paper no. 5 (Geneva: ILO, 1979).

J. M. Stopford and L. Turner, *Britain and the Multinationals* (London: Wiley, 1985).

A. Townsend and F. W. Peck, 'The Role of Foreign Manufacturing in Britain's Great Recession', in M. Taylor and N. Thrift (eds) *Multinationals and the Restructuring of the World Economy* (Beckenham: Croom Helm, 1986).

Y-L. Wong, '"Oriental Female", "Nimble-Fingered Lassie": The Ghettoisation of Women Workers in the Electronics Industry', M. Phil. Dissertation, Institute of Development Studies, University of Sussex, 1983.

3 Women's Employment and Multinationals in the Republic of Ireland: The Creation of a New Female Labour Force

Pauline Jackson and Ursula Barry

A deliberate policy of encouraging multinational companies to establish subsidiaries was adopted in Ireland in the late 1950s. This policy was a direct reversal of previous policies which had been based, since the establishment of the state in 1922, on varying levels of protection for domestic firms. This protection involved not only high tariffs on consumer goods coming into the country, but also specific controls over the ownership of industry. The Control of Manufacture Act (1934) stated that where a new company was being set up, half of the issued share capital and two-thirds of capital with voting rights must be held by the Irish citizens. Furthermore, a majority of directors of a new company had to be Irish citizens.

However, by the 1950s the economy had slid into a deep depression and emigration was rising all the time. A complete change in industrial policy took place. The 1958 White Paper on Economic Expansion spelled out in detail the proposed lines of development. Foreign investment was to be directly encouraged through a whole system of grants and incentives to multinational firms; the educational system was to be reorganised to shift resources towards the creation of a technically skilled workforce; agricultural production was to be restructured; the banking system was to be streamlined and centralised. An important aspect of the new policy was its emphasis on what was termed 'export-led growth'. Special incentives were to go to export industries and the reorganisation of agriculture was also designed to move away from the objective of self-sufficiency and concentrate on developing its export potential. This stress on exports was seen as a way to counteract the growing balance of payments crisis.

The Industrial Development (Encouragement of External Investment) Act of 1958 rendered ineffective the protectionist measures of the 1930s. It excluded from the 1934 Act companies incorporated, managed and controlled in Ireland which had export as their primary objective. This was followed by the Apprenticeship Act 1959, designed to develop key skills. This Act was later superseded by the Industrial Training Act 1967 which established a Training Board to 'provide training for any activity of industry'. The Industrial Development Authority (IDA), which had been set up in 1949, was charged with promoting the creation of new industries and attracting foreign firms. At the same time, Shannon Airport, which had been built in 1947 on the Atlantic seaboard, became the world's first free trade zone in which companies were given relief from customs duty and tax exemptions. Many of these investment incentives were later extended to whole regions of the country.

THE ROLE OF MULTINATIONALS IN THE IRISH ECONOMY

A steady stream of multinational subsidiaries was set up during the 1960s and the tempo of investment increased through the 1970s. The traditional industrial base was transformed. Already established firms were concentrated in clothing, food-processing, footwear, textiles and printing, while the new multinationals came primarily into metal manufacture and engineering (including electrical goods), and the chemicals and pharmaceutical sectors. More recently, the electronics sector has become a major area of employment.

There are about 850 multinational subsidiaries in the Republic of Ireland employing over 80 000 people. Approximately one-third of all manufacturing employment is in multinationals. As multinationals have become increasingly important in the manufacturing sector, traditional industries, particularly clothing, footwear and textiles have gone into decline. The major sectors of employment by indigenous companies are in the food industry and the metal manufacture and engineering industry. In fact, these two sectors are the only ones which include significant numbers of both multinationals and indigenous firms. In the chemicals, pharmaceuticals and electronics sectors, multinational companies are virtually in control. In the textile sector, multinational employment is based on synthetic fibres whereas indigenous companies are primarily in natural fibres. While a handful

TABLE 3.1   *Multinational companies in the Republic of Ireland by country of origin, 1983*

Country of Origin	No. of companies	No. of employed
US	325	36 000
UK	177	20 000
West Germany	122	9 700
Others	230	16 000
Total	854	81 700

SOURCE   Industrial Development Authority, 1984, p. 5.

of Irish companies have overseas investments, there are *no Irish* multinational companies.

The early years of multinational penetration of the Irish economy were characterised by investment from a variety of countries. However, during the 1970s US multinationals have dominated foreign investment, and now constitute the greatest numbers and the major employers, as is shown in Table 3.1. In the four years from 1979 to 1982 US multinational companies generated a total of 35 650 jobs, representing three-quarters of the total jobs in multinational companies. In that period 70 per cent of foreign investment came from the USA. US multinationals are mainly in the electronics, chemicals and pharmaceuticals sectors. German companies are concentrated in metals and engineering, while British and other multinationals show a wider sectoral spread.

The total value of investment in fixed assets by multinational firms between 1960 and 1982 was IR£6617 million. The US was the most important source of this investment, accounting for over 50 per cent of the total. About 80 per cent of the output of multinationals is exported. The overall value of manufactured exports has consequently risen dramatically, from a level of IR£250 million punt in 1970 to IR£3490 million punt in 1981 (Industrial Development Authority (IDA), 1984, p.5).

There is an interesting contrast between the scale of employment in indigenous and multinational companies. The majority of indigenous companies are firms employing up to 50 employees, whereas three-quarters of total employment in multinational companies is in firms employing 100 people or more. Multinational companies constitute around half of all companies in the largest size range, employment greater than 500, but only 10 per cent of companies in the lowest size range (employment less than 50).

The impact of multinational employment on the Irish economy has been enormous. The structure of manufacturing employment has been transformed. Whole new sectors of industry such as electronics, chemicals and pharmaceuticals have been created and are completely dominated by multinational companies. While traditional industries were oriented towards the domestic market, these new sectors import their raw materials and export their products. New multinationals have opened continuously but the decline in traditional industries and the constant fall in agricultural employment has meant that high levels of unemployment have been consistently recorded over the last ten years. Unemployment in the early 1980s was running at over 14 per cent of the labour force. Multinational companies tend to be more capital intensive than traditional industry.

The system of grants and incentives to multinational companies is fully managed by the Industrial Development Authority which describes itself as a 'one stop shop'. This means that multinational companies planning to set up in Ireland can carry out their negotiations with a single organisation. This autonomy, which is jealously guarded by the IDA, has meant that the process of a new multinational establishing a subsidiary in the country is not complicated by overlapping agencies, parallel power structures or bureaucratic inertia. The IDA spends about 11 per cent of the government's capital budget each year and until very recently tended to operate without critical review or assessment.

The IDA incentives system is based on a combination of tax reliefs and grants. The maximum corporation tax for a multinational company is 10 per cent and a company can depreciate 100 per cent of the total cost of fixed plant, machinery and buildings and write it off against tax in its first year of operation if it wishes. Capital grants vary by region, from as high as 60 per cent in development areas (mainly in the West of Ireland) to a maximum of 45 per cent in other regions. Up to 50 per cent of the cost of an approved Research and Development project, to a maximum of IR£250 000, is available under a recent grant scheme. The IDA also provides training grants of up to 100 per cent of the cost of agreed training programmes for workers in the new industries. Additional incentives are provided through the banking system which offers low interest loans to multinationals. Following Ireland's membership of the EEC in 1975, access to

European markets is a key factor in the location decisions of US multinationals:

> Most companies establishing in Ireland have their sights set firmly on the European market to which they have duty free access from their Irish base. Ireland's strategic location as the natural bridgehead from Europe to America and heavy dependence of foreign trade have meant that international transportation facilities are well developed.

> (IDA, *Publicity Brochure*, 1984, p. 3)

Multinationals are able to achieve very high rates of profit in Ireland, as Table 3.2 shows. In fact, US firms make their highest rate of profit in the world in Ireland. This rate of return is significantly higher than that recorded for US companies in other parts of the world, almost twice that in its closest rival. In the words of the Industrial Development Authority:

> Ireland has emerged again as the most profitable industrial location not only in Europe but the world! This is confirmed by figures published by the US Department of Commerce which reveal that the average rate of return of US manufacturing investment in Ireland in the last six years has been consistently higher than in any other country in the world.

> (IDA, *Annual Report*, 1981, p. 1)

With a rate of profit of nearly 31 per cent, clearly the cost of investment can be recuperated in a very short time: one to two years (Dowling, 1978).

Towards the end of the 1970s the National Economic and Social Council reviewed Irish industrial policy and found weaknesses in a policy which accepted multinational companies using the economy as an operations base for low-skilled assembly work. Their suggestion was to reduce the level of grants, relate grants to employment creation rather than investment value, tax exports and generally try to ensure that multinationals establish a range of activities from marketing to research and development when establishing a subsidiary plant in the country (Kennedy and Foley, 1978; National Board for Science and Technology, 1981; O'Malley, 1982; Kennedy and McHugh, 1984).

TABLE 3.2 *Average rate of profit on US capital investment in Europe and Japan*

Country	Average rate of return 1977–82 (%)
Japan	17.8
Italy	17.8
Germany	15.0
UK	14.0
Netherlands	12.6
Denmark	11.7
France	7.8
Belgium/Luxembourg	7.0
All countries	11.9
IRELAND	30.7

SOURCE Industrial Development Authority, *Annual Report*, 1983, p. 3.

WOMEN IN THE IRISH LABOUR FORCE

Women's labour force participation in Ireland is low, in particular within the age group 25–59. This is primarily due to the participation rate among married women which, even though it rose from 7.5 per cent in 1971 to over 17 per cent in 1981, remains extremely low by EEC standards. Table 3.3 gives participation rates for 1981.

Women's share of the labour force has risen over the last 20 years, from 16.3 per cent in 1961 to 28.3 per cent in 1981. The rise was limited by the fact that the marriage rate has been rising and the marriage age falling, but this trend is unlikely to continue:

With the levelling off in the marriage rate and the decline in marital fertility, it seems likely that there will be a more rapid'feminisation' of the Irish labour force in the coming years.
(Kennedy and McHugh, 1984, p. 243)

Women are primarily employees rather than self-employed or employers, and are highly concentrated in the services sector. The services sector has become the main source of women's employment over the past decade. Women's share of industrial employment fell by 3 per cent from 30 per cent of industrial sector jobs in 1971 to 27 per cent in 1981. In the industrial sector only 15 per cent of production

TABLE 3.3   *Irish labour force participation rates by age and sex, 1981*

Age Group	Men (%)	Women (%)	EEC average for women (%)
14–24	61.5	47.8	42.9
25–59	94.8	29.9	48.8
60+	41.4	7.7	5.1
Total	75.7	29.0	36.4

SOURCE   Kennedy and McHugh, 1984, p. 243.

occupations are held by women. The low representation of women
industry as a whole contrasts with their strong presence in certa
industrial occupation: 99 per cent of sewing machinists are women;
are 78 per cent of electronics assemblers and 96 per cent of assembl
workers in chemicals. In the better paid production jobs, for examp
meat-boning in the highly important beef industry, only 1 per cent
workers are women. Women's earnings in industry are about 60 p
cent of male weekly earnings. Even allowing for differences in hou
worked, in many branches of industry there is no evidence of
tendency for male/female earnings ratios to equalise.

Women predominate at the fringes of the labour market, in hom
work (especially knitting and toys) and part-time work. Cutbacks
the public sector, where nursing, social work and teaching provid
outlets for women seeking a profession, have led to the spread
contract work, temporary work and other precarious forms of er
ployment. Only 17 per cent of women 'active' in the Irish labo
force are married. This arises from a combination of factors — a leg
bar on married women working which was only lifted in 1973;
absence of legal forms of contraception (still banned to single pe
sons) and of legal abortion; and the paucity of child care facilities f
working mothers. Mothers of school-going children face the proble
that there is no schools meals service and the school day at prima
level ends at 2–2.30 pm,obliging most married women to seek pa
time work or stay out of the workforce.

Despite the passage of Equal Pay, Equal Opportunity and Mate
nity Protection legislation, after prolonged campaigns by Trade Unio
ists and Women's Groups, women are segregated in the least pai
least skilled occupations in a narrow range of branches of econom
activity.

MULTINATIONAL COMPANIES AND
EMPLOYMENT-CREATION IN IRELAND

The original intention of attracting foreign companies to Ireland was to reduce the high levels of unemployment and high rates of emigration — both of which were viewed as male problems. The presumption that foreign investment achieved this aim remained relatively unchallenged until the late 1970s. At first sight the employment impact may appear negligible. Multinational manufacturing companies employed 1–1.5 per cent of the total labour force in 1966, rising to 3–4 per cent in 1974 (Stanton, 1979) and again to 6 per cent between 1975–81. However, this is a crude measure of their impact, since the labour force has undergone some expansion since the 1970s. Women's labour force participation increased during the 1970s from 28 per cent to 29 per cent. Emigration during the 1970s reversed, with a net in-migration of former emigrants back into the country. The expansion of the labour force means that figures for the percentage of the labour force employed by multinationals underestimate the amount of job creation which has taken place. Moreover, the public sector is extremely important in Ireland, employing one out of every 3.8 persons at work (Glavey, 1981). If one excludes from the labour force the public sector employees, assisting relatives in agriculture and the self-employed, we find that multinational manufacturing companies employ 15 per cent of all private sector employees. The importance of multinationals would rise significantly if one could also calculate the numbers employed in foreign-owned banking, insurance, finance and large retail outlets. Taking manufacturing employment on its own, multinational companies employed 29 per cent of the workforce in 1973 and 34 per cent in 1980 (Telesis, 1981), amounting to over 80 000 men and women workers and employees. Almost half are now employed in American-owned subsidiaries (White, 1984).

However, the establishment of overseas companies has not been able to compensate for the losses of jobs in existing Irish industry. Table 3.4 shows that while initially new multinational job creation just about compensated for job losses in both foreign and indigenously-owned companies, by the mid-1970s job losses were outstripping the jobs created by the arrival of new subsidiaries or the expansion of existing ones. This trend prevails to the present day.

Ruane (1982) has pointed out that the net impact of this type of industrialisation may be even more negative if one takes account of

TABLE 3.4 *Job creation and job loss in Irish manufacturing*

	1969–74[1]	1973–76[2]
New jobs created by MNCs	58 500	71 150
Job losses	53 000	74 850
Net impact of MNCs	+5 500	–3 700

SOURCE 1. IDA, *News*, 1976, p. 3; 2. IDA, *Annual Report*, 1976, p. 6.

the fact that even new jobs created may subsequently be lost due to closures. She calculates that between 1973 and 1980 only 40 per cent of jobs created in overseas companies were still in existence at the end of the period. This volatility, far from developing the economy, may contribute to the destabilisation already present in the crisis of traditional industry: in car assembly, shipbuilding, glass making, carpet weaving, cigarette manufacture, milling, sweet making, sugar refining and timber.

Ruane's estimates are supported by data from *Business and Finance*, a weekly Dublin business magazine, which examined the employment record of 13 multinational companies employing 7631 persons up to 1982. Layoffs and closures had reduced employment in these companies by 54 per cent between the time of setting up and the end of the period in 1982; 11 out of 12 companies were American and engaged in the production of car parts, computers, textiles, and garments. Scattered across the country, the closures had greater socio-economic impact on the agricultural and underdeveloped areas of the West of Ireland.

Closures are not confined to any one district. The Ford Motor Company left 500 redundant in Cork; Fiat a similar number in Dublin when car assembly ended in Ireland. The Italian State company SNIA left several hundred unemployed textile workers in the town of Sligo. These three companies alone accounted for 1500 redundancies in 1982–83, a large number for a small country. Some companies, like the Dutch AKZO-owned Ferenka tyre factory, closed in controversy following a long dispute between the workers and their union and following the kidnapping of their chief executive. The US-owned Fieldcrest towel plant in Kilkenny closed even though it had received a large injection of funds from Irish banking and industrial sources.

As Table 3.5 shows, multinational investment in manufacturing is of varied importance in different sectors of industry. From the point

TABLE 3.5 *Employment in multinational companies by industrial sector, Republic of Ireland, 1982*

Sector	Total employment	Employment in MNCs	MNCs employment as % of total	Order of importance
Food	45 720	6 380	14	6
Drink/tobacco	11 430	4 080	35	3
Clothing/footwear	21 930	5 640	26	4
Textiles	14 560	5 040	35	3
Chemicals/ pharmaceuticals	14 650	9 130	62	1
Metals/engineering	67 100	38 850	58	2
Paper/printing	15 530	1 450	9	7
Non-metallic minerals	16 790	2 760	16	5
Other	16 740	8 150	48	–
Total	224 450	81 480	36	

SOURCE Calculated from IDA, *Annual Report*, 1982, pp. 17–18.

of view of employment, the most important sectors are metals/ engineering (including electronics) and chemicals, where over half of all employees are in multinational plants (62 per cent and 58 per cent, respectively).

In absolute terms, metals/engineering with 38 000 employees is most important, followed by chemicals. Clothing and footwear, along with drink and tobacco, are third and fourth in importance. Not only are chemicals and metals/engineering the most important in terms of employment, they are also the two sectors of greatest importance in terms of manufactured exports from Ireland. Electronics alone furnishes up to 20 per cent of Ireland's manufactured exports, while US involvement in chemicals has made Ireland the world's 12th largest exporter of pharmaceutical products (Department of Foreign Affairs, 1984).

However, the volatility mentioned earlier means that today's boom sectors may be tomorrow's disasters. Multinational's employment in textiles rose from 5300 in 1973 to 9300 in 1980, only to slump to 5040 in 1982.

From the point of view of many electronics and chemicals multinationals, Ireland is in competition with Asian, Latin American and Mediterranean countries for a share of footloose international investment seeking a profitable location. According to the review of Irish industrial policy, commissioned by the National Economic and Social Council, 'Ireland is similar to Singapore and Puerto Rico, which are both small tax havens used as satellite manufacturing locations for Asia and North America repectively' (Telesis, 1981, p. 135). Telesis found that of the 80 top American electronics manufacturers, 26 had subsidiaries in Ireland and six of these had already moved to Puerto Rico.

In the decade and a half from 1960–75 the numbers of jobs in Irish industry fell by 1.3 per cent (Stanton, 1979, p. 105). Over the 1970s the proportion of industrial workers with multinational employers rose steeply. The impact of multinational's manufacturing investment in Ireland has been to restrict the dynamic industrial base of the economy to just two main branches of industry (electrical/electronics and chemicals). Multinational companies have increased their share of industrial employment but industrial employment itself has contracted. The combination of these trends can be seen as a deindustrialisation of the economy and a reproduction, at the level of industry, of the tendency to mono-production already flagrantly present in Irish agriculture.

RECRUITING A WORKFORCE

Multinational companies investing in Ireland are not looking for redundant and highly skilled clothing workers or car workers — of which there is an abundance. On the contrary, their hiring preferences are very specific and they are contributing to a restructuring of the workforce by age, skill, experience and gender.

The population of Ireland is extremely young — the youngest in Europe. Multinational companies tend to recruit very young workers, as in Southeast Asia and on the Mexican border; 55 per cent of the employees of multinational companies in 1979 were under 25 years old, which is twice what one would expect from the presence of this age cohort in the industrial workforce and three times the representation of this age group in the population as a whole (IDA Survey, 1980; Central Statistics Office, 1979 and 1982).

Multinationals have a strong preference for young employees who will have less industrial and trade union experience. In 1979 school leavers and young training centre 'graduates' made up almost 23 per cent of all recruitment by new multinational plants but registered

unemployed made up only 18 per cent of recruits. The other categories of recruitment by new multinational plant in 1979 were transfers
from within industry (24 per cent), transfers from other sectors of the
economy (22 per cent), returned emigrants (4 per cent) and housewives (9 per cent) (IDA Survey, 1980).

Thus, 45 per cent of employees recruited had no previous industrial
experience: the combined recruitment categories of school leavers,
trainees and transfers from outside industry. A further point of
interest is the high proportion (36 per cent) of employees recruited
from *outside* the measured labour force. These include school leavers,
housewives and returned emigrants. None of these persons would
have been counted as in the labour force, being too young to register
as unemployed, or considered dependents of their husbands, or
resident abroad. By recruiting them, multinationals are, in effect,
increasing the labour supply, and in particular the unskilled proportion of the labour force.

The recruitment by multinational companies of persons transfering
from other sectors of the economy has special importance. Firms
located in remote rural areas recruit from among small holders in
agriculture — farmers with 20–30 acres of poor quality land, which
cannot provide an income sufficient to feed a family. Between
1961–78 the extent of part-time farming increased by 71 per cent
(Higgins, 1983). One observes this location pattern in textiles in
particular, where almost one in three multinational workers are
recruited from 'other sectors', mainly agriculture, and plants have
been located in remote western parts of the country, some six hours
drive away from the capital, Dublin.

The recruitment of persons outside the measured labour force,
including young people and housewives, reduces labour costs. The
wage earned will sometimes supplement income coming from other
family members or from agriculture. Industrial wages in rural areas
are in any case lower than in the city regions of Dublin, Cork and
Limerick. Wages paid by multinational firms tend to conform to the
'prevailing rate' — that is, the prevailing rate for that region of the
country. Where agricultural wages are low and have depressed industrial wages in the region, multinationals pay just above the agricultural wage, which, for persons like housewives and young people
with no entitlement to incomes of their own, may seem acceptable.

Start-up wages in multinational companies are often agreed before
the plant opens at private meetings between representatives of the
Irish Federated Union of Employers and one of three large general

unions. These meetings normally lead to a formal contract on wages and conditions of work fixed for the first 6–12 months of operation. Employees are then hired into the company, with obligatory union membership and fixed wages established in advance. Predictably, this leads many industrially inexperienced workers to perceive the company and union as a package deal. Leydon (1980) in her interviews with young women factory workers in the West of Ireland, found that 40 per cent of those who belonged to a union did not know its name, confirming their difficulty in distinguishing between employer and union. Other multinationals follow a strictly non-union policy, including many in the electronics sector of US origin.

WOMEN AND EXPORT-ORIENTED INDUSTRIALISATION

In the early period of export-oriented industrialisation during the 1960s, women were over-represented in multinational subsidiaries relative to their labour force participation in manufacturing. At a time when women accounted for only 25 per cent of industrial workers, they made up 39 per cent of employees in new foreign owned manufacturing plants. In the clothing sector, at a time when 69 per cent of clothing workers were female, women made up 83 per cent of employees in new foreign-owned clothing subsidiaries (Long 1976). This over-representation of women has, with rare exception (Sweeney, 1973; Wickham, 1982), been ignored in discussion of Ireland's development policies; or where mentioned (MacAleese 1977) has passed without comment. For the years 1960–73, O'Farrell notes that companies found ' . . . .more generous levels of incentive were always available to projects setting up in Designated Areas (the poorest, least urbanised and most peripheral regions of the country)'(1980, p. 143). Perrons remarks that location in a poorer region is no longer a disincentive to a company since 'access to an industrially experienced labour force is no longer looked upon as an unqualified advantage' (1981, p. 83).

The over-representation of women in foreign-owned manufacturing plants is all the more interesting when one notes that the Industrial Development Authority specifically canvassed abroad for overseas companies which would establish in Ireland and employ a majority of male workers. Indeed, up to 1975, a criteria for obtaining state grants to open a foreign-owned manufacturing plant was that a majority of the workforce would be men. Overseas companies who promised to engage a majority male workforce were the target of the Industrial Development Authority. The gender criteria was published in IDA promotional literature for distribution at their overseas offices in Europe and North America. Reviewing investment in Ireland, the American-owned First National City Bank noted that '. . .Irish public policy is strongly directed towards the development of male employment and this finds its reflection in the incentive schemes . . .' (First National City Bank, undated, p. 9).

At the beginning of the 1970s the Industrial Development Authority specifically encouraged electronics and synthetic textiles firms to come to Ireland. This has contributed to a restructuring of the gender composition of employment in both these sectors.

In the 1970s there were major job losses in clothing and textiles. Partridge (1984) found that 30 per cent of Dublin clothing firms went out of business between 1971–81. There have been some major losses in textiles, especially in carpets, but employment in textiles as a whole has expanded. This is almost exclusively due to the opening of multinational synthetic textiles plants, while Dublin clothing firms closed.

There has been much controversy as to whether the job losses are due to imports of clothing and textiles products from less developed countries. Contrary to popular myth, Fitzpatrick presents evidence that the 'major source of increased import penetration in the Irish market over the 1970s has been the UK and other EEC countries. This corresponds to the findings of studies on the issue in many Western European countries' (Fitzpatrick, 1982, p. 14).

The loss of predominantly women's jobs in clothing has been accompanied by an expansion of mainly men's jobs in new textiles companies. As the textiles plants are in rural areas, the city clothing workers remain unemployed. The gender restructuring which these changes have entailed is shown in Table 3.6.

Over a 13-year period there has been a 14 per cent drop in women's employment and a 42 per cent rise in men's employment, largely due to the arrival of foreign synthetic fibres plants such as the US Burlington, Fieldcrest and Wellman; the Italian SNIA, the Japanese Asahi plants and the German Nino company. What is patently clear is that multinational investment is not 'gender blind'. In the absence of an indigenous Irish synthetic textiles industry, overseas companies carried into the labour force a specific gender division of labour established elsewhere.

Overall, the proportion of women working in manufacturing

TABLE 3.6   *Composition of labour force in textiles and clothing, Republic of Ireland*

	1966	1971	1979
Total employment	34 748	36 154	41 646
Women as % of total	69	66	55

SOURCE   Deeny, 1971, p. 16: National Board for Science and Technology, 1981, p. 84.

TABLE 3.7   *Women as a percentage of the labour force in the electronics and electrical industry, Republic of Ireland, 1973–83*

	1973	1975	1977	1979	1981	1983
Foreign-owned electronics plants	62	55	56	56	52	51
Foreign-owned electrical plants	51	49	51	52	51	51
Indigenous-owned electrical and electronics plants	37	35	35	32	32	33
Total manufacturing	–	29	27	27	27	28

SOURCE   Calculated from data supplied by Industrial Development Authority, and Central Statistics Office, 1981 and 1982.

remained relatively stable in Ireland during the 1970s at 29–27 per cent. The expanding labour force participation of women has been oriented more to the services sector. Yet foreign electronics companies have shown a marked preference for women as production workers. So, in 1979, when women were only 27 per cent of the manufacturing workforce, we find that 56 per cent of foreign companies' electronics employees were women. This is all the more noteworthy when one recalls that the proportion of women employed in all manufacturing in Ireland is very small and getting smaller all the time.

Table 3.7 shows the proportions of women in electrical and electronics companies and their share of manufacturing employment as a whole for the period 1973–83. Women are the majority of the workforce in both foreign electrical and electronics companies for all years for which comparisons are made. Compared with indigenous companies in these sectors, the multinational employer preference for women still holds true. The long-term trend shows a decline in women's share of electrical and electronics jobs. However, in the period 1975–79, women's share of foreign electrical and electronics jobs rose slightly in contrast to a fall within indigenous companies and manufacturing as a whole.

The peak of women's share of employment in electronics subsidiaries occurred when foreign companies began to open plants in Ireland in the early 1970s. There were just three major US plants in 1973: The Digital Equipment Company and two subsidiaries of the General Electric Company. During 1974 and 1975 the absolute numbers of workers in electronics fell. This hit women harder than men and their employment fell correspondingly by 6 per cent in electronics. Subsequently, although women's share of employment settled at just over 50 per cent, their absolute numbers rose as more and more New England and Californian subsidiaries were opened. Some, like Apple, General Electric, Digital, Westinghouse, Atari and Varian Associates, opened up several plants at different locations. Others, like Mostek, Floating Point, Amdahl, Perkin Elmer, Wang and Zenith, have been content with just one. During 1979–80 a US electronics subsidiary was opening a plant in Ireland at the rate of one every six weeks!

Electronics and electrical companies from overseas now provide 12 per cent of women's jobs in manufacturing — a proportion that has been rising over the decade and which is likely to continue to rise as electronics replaces clothing jobs as the main 'work for women' in manufacturing.

The numbers of women employed in indigenous electronics companies is extremely small. Electronics employment is virtually synonymous with employment by a multinational. The latter, in turn, is virtually synonymous with an American employer. The distribution of women electronics workers by country of origin of employer is shown in Table 3.8. The weight of US investment has shifted slightly in favour of investment from Japan and Germany but the majority of Irish women electronics workers are employed by subsidiaries of firms based in New England or California.

For women clothing workers the chance to work in an electronics plant is an opportunity not to be missed. The environment is less dusty and apparently cleaner. There is no piece work and there is more likelihood of cloakrooms, new toilets and a canteen. Electronics

TABLE 3.8   *Distribution of Irish women electronics workers by country of origin of employer*

Country of Origin	1973		1983	
	No. of women employed	Share of total (%)	No. of women employed	Share of total (%)
USA	1 934	99.3	3 940	84
Germany	7	0.3	393	8
Japan	7	0.3	219	5
Other	0	0	136	3
Total	1 948	100	4 688	100

SOURCE   Calculated from data supplied by Industrial Development Authority.

and electrical multinationals employ a growing proportion of Irish women industrial workers. Their importance as employers of women workers is likely to increase as the proportion of women employed in other branches decreases. Electronics exports account for 20 per cent of manufactured exports from Ireland and this, among other factors, make women electronics workers strategic in the Irish economy. Inside the electronics sector women occupy a specific gender defined place in the occupational hierarchy.

OCCUPATIONAL SEX SEGREGATION IN ELECTRONICS

Women are confined to the lowest paid and lowest status jobs in the sector, jobs with little or no chance of promotion and which are classed as semi-skilled or unskilled. The extent of sex segregation can be ascertained by examining the results of an employment survey carried out by AnCO, the Industrial Training Authority, for the purposes of establishing training needs in industry. The survey covered 74 companies which corresponds to all foreign and indigenous companies employing more than ten persons in 1981. All employees were allocated to one of 88 different occupational categories: 71 per cent of women electronics workers fitted into just five of the 88 categories, an astonishing example of sex segregation at work. The five categories were: mechanical assembly, electronic assembly, keyboard operator, bookkeeper, secretary-receptionist.

Table 3.9 summarises the results of the AnCO survey by broad

TABLE 3.9   *Occupational segregation in the Irish electronics industry, 1981*

Occupational category	Women's share of employment (%) in each occupation	Distribution of women employees between occupations (%)
Manager/supervisor	10.6	2.6
Technologist	2.2	0.1
Technician	3.8	0.9
Professional/administrative/ clerical	57.3	18.4
Production operative	70.5	75.7
Other workers	35.0	2.3

SOURCE   Calculated from AnCO (Industrial Training Authority), 1982.

occupational group. It shows that 70 per cent of production operatives are women — a very high proportion given the low proportions of women in manufacturing as a whole. Very few women are in managerial, technical, or supervisory occupations. Indeed, there were no women in any skilled production occupations. In terms of occupational sex segregation, women are clearly and unambiguously in a subordinated position.

Almost 76 per cent of all women in the electronics industry are in unskilled production jobs, while not one women in a hundred holds a technical, technological or skilled position; 94 per cent of all women in electronics are restricted to just two out of eight broad occupational categories.

By contrast, in printing and paper, where 90 per cent of employees have non-multinational employers, one finds higher proportions of women holding technical, technological and skilled posts and a greater diffusion of women among broad occupational groups in the industry. Although many factors may account for this variation, different recruitment strategies pursued by foreign and indigenous industries would be an important factor to consider.

UNIONISATION AND WAGE LEVELS IN ELECTRONICS

Women in foreign electronics companies are less likely to be unionised than women in other foreign and indigenous branches of manufacturing. This is not always for lack of trying on the part of general unions like the Irish Transport and General Workers Union and the Federated Workers Union of Ireland. Many multinational electronics companies are non-union employers in the USA and do not expect or plan to recognise trade unions among the workforce in Ireland. The absence of strong unionisation; the industrial inexperience of the workers; the difficulties women workers find in organising under the best conditions; as well as rising unemployment, are all factors contributing to low wages in Irish electronics multinationals compared to the prevailing rate in the multinational's country of origin. The low gross pay of women workers is further eroded by high levels of taxation on the weekly pay of young single women living at home with their parents who are ineligible for most tax allowances which would exempt their wages from penal levels of taxation.

Ireland was extremely popular among US electronics companies as a production base during 1983 according to the publication *Electronics Location File*. Its findings were reported as follows:

> The availability of a skilled labour force and good labour relations were cited . . .as important reasons for Ireland's popularity. Ireland also scored well on its comparatively low wage levels and good financial aid . . . .Pay levels for electronics personnel in Ireland are often below those in other European countries, while Ireland's incentive package is renowned for being among the most generous in Europe.
>
> (*Irish Times*, 1984)

However, despite the flood of investment, unemployment continues to rise and is cited as a contributory factor in keeping Ireland's wage levels low. In 1983 'Ireland's average wage was $5.76 an hour, compared with West Germany's $11.78 an hour and Britain's $7.26. Only Greece and Spain have lower average wages than Ireland' (Tuller, 1983). The relatively low wages; the predominance of women as production workers; the polarised occupational sex segregation of women employees; the low level of unionisation among workers in multinational electronics companies: all combine to suggest that the impact of multinational companies on women's employment in Ireland has been to perpetuate and even extend the subordinate position of the Irish woman industrial worker into a new generation of young women wage labourers and into relations with a new generation of technology.

CONCLUSION

Industrial policy in Ireland has been based on encouraging multinational companies to open subsidiaries since the late 1950s, using a comprehensive system of grants, tax concessions and other incentives, administered by a single agency, the Industrial Development Authority. Over 850 multinational subsidiaries have been opened over the last 25 years, employing one-third of the manufacturing workforce. American multinationals are the leading source of foreign investment, followed by those from Britain and Germany. Multinational companies are concentrated in three main sectors: chemicals/pharmaceuticals, electronics and metals/engineering. The first two of these are wholly new productive sectors dominated by multinational companies. The rate of profits generated by American multinationals in Ireland is over 30 per cent, the highest in the world; a rate almost double that achieved in other European countries and almost three times the world average. Multinationals tend to employ a larger labour force than indigenous companies and are capital intensive and export-oriented. US multinationals establish subsidiaries in Ireland with a view to penetration of the EEC market.

Little critical assessment of the impact of multinational companies was carried out until the last five years; since then, analysts have highlighted the level of closures, the low technological content of the production processes, the high level of the cost-per-job and the volatility of a development policy based on multinationals. Recruiting extensively among the young and the industrially inexperienced, multinationals have failed to have a significant impact on the unemployment problems their presence was intended to resolve and have tended to enlarge an already expanding supply of labour.

In electronics and electrical engineering US multinational companies have shown a preference for employing women. This has counteracted the decline in women's share of employment in textiles and the overall effect has been to slow down the rate of de-industrialisation of women's work. Employment patterns in multinational companies have been marked by the persistence of an already strong occupational sex segregation of women into a few categories of low paid, low-skill jobs. In electronics 78 per cent of women employees are in what is classed as unskilled production work.

Electronics and electrical engineering jobs are tending to replace those in clothing and textiles as the key industrial jobs for women. Multinational manufacturing companies have thus restructured the

workforce, but continue to display a high level of volatility and a
unlikely to provide a stable source of jobs for women in the futur

REFERENCES

AnCO (The Industrial Training Authority), *Manpower Survey, 1981* (D
    blin: AnCO, 1982).
Business and Finance (Dublin), vol.19 (1982) no.12.
Central Statistics Office, *Labour Force Survey, 1979* (Dublin: CSF, 1979)
Central Statistics Office, *Census of the Population, 1981* (Dublin: CS
    1982).
J. Deeny, *The Irish Worker — A Demographic Study of the Labour Force
    Ireland* (Dublin: Institute of Public Administration, 1971).
Department of Foreign Affairs, *Ireland Today*, Bulletin 984 (Dublin: DF
    1984).
J. Dowling, 'Financing the Multinationals', *Business and Finance*, vol.
    (1978) no. 19.
First National City Bank, *Investment in Ireland* (n.d.).
J. Fitzpatrick, 'Trade Between a Newly Industrialised and Newly Industri
    lising Countries: The Case of Ireland', Paper presented to Developme
    Studies Association Conference, Dublin, 23–25 September 1982.
F. Glavey, 'Civil Servants: How Many and What Do They Do?' (Dubli
    Department of the Public Service, 1981).
J. Higgins, *A Study of Part-time Farmers in the Republic of Ireland* (Dubli
    An Foras Taluntais, 1983).
Industrial Development Authority, *Annual Reports* (Dublin: IDA, 197
    1981, 1982, 1983).
Industrial Development Authority, *News*, vol. 2 (1976) no. 7.
Industrial Development Authority, *Publicity Brochure* (Dublin: IDA, 1984
Industrial Development Authority, *Overseas Companies in Ireland* (Dubli
    IDA, 1984).
Industrial Development Authority, *Survey of Recruitment Patterns and A
    Structure of Workforce in New Industry Grant Aided Companies* (Dubli
    IDA, 1980).
Irish Times, 'US Electronics Firms Favour Ireland' — Survey', 23 Mar
    1984.
K. Kennedy and A. Foley, 'Industrial Development', in B. R. Dowling a
    J. Durkan (eds) *Irish Economic Policy — Review of the Major Issu
    (Dublin: ESRI, 1978).
K. Kennedy and D. McHugh, 'Employment', in J. O'Hagan (ed.) *T.
    Economy of Ireland* (Dublin: Irish Management Institute, 1984).
M. Leydon, *A Study of Young Women Industrial Workers in the West
    Ireland* (Dublin: AnCO, 1980).
J. Long, 'Foreign Direct Investment in an Underdeveloped European Eco
    omy — The Republic of Ireland', *World Development*, vol. 4 (1976) no.
D. McAleese, *Profile of Grant Aided Industry in Ireland* (Dublin: ID
    1977).

National Board for Science and Technology, *Microelectronics — The Implications for Ireland* (Dublin: NBST, 1981).

P. N. O'Farrell, 'Multinational Enterprises and Regional Development: Irish Evidence', *Regional Studies*, vol. 14 (1980) no. 6.

E. O'Malley, 'Late Industrialisation and Outward Looking Policies in the Republic of Ireland', Paper presented to Development Studies Association Conference, Dublin, 23–25 September 1982.

P. Partridge, 'The Clothing Industry in Inner-City Dublin' (Dublin: Department of Geography, University College, 1984).

D. C. Perrons, 'The Role of Ireland in the New International Division of Labour — A Proposed Framework of Regional Analysis', *Regional Studies*, vol. 15 (1981) no. 2.

F. Ruane, 'Irish Industrial Policy', Paper presented to Seminar of the Statistical and Social Inquiry Society of Ireland (Dublin: ESRI, 1982).

R. Stanton, 'Foreign Investment and Host Country Politics: The Case of Ireland', in D. Seers, B. Schaffer and M-J. Kiljun (eds) *Underdeveloped Europe: Studies in Core-Periphery Relations* (Brighton: Harvester Press, 1979).

J. Sweeney, *Foreign Companies and the Industrialisation of the Republic of Ireland*, Thesis, Department of Economics, University College, Dublin, 1973.

Telesis Consultancy Group, *Review of Irish Industrial Policy* (Dublin: National Economic and Social Council, 1981).

D. Tuller, 'American Business Finds Ireland', *New York Times*, 21 August 1983.

A. Wickham, 'Women, Industrial Transition and Training Policy in the Republic of Ireland', in M. Kelly, L. O'Dowd and J. Wickham (eds) *Power, Conflict and Inequality* (Dublin: Turoe Press, 1982).

P. White, Special Supplement to *Irish Times*, 2 June 1984.

4 Women's Employment and Multinationals in the Federal Republic of Germany: the Job-Export Question

Sabine Gensior and Bärbel Schöler

Multinational enterprises (domestic and foreign ones) are of growing importance in determining the direction and speed of industrial structural change in the Federal Republic of Germany[1]. With rising unemployment there has been increasing public concern about possible employment effects of foreign investment. This has mainly focused on the question of a possible export of jobs resulting from foreign investment by German firms rather than on the employment impact of inward investment by foreign firms.

This chapter attempts to shed some light on the implications of multinationals for women's employment and the sexual division of labour, by drawing on official statistical data and some relevant case studies on the development and present structure of women's employment and on the activities of German and foreign multinational companies.

THE ROLE OF MULTINATIONALS IN THE FEDERAL REPUBLIC OF GERMANY

German and foreign multinationals are very important employers in the West German economy. Olle, in his recent study (ILO, 1984) indicated that at the beginning of the 1980s about 60 per cent of those employed in the manufacturing sector worked in the internationalised sector of the economy. According to this estimate, which is based on a survey of 65 German and 47 foreign multinationals, almost 1.2 million people worked in foreign enterprises and about 3.2

million in the domestic plants of German multinationals. Some figures for 1974, taken from a survey study of 39 German and 34 foreign multinationals (Jungnickel *et al.*, 1977), are considerably lower, with approximately 1.9 million people working in the internationalised sector, amounting to about 24 per cent of all people employed in the manufacturing industries. Only about 0.5 million people worked for foreign multinationals while nearly 1.5 million were employed by German-owned multinationals. However, not all of this difference can be attributed to growth of multinationals as the sources and the statistical base of the two sets of estimates are different.

Ranked by the number of their domestic employees the most important German multinationals are at present:
– AEG-Telefunken AG, Robert Bosch GmbH, Siemens AG (electrical engineering, data processing);
– BASF AG, Bayer AG, Hoechst AG (chemicals, pharmaceutical industry, plastics);
– Daimler Benz AG, Volkswagenwerk (motor vehicle construction);
– Friedrich Krupp GmbH, Mannesmann AG (iron/steel, machinery construction);
– Reemtsma (food, drink and tobacco);
– Freudenberg & Co., Triumph International (leather, textiles and clothing).
Some of the most important foreign multinationals are:
– Esso (US), Shell (UK, Netherlands), (petroleum processing);
– Adam Opel AG (US), Ford (US), (motor vehicle construction);
– Nestle (Swiss), Unilever (Netherlands, UK), Philip Morris (US), (food, drink and tobacco);
– Philips (Netherlands), IBM (US), (electrical engineering/data processing).

Whereas foreign firms have been established in the Federal Republic for years, German enterprises switched to large-scale production abroad only in the course of the 1970s. A reversal in current investment flows took place in 1974, when for the first time new German direct investment abroad slightly exceeded that of foreign enterprises flowing into Germany. By 1981 the value of the overseas assets of German firms exceeded the value of German assets of foreign firms (Deutsche Bundesbank, 1984).

The reversal in the net balance of direct investment in the mid-1970s partially resulted from the decline in direct foreign investment in the Federal Republic and partially from the expansion of

direct German investment abroad. The country most involved in th
change was the United States of America. On the one hand the U
was the favourite target country for German investment abroad –
with restrictions on access to the US market and the changed rel
tionship of the Deutschmark to the dollar making an inward inves
ment strategy more profitable than exporting. On the other hand U
firms reduced their investment in Germany. From 1975 to 1977 th
only invested half as much as in the period 1972 to 1974 (Deutsch
Bundesbank, 1983). As in the case of German investment in the U
the changed rate of exchange — besides other reasons — may hav
played a significant role in explaining the fall in foreign investmen
especially that of US firms.

Availability of data

The lack of good data on many aspects of the performance ar
economic activities of multinationals in the 1970s was pointed out :
an ILO review of studies of multinational enterprises in German
(ILO, 1979). Gaps in the official statistics continue to exist. Sind
1976 the Federal Bank has carried out an annual direct foreig
investment survey, but this survey fails to record much foreig
investment by small and medium-sized German firms. It includ
only investments with a German participation of 25 per cent; that i
the minority holdings of smaller and medium-sized enterprises a
not included, although such firms are responsible for a considerab
share of foreign production in some sectors (Fröbel *et al.*, 1977).
further deficiency of these statistics is that they do not contain ar
information about the operations of German multinationals withi
Germany since they only cover foreign investments of Germa
multinationals. Data on turnover, number of employees and so o
are shown only for the foreign establishments of German multina
tionals and for the German establishments of foreign multinational:
    Another problem area is related to the question of how to defin
the internationalisation of production. The official statistics assum
formal ownership to be a characteristic feature of the internationalis
ation of production. In the last few years, however, the inter
nationalisation of the activities of German and foreign firm
increasingly appears to have taken alternative forms, different fror
formal capital participation. Control and influence over the manage
ment of the foreign enterprise is assured not through direct inves
ment but through a variety of subcontracting procedures, making

possible to produce abroad with formally independent units. Such new forms of internationalisation are spreading, especially in developing countries, in sectors such as plant engineering and construction and in some branches of the consumer goods sector such as the textile and clothing industry and the electronics industry. Given that the official statistics on direct investment do not contain figures on these new forms of internationalisation, they give only a partial picture of the real state of the international links between firms.

These limitations should be borne in mind when considering statistics derived from the annual survey carried out by the German Federal Bank. We have supplemented these statistics with data from the recent ILO survey study carried out by Olle (ILO, 1984).

German multinational companies

The Federal Bank's survey shows that in 1982 75 per cent of the total value of stocks of German foreign investment was held in other industrialised western countries; 26 per cent in the USA and 42 per cent in Western Europe. The share of developing countries, including OPEC countries, was only 18 per cent (Deutsche Bundesbank, 1984). Data on the yearly investment flows supplied by the German Federal Ministry of Economics show a rather higher share — about 30 per cent — for developing countries for the period 1973 to 1977, then a sharp decline to nearly 13 per cent in 1979–80 and an increase to about 23 per cent in 1982 (ILO, 1984). Within the industrialised countries investments in the USA showed by far the highest growth rate between 1976 and 1982 (323 per cent). Among the developing countries the growth rate was highest for the Asian countries. Nearly 60 per cent of German direct investment abroad is in the manufacturing sector. About three-quarters of the manufacturing investment is spread over only four branches: chemicals, electrical engineering, vehicles, and machinery construction.

The distribution of manufacturing investment between industrialised and developing countries is shown in Table 4.1. Shares have been calculated on the basis of data from the Federal Bank and have been compared to the shares derived by Olle (Olle, 1983).

It is noteworthy that for all branches the Federal Bank data suggest considerably lower shares than those given by Olle (Olle, 1983). Besides the different time period, a different classification of developing countries may play a role in explaining these divergences. Furthermore, the Federal Bank data refer to stock values of German

TABLE 4.1   *Share of developing countries* in West German direct foreig*
investment

Industry	Share of developing countries (%) 1982	Average share of developing countries (%) 1972–80
Chemicals	18	25
Machinery construction	17	24
Motor vehicles	27	41
Electrical engineering	18	30
Precision instruments	–	13
Clothing	–	57
Textiles	–	26
Manufacturing total	18	25

* Excluding OPEC countries.
SOURCE 1982 figures calculated from data in Deutsche Bundesbank, 198
1972–80 figures estimated in Olle, 1983.

assets, while the Olle figures are for the value of flows. According
Olle's data the industry with highest share of investment in develo
ing countries is the clothing industry with 57 per cent of its investme
in developing countries; followed by the motor vehicle industry ar
— to a far lesser degree — the electrical industry. This high sha
seems to correspond with the findings of Fröbel *et al.* according
which 50 to 60 per cent of the foreign production of German texti
and clothing enterprises is in the developing countries.

The Federal Reserve Bank provides data on the overseas emplo
ment of German multinationals, compared to industrial employme
in the German economy (see Table 4.2). The figures show th
predominant role of the chemical industry in German firms' oversea
employment; motor vehicles and electrical engineering are the ne
most important. The figures for the textile and clothing industry a
much lower. The relative importance of overseas employment seem
however, to have been rising in this industry. Fröbel *et al.* estimate
that in 1974–75 German overseas employment in textiles and clothin
amounted to 8.6 per cent of those employed inside Germany in th
industry. The figure for 1982 in Table 4.2 is 11.8 per cent. Mo
probably the real increase is much higher than is shown by this dat
as studies show that production abroad in this branch is large
carried out with new forms of internationalisation (subcontractin

TABLE 4.2 *Overseas employment of West German multinationals, 1982*

Industry	Employment (000s)		
	West German enterprises abroad A	All enterprises in West Germany B	A as % of B
Chemicals	332	579	57.3
Machinery construction	128	991	12.9
Motor vehicles	229	793	28.9
Electrical engineering	235	1 024	23.0
Food, drink and tobacco	32	498	6.4
Textiles and clothing	55	468	11.8
Manufacturing total	1 255	6 960	18.0

SOURCE Deutsche Bundesbank, 1984; Statistiches Bundesamt, 1982.

with formally independent units) rather than direct investment.

There is evidence to suggest that the overseas production of German multinationals is somewhat more labour-intensive, on average, than their domestic production. Overseas employment as a proportion of domestic employment tends to be higher than overseas turnover as a proportion of domestic turnover (ILO, 1984, p. 14). As already noted, the most up-to-date estimate puts the domestic employment of German manufacturing multinationals at about 3.3 million in 1980. This corresponds to a share of total employment in the manufacturing sector of about 46 per cent.

Foreign-based multinational companies

At the end of 1982 the total amount of foreign direct investment in Germany came to 100.7 billion DM, compared with 109 billion DM of German direct investment abroad. About 75 per cent of the foreign investment came from only four countries, namely the USA (the single largest source with about 42 per cent), Switzerland, The Netherlands and Great Britain. A comparison with the origins of foreign direct investment in 1976 reveals that the relative importance of different countries has not changed very much. Japanese investors have expanded their participation in the German economy during the last few years, though in 1982 it amounted to only 4 per cent of the total value of foreign investment in the West German economy.

The activities of foreign multinationals are concentrated — just

TABLE 4.3   *Employment of foreign multinationals in West Germany, 1982*

Industry	Employment (000s)		
	Foreign multinationals A	All enterprises in West Germany B	A as % of B
Chemicals	126	579	21.8
Petroleum refining	25	41	60.9
Electrical engineering	215	1 024	21.0
Textiles, clothing, leather	28	474	5.9
Food, drink, tobacco	89	498	17.9
Manufacturing total	1 094	6 960	15.7

SOURCE   Deutsche Bundesbank, 1984; Statistiches Bundesamt, 1982.

like German direct investment — in the manufacturing sector. More than half of foreign investment was in this sector in 1982. Within the manufacturing sector the four most important recipients are petroleum refining (with 19 per cent), electrical engineering (with 18 per cent, much of it in office machinery), chemicals (with 17 per cent) and motor vehicles (with 10 per cent).

The volume of foreign capital flows has been declining since the mid-1970s. Commenting on this the Federal Bank suggested that perhaps certain industries had reached saturation point and were unable to absorb any further foreign capital (Deutsche Bundesbank, 1983). Additionally it was reasoned that many of the foreign subsidiaries in West Germany can now expand based on the profits gained from their operations there, without new capital from the parent abroad. In this context it should be pointed out that in the Federal Republic of Germany there has not been any policy of encouraging foreign investment with special grants and incentives to foreign multinationals as has been the case in Ireland and parts of Great Britain. In contrast, policy in the Federal Republic encourages German firms to invest abroad, especially in developing countries (Olle, 1983). Nevertheless, according to calculations made by the Federal Bank for 1980 (Deutsche Bundesbank, 1983), almost a quarter of enterprises in the manufacturing sector are owned by foreign capital.

The relative importance of foreign multinationals in manufacturing employment in 1982 is shown in Table 4.3. Almost 16 per cent of employees in the manufacturing sector worked for foreign multinationals. Within this total there are particular concentrations in certain subsectors, notably petroleum refining and data processing equipment where more than half of employment is in foreign multi-nationals. There is evidence that foreign multinationals operate with a higher labour-intensity than the average for the industry concerned. Their share of turnover tends to be higher than their share of employment (ILO, 1984, p. 13).

WOMEN IN THE WEST GERMAN LABOUR MARKET

According to the results of the micro census of April 1983 there are 11 092 000 economically active women in West Germany, which corresponds to a share of 34.6 per cent of total female population and 50.7 per cent of the female population of working age (15 to 65 years). Women's share of paid employment amounts to 38.9 per cent. Since 1970 women's participation rate has increased. In 1970 46.6 per cent of the female population of working age was economically active; by 1982 this had risen to 51 per cent. Analysis of employed women according to family status shows that the number of married women in paid employment, as well as of women with children under 18 years, significantly increased during the last ten years.

It is anticipated that this trend of growing economic activity of women will continue in spite of the unfavourable labour market situation. During the period of continuous high unemployment since 1975 women's share in total unemployment continuously rose from 39.5 per cent (1975) to 46.8 per cent (1983), which means — as compared to women's share of employment — a pronounced over-representation of women among the unemployed. This is due to the fragmentation of the labour market into a primary, skilled labour market segment with secure men's jobs on the one hand and a secondary, unskilled labour market segment with insecure women's jobs on the other. Management strategies for recruitment, training and remuneration are decisive for maintaining this fragmentation (Gensior and Lappe, 1983).

Sectoral distribution of women's employment

The most important features of the sectoral structure of women's employment are shown in Table 4.4. The majority of women are employed in services, with just over 25 per cent in manufacturing, and a small minority in other sectors. The number of women

TABLE 4.4   *Sectoral distribution of women's employment in West Germany*

Sector	Women's employment (000s)		Sectoral share of women's employment (%)	Change 1970 to 1982 (%)
	1970	1982	1982	
Agriculture, forestry	1 248	655	6.4	−48
Energy, mining	38	49	0.5	+29
Manufacturing	3 028	2 596	25.5	−14
Building, construction	126	169	1.7	+34
Distribution	1 681	1 818	17.4	+ 8
Transport, communication	241	325	3.0	+35
Finance, insurance	286	441	3.8	+54
Other services	2 861	4 130	36.9	+44
Total	9 519	10 182	100.0	+ 7

SOURCE   Statistisches Bundesamt, 1982; Lappe, 1981.

employed in service activities has grown rapidly over the last 12 years, while the number employed in manufacturing has fallen by 14 per cent. However, according to recent research (Ifo-Institut für Wirtschaftsforschung, 1982) future rationalisation will be concentrated on the application of new technology within services; heavy job losses and/or de-skilling are expected for women in many service occupations.

Since multinationals' activities are concentrated in the manufacturing sector, we will focus on women's employment in particular branches of this sector. The structure of women's employment within the manufacturing sector is shown in Table 4.5. The sectors with the highest numbers of women in absolute terms are the textiles and clothing industry, the electrical engineering industry and the food, beverages and tobacco industry. Women are a high proportion of the labour force in leather goods, textiles and clothing; food, beverages and tobacco; musical instruments, toys and jewellery; electrical engineering, and precision engineering and optics.

A comparison of trends in women's employment by industrial branches for 1970 and 1980 shows that women's share of employment has behaved in different ways in different branches, increasing in leather goods and textiles, decreasing in electrical engineering and clothing, and remaining constant in food, drink and tobacco (Ifo-Institut für Wirtschaftsforschung, 1982).

TABLE 4.5   *Women's employment in manufacturing, West Germany, 1980*

Sector	Employment (000s)		Female employment share (%)	Distribution of employed women by sector (%)
	Total	Women		
Chemicals, mineral oil	709.6	187.7	26	7
Rubber, plastics, asbestos	309.7	101.0	33	3
Stoneware, glassware	389.4	78.9	20	3
Iron, non-ferrous metals	1 258.6	232.8	18	8
Steel	385.1	48.2	13	1
Machinery construction, office machinery	1 189.8	216.6	18	8
Motor vehicles	1 050.3	166.0	16	6
Shipbuilding, aerospace	120.8	16.0	13	1
Electrical engineering*	886.8	316.5	36	11
Precision instruments, optics	183.0	75.9	41	3
Other metal products	340.8	105.0	31	4
Musical instruments, toys, jewellery	84.3	45.1	53	2
Timber, furniture	534.6	102.4	19	4
Paper	161.0	57.6	36	2
Printing, publishing	241.9	84.6	35	3
Leather	133.1	75.6	57	3
Textiles	480.2	277.8	58	10
Clothing	323.2	242.7	75	9
Food, drink, tobacco	892.0	344.9	39	12
Manufacturing Total	9 674.2	2 775.3	29	100

*   The figures for the electrical industry are likely to be too low; they are estimated on the basis of the number of persons employed who are subject to social insurance.

SOURCE   Batelle-Institut und Infratest, 1982.

The increase in the female share of employment in the leather goods and textiles industries was based on a decrease in total employment and a below-average decrease in women's employment. The reasons for this comparatively favourable development of women's employment in crisis-branches such as the textile industry are unclear. More detailed micro-level studies are required to establish an explanation. The electrical engineering industry and the clothing industry have both registered a decline in their female share of employment, based on a decrease of total employment in these branches and an above-average decrease in women's employment.

Occupational distribution of women's employment

Research on women's occupational patterns in West Germany stresses the higher concentration of women — compared with men — in fewer occupations (Lappe and Schöll-Schwinghammer, 1978; Battelle Institut, 1982; Ifo-Institut für Wirtschaftsforschung, 1982). Thus, about 75 per cent of women's employment is concentrated in only 15 occupations, with about a quarter of women concentrated in office occupations.

Women are predominantly working in unskilled positions and often below the level for which they are qualified. A prominant example is that of machinists in the clothing industry (Diezinger *et al.*, 1979 and Lappe, 1981). An analysis of jobs within the manufacturing sector (Ifo-Institut für Wirtschaftsforschung, 1982) showed that women are over-represented in those jobs which have decreased heavily as a consequence of technical change whereas they are distinctly under-represented in the expanding occupational fields. Jobs which have been reduced during the last decade, and where the female share of employment is considerable, include assembly work and supply and storage of materials.

THE IMPACT OF MULTINATIONALS ON WOMEN'S EMPLOYMENT

An analysis of statistics on women's employment and the operations of multinationals in West Germany shows that multinationals are likely to have a significant impact on women as workers in certain sectors of manufacturing. About a quarter of all economically active women are in manufacturing while 57 per cent of German direct investment overseas and 55 per cent of foreign direct investment are in this sector. But a substantial overlap is to be found only in the electrical engineering/electronics industry and, to a lesser extent, in textiles, clothing, and food, drink and tobacco.

TABLE 4.6   *Employment trends in selected industries, West Germany, 1976–82*

Sector	Employment (000s)		Change 1976 to 1982	
	1976	1982	(000s)	(%)
Electrical engineering	1 047	979	− 68	− 6.5
Textiles and clothing	618	470	−148	−23.9
Food, drink, tobacco	512	472	− 40	− 7.8
Motor vehicles	702	788	+ 86	+12.3
Chemicals	570	561	− 9	− 1.6
Manufacturing total	7 452	6 994	−458	− 6.1

SOURCE   ILO, 1984.

A full evaluation of the consequences of multinationals activities for the level and structure of women's employment is not possible at present, given the data situation and the present state of research; but we can consider some employment trends in the above mentioned manufacturing sectors.

Table 4.6 shows the trends in employment for the manufacturing sector as a whole and in the three branches of particular importance to women, between 1976 and 1982. Similar figures for foreign-owned multinationals are given in Table 4.7. The decline of manufacturing employment in foreign multinationals was far more pronounced than the decline in manufacturing as a whole (13.7 per cent as compared to 6.1 per cent), but the picture for the sectors where women are concentrated is somewhat different from that for manufacturing as a whole. Employment showed no change in foreign enterprises in electrical engineering and food, drink and tobacco as opposed to a considerable decline for total employment in these industries. In the textile and clothing industry the decline in employment was less pronounced in the foreign enterprises than for the sector as a whole.

In the three selected branches with large numbers of women employees the foreign enterprises are maintaining employment much better than domestic enterprises. There are, however, branches with just the opposite trends, such as the vehicle construction and machinery construction industries (ILO, 1984, p. 19).

Table 4.8 shows employment-related data for two sample surveys of German multinationals (excluding the textile and clothing industry) and two different periods. For the period 1974–80 domestic

TABLE 4.7   *Employment trends of foreign multinationals, West Germany,*
1976–82

Sector	Employment (000s)		Change 1976 to 1982	
	1976	1982	(000s)	(%)
Electrical engineering	215	215	0	0
Textiles and clothing	31	25	− 6	− 19.4
Food, drink, tobacco	89	89	0	0
Manufacturing total	1 268	1 094	− 174	− 13.7

SOURCE   Deutsche Bundesbank, 1984.

TABLE 4.8   *Employment trends of selected West German multinationals,*
1974–82

Manufacturing sector	49 Enterprises*		
	Employment (000s)		Change
	1974	1980	1974 to 1980 (%)
Total employment	2 326.4	2 573.4	+ 8.0
Overseas employment	560.7	735.4	+ 31.0
Domestic employment	1 765.7	1 778.0	+ 0.7
Average for total manufacturing sector†			− 8.5
Manufacturing sector	65 Enterprises*		
	Employment (000s)		Change
	1980	1982	1980 to 1982 (%)
Total employment	2 983.2	2 855.0	− 4.3
Overseas employment	834.7	785.1	− 5.9
Domestic employment	2 148.5	2 069.9	− 3.7
Average for total manufacturing sector†			− 5.8

* Sample does not include enterprises in textiles and clothing and mineral oil industries.
† Excluding textiles and clothing and mineral oil industries.

SOURCE   ILO, 1984.

employment showed little change and thus developed in a comparatively favourable manner, as compared to the fall in employment in all manufacturing enterprises (excluding textiles and clothing) by 8.5 per cent. This corresponds to previous studies (for example, ILO, 1979), which found that domestic employment trends of German multinationals were more favourable than for manufacturing as a whole. But while domestic employment stood still, employment in overseas plants of German multinationals increased by just over 30 per cent. In the early 1980s employment trends were reversed; employment declined both at home and abroad, with a somewhat larger decline abroad.

The 'Job-Export' question

The question of whether domestic employment declines because of the growing internationalisation of production is still the most important issue in German discussions about the employment effects of multinationals. Data in Table 4.6 and Table 4.9 show that in the three sectors of importance for women's employment, German multinationals have expanded their employment abroad while total domestic employment in these sectors has registered pronounced declines. However, there is no comparable data on domestic employment of German multinationals in these sectors.

According to previous studies (ILO, 1979) employment abroad and domestic employment of German multinationals up to the mid-1970s developed in a parallel way; that is, in both cases there was an increase in employment, though with higher growth rates in foreign employment. Thus it was concluded that while there was a considerable discrepancy between the rates of change in domestic and foreign employment, both were positive so that these data alone could not sustain the 'job-export' thesis (ILO, 1979).

Neither do the data on the employment trends between 1976 and 1982 (Tables 4.6 and 4.9) sustain job exports as the main explanatory variable for the decline of domestic employment: in absolute terms the increase in employment abroad is far too low to explain the whole of the decline in domestic employment in the respective branches. Table 4.8 reveals that the employment effects of multinationals cannot simply be subsumed under a term like 'job-export': employment abroad between 1980 and 1982 fell by even more than domestic employment during this period. Cutbacks of employment in foreign locations particularly took place in developing countries, which may

TABLE 4.9   *Overseas employment of West German multinationals, selected manufacturing industries, 1976–82*

Sector	Employment (000s)		Change 1976 to 1982	
	1976	1982	(000s)	(%)
Electrical engineering	187	235	+ 48	+ 26
Textiles and clothing	45	55	+ 10	+ 22
Food, drink, tobacco	23	32	+ 9	+ 39
Chemicals	195	332	+ 137	+ 70
Motor vehicles	185	229	+ 71	+ 45
Manufacturing total	922	1 255	+ 333	+ 36

SOURCE   Deutsche Bundesbank, 1984.

be an indication of a change in the strategies of international restructuring of manufacturing (ILO, 1984). Moreover, German industrial enterprises engaged in production abroad predominantly take over existing companies. The increase in the number of people employed abroad by German multinationals between 1974 and 1980 is not synonymous with the creation of new jobs. According to Olle more than 80 per cent of this increase is due to the takeover of existing firms (ILO, 1984).

It is true that those branches which are major employers of women (with a female share in employment in 1980 between 40 per cent and 75 per cent) belong to the group of industries with the most pronounced decline in domestic employment since the mid-1970s (see Table 4.6). Of the four branches covering 50 per cent of the employment cutbacks between 1976 and 1982, three were 'female intensive', namely, the textile and clothing industries and the electrical engineering industry. However, the rate of employment growth in German industrial enterprises abroad (see Table 4.9) during this period was highest in branches which are not female-intensive, such as chemical and vehicles. The increase in employment abroad in the female-intensive branches fell far short of the considerable declines in the respective domestic branches.

In our view it makes sense to speak of job *exports* only if there is a real domestic alternative to relocating production facilities. Protectionism and a high degree of international competition often force enterprises to seize market opportunities by shifting production to foreign locations nearest to the target market (either by establishing subsidiaries or through commercial links such as subcontracting).

Thus, the term 'job-export' should be only applied to that share of domestic jobs which could have been maintained or created if the respective firms had *not* relocated production abroad.

The extent of reimportation of products being manufactured at foreign locations is of great importance when estimating the displacement of domestic jobs — employment effects are particularly negative if the degree of reimportation is great, which it may be in clothing and entertainment electronics. The same applies to a substitution of exports by production abroad. On the other hand, positive employment effects are to be expected in the case where production abroad stimulates exports as has been reported for parts of the chemical industry, for the electrical/electronic industry, and for vehicles and machinery construction.

The Centre for Socio-Economic Research on Labour in West Berlin has calculated the extent of 'job-exports' for West Germany for the period 1975–80, taking account of the factors mentioned above (Olle, 1983). According to these calculations an export of about 50 000–60 000 jobs took place as a consequence of German direct investment in developing countries. The employment impact of German direct investment in Western industrialised countries is, according to this study, more negative. The majority of the jobs exported are in labour-intensive consumer goods industries, above all in the clothing industry.

Attractions of cheap female labour

The limitations of statistical data are particularly acute in the textile and clothing industry, where overseas production is carried out to a large extent not through direct investment but through other forms of internationalisation, such as industrial co-operation agreements, and subcontracting certain parts of the production process (Fröbel *et al.*, 1977). A recent estimate claims that production abroad by subcontracting with formally independent firms in developing countries is about six times as high as production abroad by direct investment in developing countries (Olle, 1983).

According to reports of the textile and clothing employers federation some German enterprises have reached shares of production abroad in total production of up to 80 per cent. The extent of reimportation into West Germany is extremely high. A recent prominent example of job exports is provided by the German multinational Triumph International. Out of 20 000 Triumph employees in the world today no more than 20 per cent are still employed at home. According to the trade union for textiles and clothing, about 60 000 jobs have been lost in the period up to 1980 as a result of relocation of production abroad.

The motive of reducing labour costs plays a predominant role in the production location decisions of German textile and clothing enterprises (unlike most other industries where such motives as market access and maintaining export shares are the leading determinants of direct investment). The wish to take advantage of the low wages in developing countries also explains the comparatively high share of investment in this branch which goes to developing countries. The textile and clothing industry with its traditionally high female share of employment appears to have been particularly affected by employment cutbacks resulting from large-scale relocations of production to low-wage countries.

Businessmen in the clothing sector interviewed during a comprehensive study on women's working conditions in industry (Lappe and Schöll-Schwinghammer, 1978; Lappe, 1981) stated that shifts abroad were profitable only in the case of mass production goods; skilled workers for the production of branded goods were lacking abroad. Only labour-intensive jobs were shifted abroad; since labour-intensive jobs were predominantly held by women, women would be affected by these shifts more than men. A clothing enterprise owning five establishments abroad and placing orders to low-wage countries indicated that it uses the threat of a further shift of production abroad in order to exercise pressure when there are demands for wage increases at home.

The same study concluded that the bulk of working women in the industrial sector are concentrated in production processes which are characterised by mechanisation blocks such as assembling processes in electrical engineering, and machining in the clothing industry; or in which mechanisation and automation have created de-skilled, machine minding jobs, such as in textiles. On the whole these jobs, almost exclusively done by women, require only a low level of formal qualifications and are classified as unskilled or semi-skilled.

Thus, given the increase in real labour costs at the beginning of the 1970s in West Germany, as in other Western European countries, and the intensive use of female labour in the production processes mentioned above, a low level of mechanisation and low qualification requirements are important factors contributing to relocation of production facilities abroad, especially to low-wage countries. In particular this applies to labour-intensive industries such as the textile and clothing industry and the electrical engineering industry.

Recent trends in international industrial restructuring

Since the beginning of the 1980s there have been signs of a change in the strategies of relocation as a result of new technologies (for a comprehensive discussion of such changes and the implications for the international division of labour, see Ernst, 1981). Major innovations in the field of information technology during the last few years make it possible, for instance, to introduce industrial automation systems to previously very labour-intensive assembly activities and even to small and medium batch production. This will have considerable implications for industrial production sites in the Third World with concomitant effects on production and employment in the industrialised countries.

In the case of the production of micro-electronic circuits, for instance, the availability of new techniques for automating the formerly highly labour-intensive assembly and testing of chips has already ended much of the growth of employment in electronics components assembly in developing countries. In the clothing industry various steps of production which used to be labour-intensive (such as monitoring the quality of fabrics, design, pattern-making and cutting) are increasingly penetrated by new modes of highly automated production (such as the application of Computer Aided Systems for design, pattern-making and quality control). But what is even more decisive is that the introduction of Flexible Manufacturing Systems (FMS) into clothing manufacturing could become possible. A concomitant application of Computer Aided Manufacturing Systems could in the future decisively change the economics of clothing, decreasing the comparative advantage of clothing manufacturing located in Third World countries.

Significant changes in the pattern of demand are also discernible which may facilitiate a retransfer of production to industrialised locations. Some German clothing firms are increasingly trying to meet such consumer demands for increased quality and reliability by manufacturing more branded goods, preferably at domestic sites where skills and new technology are available. Similar examples can be given for the production of consumer durables in the electrical industry and for the field of entertainment electronics.

The implications of such changes in the strategies of international restructuring for women's employment in Germany are difficult to assess at present. Yet we can anticipate some negative effects. In the face of pressures resulting from world market competition, multi-nationals will intensify investment in modernisation and rationalis-ation, for instance, in the automation of assembling and packaging processes, up to now technological gaps where almost exclusively women had been working (Gensior, 1984). Even if production is relocated in Europe, this will not regenerate the previous level of manufacturing employment for women.

NOTES

1. This is an edited and shortened version of a longer paper which is available as a Working Paper, no. 1, Project on Women and Multination-als — Europe, School of Development Studies, University of East Anglia.

REFERENCES

Battelle-Institut und Infratest, *Technik und Frauenarbeitsplätze* (Bericht für das Bundesministerium für Forschung und Technologie, 1982).

Deutsche Bundesbank, 'Struktur der Kapitalverflechtung der Unternehmen mit dem Ausland', *Monatsberichte der Deutschen Bundesbank*, nr. 5 (1983).

Deutsche Bundesbank, 'Die Entwicklung der Unternehmen mit dem Aus-land nach Ländern und Wirtschaftszweigen 1976 bis 1982', *Statische Beihefte zu den Monatsberichten der Deutschen Bundesbank*, Reihe 3, Zahlungsbilanzstatistik, nr. 4 (1984).

A. Diezinger und R. Marquardt, 'Zur beruflichen Sozialisation von Frauen', in R. Grosskurth (Hg.) *Arbeit und Persönlichkeit* (Hamburg: Reinbek, 1979).

D. Ernst, 'Industrial Redeployment and Control over Technology — Conse-quences for the Third World', in D. Ernst (ed.) *Industrial Redeployment and International Transfer of Technology*, Vierteljahresberichte, nr. 83 (Bonn: Friedrich-Ebert-Stiftung, 1981).

F. Fröbel, J. Heinrichs und O. Kreye, *Die neue internationale Arbeitsteilung* (Hamburg: Reinbek, 1977).

S. Gensior, 'New Technologies — Possibilities for a New Valuation of Women's Work', IFIP Conference on 'Women, Work and Computeriz-ation', Riva del Sole, 1984.

S. Gensior und L. Lappe, *Arbeitsmarkt und Frauenerwerbsarbeit* (Pader-born: Arbeitskreis SAMF, 1983).

Ifo-Institut für Wirtschaftsforschung und Institut für Sozialforschung und Gesellschaftspolitik, *Techknik und Frauenarbeitsplätze* (München: Gutachten in Auftrag des Bundesministers für Forschung und Technologie, 1982).

International Labour Office, *Employment Effects of Multinational Enterprises: A Survey of Relevant Studies Relating to the Federal Republic of Germany*, Multinational Enterprises Programme, Working Paper no. 2 (Geneva: ILO, 1979).

International Labour Office, *The Development of Employment in Multinational Enterprises in the Federal Republic of Germany — Results of a New Survey (1974–1982)*, Multinational Enterprises Programme, Working Paper no. 33 (Geneva: ILO, 1984).

R. Jungnickel, H. Krägenau, M. Lefeldt und M. Holtus, *Einfluss multinationaler Unternehmen auf Aussenwirtschaft und Branchenstruktur der Bundesrepublik Deutschland* (Hamburg: HWWA — Institut für Wirtschaftsforschung, 1977).

L. Lappe, *Die Arbeitssituation erwerbstätiger Frauen* (Frankfurt/New York: Campus, 1981).

L. Lappe und I. Schöll-Schwinghammer, *Arbeitsbedingungen und Arbeitsbewusstsein erwerbstätiger Frauen* (Göttingen: Campus, 1978).

W. Olle, 'Deutsche Direktinvestitionen in Entwicklungsländer — "Arbeitsplatz export" in Niedriglohnländer?', *Arbeitspapier Nr. 6*, der Seminarreihe 'Weltwirtschaft, Entwicklungspolitik und Arbeitsplatzsicherung' (Bonn: Friedrich-Ebert-Stiftung, 1983).

Statistiches Bundesamt, *Beschäftigung, Umsatz und Energierersorgung der Unternehmen und Betriebe von Bergbau und vom Verarbeitenden Gewerbe*, Fachserie 4, Reihe 4.1.1 (1982).

5 The Cutting Edge: Multinationals in the EEC Textiles and Clothing Industry
Diane Elson

The largest textile and clothing multinational in the world is the British-owned firm of Courtaulds. The Chairman of the company said in a recent interview:

> On the whole, the UK is not a good base from which to manufacture and compete internationally. There is no barrier, in my mind, to where we manufacture our goods. The market is a totally international one, and we must concentrate on scale, efficiency, and the development of the product. . . . It is a difficult point to get across. But in the long term, or even in the medium term, you do nobody any good by being insular in your outlook and preserving UK manufacturing, if that is going against the direction in which the market is moving. (Greater London Council, Industry and Employment Branch, 1986).

This chapter examines the ways in which multinationals in the textile and clothing industry have restructured women's employment in the Europe of the Nine (that is Germany, France, United Kingdom, Italy, Netherlands, Belgium, Luxembourg, Ireland and Denmark).[1]

The textile and clothing industry is the major source of industrial employment for women in the European Economic Community. In 1983, the last year for which complete figures are available,[2] almost 22 per cent of women in paid employment in the Europe of the Nine worked in industry. Of them, about 8.7 per cent were employed in textiles and 13.8 per cent in clothing, including footwear. The only other industry of anything like the same importance for women's industrial employment is electrical engineering, accounting for about 10.9 per cent of women's industrial employment. Not only is the textile and clothing industry important to women: women are important to it. In 1983 women accounted for 55 per cent of the textile labour force and just over 78 per cent of the footwear and clothing labour force in the Europe of the Nine. This is much higher than the industrial average of about 23 per cent.

However, job opportunities for women in this industry have been declining, as the level of employment in the industry has fallen substantially. Between 1975 and 1983 textile employment in the Europe of the Nine declined from 1 983 000 to 1 343 000, a loss of 640 000 jobs; about 32 per cent of the 1975 total. In the same period employment in clothing and footwear declined from 1 906 000 to 1 492 000, a loss of 414 000 jobs; about 22 per cent of the 1975 total. Women's share of employment in the textile sector as a whole has fluctuated slightly during the period, starting at 55.7 per cent in 1975, falling to 52.7 per cent in 1977, but rising thereafter to 55.0 per cent in 1983. In clothing and footwear the evidence points to a slight rise in women's share of employment, up from 75.5 per cent in 1975 to 78.4 per cent in 1983. In some sub-sectors of the textile industry, however, women seemed to have suffered a greater decline in employment than men. In the UK cotton and allied fibres industry, men's employment declined by 66.3 per cent between 1969 and 1983, while women's employment declined by 81.1 per cent (Lloyd and Shutt, 1983).

The decline in employment in the Europe of the Nine is part of a global relocation of production in textiles and clothing (Cable and Baker, 1983). As Table 5.1 shows, output has stagnated and employment has declined in the developed market economies as a group; but both have risen in the developing countries and the centrally planned economies. The rise in employment has been fastest in the developing countries, and the rise in output fastest in the centrally planned economies.

The most rapid rises in employment in the developing countries have been concentrated in a few countries in the Far East, and the southern Mediterranean. Employment in South Korea rose by 111 per cent in textiles and 224 per cent in clothing between 1971 and 1978; in Hong Kong employment in clothing increased by 138 per cent between 1970 and 1980; and in Singapore employment in clothing increased by 174 per cent between 1970 and 1979. Cyprus enjoyed an increase in textile employment of 55 per cent and in clothing of 52 per cent between 1978 and 1980, and Portugal's clothing employment increased by 71 per cent from 1971 to 1978 (ILO, 1984, pp. 29–33).

TABLE 5.1   *Average annual growth rates of output and employment, textile and clothing industries, 1973–80*

	Textiles		Wearing Apparel, Leather, and Footwear	
	Output (%)	Employment (%)	Output (%)	Employment (%)
Developed market economies	0.1	–3.0	0.3	–1.4
Developing countries	2.1	2.2	2.9	5.7
Centrally planned economies	4.2	0.4	4.9	0.7

SOURCE   UNIDO, 1983, Table III.10, p. 75.

MULTINATIONAL COMPANIES AND THE SEARCH FOR CHEAP LABOUR

It has been suggested that multinational companies have played a significant role in the global relocation of employment and production, even though multinationals are not as important in textiles and clothing as they are in many other branches of manufacturing (ILO, 1984). It has been argued that, given the relatively labour-intensive character of textile and clothing production, multinational companies have adopted the strategy of moving production out of Europe and North America, attracted by cheaper labour in the developing countries (Fröbel, Heinrichs and Kreye, 1981; Safa, 1981; Sinclair, 1982; Rhodes, Wield and Heyzer, 1983; Robert, 1983; Chisholm, Kabeer, Mitter and Howard, 1986; Greater London Council, Industry and Employment Branch, 1986).

Undoubtedly there is a considerable gap in labour costs between the developed market economies and the developing countries. The United Nations Industrial Development Organisation estimates that in 1978 average hourly gross wages[3] in the textile industry in the developed market economies were 8.5 times higher than in the developing countries (UNIDO, 1983, p. 236). Table 5.2 gives hourly gross earnings in US dollars in the textile industry in 1980 for selected developed and developing countries. It is clear that in some cases the gap may be much bigger than the UNIDO average figure. Gross hourly earnings in West Germany, for instance, are 24 times higher than in Thailand. The total labour cost gap is likely to be even greater because of the burden of social payments in West Germany. In the

TABLE 5.2 *Labour costs in the textile industry, 1980*

	Gross earnings* ($ per hour)	Index of earnings (US = 100)	Firms' social payments[†] (%)
USA	5.29	100.0	20.4
West Germany	8.00	151.2	25.2
France	5.04	95.3	56.9
UK	5.11	96.6	10.2
Ireland	4.50	85.1	14.0
Portugal	1.44	27.7	16.7
Morocco	0.72	13.6	18.1
Tunisia	0.94	17.8	n.a.
Hong Kong	1.85	35.0	3.2
Singapore	0.94	17.8	**
South Korea	0.78	14.7	n.a.
Thailand	0.33	6.2	n.a.

* Gross earnings is defined as basic wages plus all other payments made to workers in a medium sized plant working on a three shift basis.
[†] Firms' taxes and social service payments including payroll taxes and social insurance contributions, as a percentage of gross earnings. ** In the case of Singapore, the social payments are included in the gross earnings figures.
SOURCE   Cable and Baker, 1983, Table 49, p. 53.

developing countries in Table 5.2, with the exception of Singapore, social payments tend to be low (specific figures are unfortunately only available for Morocco and Hong Kong). The gap between West Germany and North Africa is lower: hourly earnings are 11 times higher in West Germany than in Morocco, and 8.5 times higher than in Tunisia. The earnings gap between France and North Africa is even lower — but the burden of social payments is much higher in France. The UK has considerably lower wage costs than Germany and France. Earnings in the UK are only 2.8 times earnings in Hong Kong, which has the highest earnings among the developing countries in the table; taking account of social payments would widen that gap somewhat.

It is more difficult to make comparisons for the clothing industry because the large numbers of small firms make data collection difficult. Table 5.3 gives some estimates for average hourly earnings in the clothing industry for a more limited selection of countries. Average earnings are lower in clothing than in textiles; there may also be a tendency for the gap between developed and developing countries to be wider than in textiles. Comparing the USA with Hong Kong,

TABLE 5.3   *Average hourly earnings in the clothing industry*

	Year	US $
USA	1980	4.57
Hong Kong	1980	1.03
South Korea	1980	0.59
Philippines	1978	0.17
Singapore	1980	0.80
Sri Lanka	1981	0.12

SOURCE   Edgren, 1982, p. 20.

South Korea and Singapore, hourly earnings in textiles are 2.9 times those in Hong Kong, 6.7 times those in South Korea, and 5.6 times those in Singapore; but in clothing they are 4.4 times those in Hong Kong, 7.7 times those in South Korea, and 5.7 times those in Singapore (calculated from figures in Tables 5.2 and 5.3).[4] A comparison of average hourly wages in the UK and Hong Kong clothing industry (Chisholm, Kabeer, Mitter and Howard, 1986, p. 39) suggests wages in the UK are about 4 times those in Hong Kong, which again is higher than the ratio for textiles of 2.8. This may reflect the higher proportion of semi-skilled women workers in clothing than in textiles. Some case studies of other industries suggest that the wage gap between developed and developing countries may be greater for semi-skilled women and unskilled female workers than for other groups (see chapter 7 of this volume). Unfortunately, no international comparisons are available for the textile and clothing industry disaggregating earnings data by gender and skill level. At this stage it seems reasonable to hypothesise that women's semi-skilled and unskilled labour in the developing countries is particularly cheap, but the testing of this hypothesis requires further research.

There is evidence that at least one major textile and clothing multinational, Scottish-based Coats Patons, does regularly compare the labour costs of thread production at various sites around the world for use as a management tool in making production and investment decisions (*Financial Times*, 29 June 1981). Moreover, it is well known that Triumph International, the German-owned underwear producer, has extensively relocated production away from its home base to export platforms in the developing countries. In 1965 the company employed 18 000 people (the vast majority women) of whom 13 200 were in Germany and 4800 abroad. By 1983 total employment was up to 19 370, but only 2600 were employed in Germany and 16 770 were employed abroad. Employment in the Federal Republic of Germany has thus fallen from 75 per cent of the total in 1965 to only 13 per cent in 1983 (ITGLWF, 1984, p. 70). Plants have been opened in Brazil, Argentina, Thailand, the Philippines, Malaysia and Pakistan. The company also has extensive co-production agreements with Hungarian enterprises. Wage costs have been suggested as the crucial factor in the move abroad (Fröbel, Heinrich and Kreye, 1981, p. 125).

It seems clear that Triumph International has transferred jobs abroad, in the sense that it has closed down plants in Germany and drastically reduced employment there, while opening up plants abroad and rapidly expanding overseas employment. It cannot be argued in this case that while employment has expanded abroad, it has also expanded domestically. However, it might be argued that the company had little alternative; that the only way to preserve its profitability, and hence retain at least some jobs in its home country, was to transfer most of its employment abroad. A few studies do exist which try to test such hypotheses, and they have generally concluded that only a fraction of the jobs lost in home countries might actually have been saved had the multinational pursued different strategies (ILO, 1984, p. 20). However, the methodological basis for any such studies is highly debatable, since it is not clear which are the appropriate counter-factual assumptions (ILO, 1981, pp. 78–86).

This chapter will therefore not attempt to assess the extent of 'avoidable' job export arising from the actions of multinationals in the EEC textile and clothing industry. Rather it seeks to assess whether the role of multinational firms in the EEC textile and clothing industry can be adequately explained in terms of a model which places the main emphasis on multinationals moving their plant out of the EEC in search of cheap female labour in the southern Mediterranean, Eastern Europe, Latin America and the Far East. Or are the patterns of multinational operations and the strategies they pursue more complex than that?

THE IMPORTANCE OF MULTINATIONALS IN THE EEC TEXTILE AND CLOTHING INDUSTRY

There are no statistics which can immediately tell us what proportion of employment and output in the EEC textile and clothing industry is accounted for by multinationals, so a qualitative picture has to be pieced together from a diversity of sources. The traditional view of the industry is that apart from a few large international firms producing artificial fibres, most of the industry consists of a large number of small and medium sized firms operating on a purely national basis.

Most textile and clothing enterprises appear to have made only limited use of direct foreign investment abroad in the last 10 to 15 years (OECD, 1983, p. 57). However, other forms of internationalisation of production have been important, such as co-production deals with enterprises in Eastern Europe and Yugoslavia; offshore processing, in which raw materials and components are sent 'off shore' for making up by firms which are not necessarily subsidiaries of the supplier of inputs; and international commercial subcontracting in which European principals place contracts with firms oversea for the supply of specified items which they then market. These forms of internationalisation of production are mainly concentrated in clothing and knitwear.

Offshore processing (or outward processing as it is sometimes called) has been encouraged in some countries by special provisions in the tariff structure. These allow for the reimport of the processed goods at advantageous rates because tariffs are only levied on the value added offshore, and not on the total value of the product including the materials and components originally sent offshore.

In the EEC, Germany and The Netherlands have had such special provisions for several years. In 1978 12.5 per cent of imports of clothing into Germany came in under the offshore processing provisions (OECD, 1983, p. 27). The bulk of German offshore processing takes place in Eastern Europe and Yugoslavia though some is in North Africa. France is a relative newcomer in the offshore processing field but between 1977 and 1979 the share of offshore processing in total imports of ladies clothing increased from 5 per cent to more than 7 per cent. The most rapidly expanding suppliers were Morocco Tunisia and Portugal (OECD, 1983, p. 61). In The Netherlands nearly 15 per cent of all clothing imports in 1975 came from Eastern Europe and most of them had been manufactured under outward processing arrangements (ILO, 1980, p. 15). According to official sources, the UK has no important involvement with offshore processing (OECD, 1983, p. 61). The UK has no special tariff provision for offshore processing, and hence collects no official data on it. Nevertheless, UK firms do send garments abroad for making up especially in Mediterranean countries such as Malta and Cyprus

(Phizacklea, 1984; Chisholm, Kabeer, Mitter and Howard, 1986). However, it is impossible to quantify the extent of this practice. No general statistics are available on forms of international commercial subcontracting from EEC countries which do not entail the outward shipment of materials, though such commercial subcontracting is probably substantial.

The development of these forms of internationalisation blurs the distinction between uninational and multinational firms. If a simple 'threshold' definition of the multinational enterprise is used, such as 'a multinational enterprise is one which owns or controls income-earning assets in more than one nation', then many medium and small EEC clothing firms would qualify as multinationals because through offshore processing or international subcontracting they do control income-earning assets abroad. Provision of credit, raw materials, technical assistance and quality supervision may make control over the subcontractor almost complete, though there is no obvious formal relationship. A recent study of the German clothing industry concluded that while German clothing firms are only moderately involved in direct foreign investment through their own subsidiaries, they have at least one-third of their production done abroad through subcontracting arrangements; of this overseas production, the amount carried out through legally independent companies in developing countries is about six times the amount of their own production in foreign subsidiaries (ITGLWF, 1984, pp. 3–4). A typical case would be the Seidensticker Group, producing shirts and women's wear. Since 1975 80 per cent of their shirts have come from abroad, but the company does not *own* any production facilities in low-wage countries.

If we adopt a more restricted definition of 'multinational' in which a company must legally own subsidiaries in other countries to count as a multinational, then, of course, the number of multinationals is much smaller. A distinction may be drawn between textile and clothing multinationals and artificial fibre multinationals. The latter are really part of the chemical industry, and only a small part of their total output consists of fibres. The distinction is not quite water tight because Courtaulds, the world's largest textile and clothing multinational, is also a major producer of artificial fibres.

Artificial fibre production is dominated by multinationals. The 12 biggest companies account for roughly 60 per cent of world fibre production (ITGLWF, 1984, p. 77). The largest artificial fibre companies active in the EEC are Enka (owned by the Dutch company

TABLE 5.4   *Employment in artificial fibre production in selected EEC countries*

	1976	1982
Benelux	13 545	8 620
France	18 400	8 567
Germany	40 200	27 200
Ireland	800	1 540
Italy	38 300	22 952
UK	32 979	11 236

SOURCE   ITGLWF, 1984, p. 94.

AKZO); Rhone Poulenc (French); ICI (British); Hoechst (German); Montefibre (Italian); Sniafibre (Italian); Bayer (German); Du Pont (American) and Monsanto (American). Each has plants in other EEC countries as well as in their home bases and outside Europe. The world recession has seen the development of massive over capacity in artificial fibres, and these firms have shed thousands of jobs in the 1970s as reflected in the figures in Table 5.4. The only exception is Ireland where total employment rose between 1976 and 1982. A Japanese multinational, the Asahi Chemical Industry Company, began operating two plants in Ireland in 1977, making and spinning acrylic fibre. The spinning plant employs about 200 people, with women in the majority; far fewer women are employed at the fibre processing plant (about 300 employees) (ILO, 1984, p. 54 and pp. 157–199). The availability of cheap female labour was not the motivation for the move: the key factor was securing a foothold in the European market. It has also been suggested that a more lenient anti-pollution policy and generous tax incentives played a part (ITGLWF, 1984, p. 24). For reasons of space, we shall not consider the artificial fibre multinationals in any more detail.

The textile and clothing multinationals are far less dominant, and account for a much smaller share of output and employment in their industry. There are no figures available for all the EEC countries which directly show the proportions, but the evidence in Tables 5.5 and 5.6 give some indications. Table 5.5 shows concentration characteristics, and while large firms are not necessarily multinational firms, there is considerable overlap. The European country with the greatest concentration is the UK. Table 5.6 shows the importance of multinationals in the UK textile industry, and in the clothing, leather

TABLE 5.5   *Concentration characteristics of selected European textile industries*

	Germany (1976)	France (1978)	Italy (1978)	UK (1978)
Employment (000s)				
Largest 3 firms	21	68	16	199
Largest 5 firms	32	83	24	256
Largest 10 firms	57	94	37	304
Ratio of employment in largest firms to total textile employment (%)				
Largest 3 firms	6	12	5	44
Largest 5 firms	10	14	8	56
Largest 10 firms	17	16	12	67
Total number of firms with turnover exceeding US $ 500 million	0	4	0	5

SOURCE   OECD, 1983, p. 26

TABLE 5.6   *Distribution of textile and clothing employment by type of firm, UK, 1975*

	UK national firms (%)	UK multinationals (%)	Foreign multinationals (%)
Textiles	69	27	4
Leather, clothing and footwear	80	18	2

SOURCE   Calculated from Stopford, 1979, Table 15, p. 40.

and footwear industry.[5] In the UK multinationals are more important in textiles than in clothing, and UK multinationals are more important than foreign multinationals. The pattern for other EEC countries is likely to be the same, with national firms playing an even larger role.

The presence of foreign multinationals should be noted. This means it is not simply a matter of each country's own multinationals deciding whether to locate its plant at home or in a 'cheap labour'

TABLE 5.7   *Major textile and clothing multinationals in the EEC*

Company	Country of origin	No. employees in 1980	Areas of overseas investment within EEC
Courtaulds	UK	153 003	Ireland, France, Italy, Germany
Coats Patons	UK	60 000	Belgium, Germany, Italy
Tootal	UK	29 400[1]	Ireland, Germany, Netherlands
Agache Willot	France	44 700[2]	Germany, Belgium, Italy, UK
Prouvost	France	28 100[2]	Belgium, Germany
Dollfus-Mieg	France	20 955	Belgium, Italy, Denmark, Germany
Bidermann	France	n.a.	UK, Belgium
Triumph	Germany	19 370[3]	UK, France, Italy
Freudenberg	Germany	23 900	UK, Belgium, France
Nino	Germany	n.a.	Ireland, France, Italy, Netherlands
Levi Strauss	USA	48 000	Belgium, UK, France
Blue Bell	USA	35 000	Belgium, UK
Vanity Fair	USA	19 400	UK, Germany, Ireland, France
Burlington Industries	USA	65 000	Germany,[4] France,[4] UK,[4] Ireland, Italy

1. Employment data is for 1980–81, taken from Tootal Annual Report.
2. Data is for 1982, from ITGLWF, 1984, p. 63.
3. Data is for 1983, from ITGLWF, 1984, p. 70.
4. Since 1979, Burlington has moved out of Germany, France and the UK.
SOURCE ITGLWF, 1984; ILO, 1984, p. 18, for employment data, except where noted.

country in the Far East, or Eastern Europe, or the Mediterranean. Many of the major EEC multinationals have plants in other EEC countries; and there has been inward investment from US multinationals.

The most important textile and clothing multinationals operating in the EEC are listed in Table 5.7. They can be divided into clothing firms and firms which engage in a whole range of activities including production of fibres and fabrics, household linens and furnishings, and clothing. In the first category come the jeans multinationals, Levi Strauss, Blue Bell and Vanity Fair; and Bidermann (making up-market men's and women's clothing and uniforms) and Triumph (specialising in underwear). In the second category come Courtaulds (which also has extensive chemical interests and is the only artificial fibre manufacturer in this group), Coats Patons, Tootal, Agache Willot, Prouvost, Dollfus-Mieg, Freudenberg, Nino and Burlington.

Only five of these companies are included in the 500 largest multinationals analysed in Stopford and Dunning, 1983; namely, Courtaulds, Coats Patons, Burlington, Levi Strauss and Blue Bell. As multinationals go, most of them are quite small, and the foreign operations of some of them are quite limited.

THE ROLE OF AMERICAN MULTINATIONALS

The American firms are in Europe principally for access to European markets, though they show a clear tendency to locate their plant within Europe in areas where wages are lowest and governments offer substantial incentives for firms setting up plants; for instance, the Levi Strauss factories in the UK are in the economically depressed north — in North Shields, Glasgow and Dundee. Levi Strauss, together with the other two big jeans multinationals, Blue Bell (makers of Wrangler) and the Vanity Fair Corporation (makers of Lee Jeans) plan their operations on a worldwide scale, taking advantage of new technology to economise in skilled male labour in design, pattern making and cutting; and of locations where female labour is cheap and ununionised for making up. The workforce in jeans factories is predominantly female — as much as 80–90 per cent of the labour force (Bradley, 1983).

Levi Strauss, the world's largest clothing firm, had 104 manufacturing plants in 1983. Of these, 66 were in the USA, mainly in the southern states, and 38 were abroad — 15 of them in Europe; in Belgium, the UK and France. To some extent the 'search for cheap female labour in developing countries' model does fit Levi Strauss: the company has a very large plant in Mexico[6] and plants in Southeast Asia co-ordinated from Hong Kong. A plant was opened in the Philippines in 1972 to produce for both the European and the local market; 95 per cent of the labour force are young women, mostly in their early 20s, who have migrated from rural areas (Enloe, 1983). Production in the Philippines begins with cutting denim cotton imported from Japan according to patterns sent from the company headquarters in San Francisco. All the cutters are men, as is typical in garment production. Using machines imported from the USA and thread made by a Philippines subsidiary of the British multinational, Tootal, women stitch jeans. Special equipment is used to insert copper rivets at stress points, and to install zippers. Finally the jeans are washed and pressed; all the pressers are men. The cutters and pressers are the highest paid workers in the factory. The average pay for all the shop-floor workers in the factory in 1980 was $22 a week. Levi Strauss also has jeans produced in Hungary under a co-production agreement.

Trade unions are recognised in some Levi Strauss factories and according to the International Textile, Garment and Leather Workers Federation, the company does not engage in massive anti-union campaigns (ITGLWF, 1984, p. 50). However, according to grass roots union activists in the USA, the company has employed 'industrial relations consultants' (described by the workers as 'union busters') to undermine the strength of particularly well organised sections of workers. It is claimed that of Levi's 66 plants in the USA, only about 20 were unionised by the early 1980s and that Levi's has a goal of no unions in any of Levi's plants in the USA by 1990 (Chapkis, 1983). Recently, Levi Strauss has been hit by changes in consumer tastes away from blue jeans and has closed 10 per cent of its production capacity in the highest labour cost areas of the USA and Europe.

The second largest firm in blue jeans is Blue Bell, makers of Wrangler Jeans. In 1983 it employed 27 000 people in 95 plants and 49 warehouses. Within the USA its operations are concentrated in locations where labour is cheaper — 21 of its operations are in North Carolina, and five in Puerto Rico — but it has no plants in Latin America or Southeast Asia. In Europe it has factories in Belgium, the UK, Spain and Malta. According to the International Textile, Garment and Leather Workers Federation, it is determinedly non-union (ITGLWF, 1984, p. 50). Blue Bell has extensive licensing agreements, whereby it sells for royalties the right to produce goods under its trade mark to independently-owned companies in about 50 countries. For instance, it has a licensing agreement with the Japanese textile multinational Toyobo, which makes both fabrics and garments, and has overseas interests in both Latin America and Southeast Asia.

The third biggest jeans multinational is the Vanity Fair (VF) Corporation. In 1980 it had 34 factories in the USA and 19 abroad, in Canada, Belgium, the UK, Ireland and Hong Kong, employing in all about 18 500 workers (Counter Information Services and War on

Want, 1981). The company also has joint ventures and affiliates operating in Australia, Africa, Asia, Brazil, Finland, Japan, South Africa and Spain. Within Europe location decisions have been affected by government investment incentives, as well as labour costs. In 1970 the company set up a factory at Greenock, Scotland, employing 240 workers, mainly women, in an area of high unemployment. The building was provided by the local authority free of rent and rates for the first three years; and the British Government provided investment grants which covered 40 per cent of the cost of plant and machinery. Wages were subsidised under a Regional Employment Premium; cheap loans were available and there were substantial tax rebates. Three-quarters of production was exported, mainly to Scandinavia. In 1981 the company announced the closure of the Greenock factory, even though its productivity record was as good as or better than that of the other company plants in the UK. The company preferred to concentrate production in Northern Ireland, where it had sewing factories and where it had recently opened a cutting factory and a distribution centre. In Northern Ireland the incentives for investors were even more generous (Counter Information Services and War on Want, 1981).

Trade union activities are not encouraged in the VF Corporation's plants in the USA, which are mainly in the South. However, the Greenock plant, known as the Lee Jeans factory, was organised by the National Union of Tailor and Garment Workers. The Greenock women responded to the closure announcement with a factory occupation that lasted seven months.[7] They felt that there was little chance of finding alternative employment, and with high levels of male unemployment, many families were wholly dependent on women's earnings. They were also convinced that their productivity was as high as that of the factories in Ireland. They felt they were unfairly being made redundant by a company strategy decided at headquarters in Pennsylvania, USA, which took no account of the contribution they had made to the company's profits. If orders for jeans were falling because of the recession, then their proposal was for work sharing throughout all the UK plants, and requests for a temporary employment subsidy from the government's programme of assistance to depressed regions.

The opposition of the Lee Jeans women to the closure of their factory attracted local and national trade union and public support. The women were unable to convince the VF Corporation to change its plans, but their actions did pressure the company to sell the plant to a group of former managers (who had formed a company called Inverwear) rather than transfer the machinery to their other factories in Northern Ireland. All the 140 women who had sustained the occupation through to the end were employed in Inverwear. A key factor in securing this result was the adverse publicity Lee Jeans received, which the company was worried would affect sales of their product.

It appears that the combination of worker militancy and the adverse publicity Lee Jeans was receiving from the War on Want/ CIS report, caused them finally to capitulate. Even large companies are vulnerable to bad press, particularly when it might make consumers think twice about buying their product.

(Bradley, 1983)

The jeans multinationals produce long runs of products in relatively standardised form, and as a result have been able to take advantage of new micro-electronic based technology which requires high initial outlays. Computer aided interactive graphics and numerically controlled machine tools have had considerable impact on pattern grading, marking and cutting, leading to considerable increases in the speed and accuracy of the pre-sewing stage of production. Most of this equipment is in the price range $250 000–$600 000, so it only makes economic sense for large multi-plant firms, with turnovers starting at $20 million (Rush and Soete, 1984). This kind of equipment economises on male labour, and in some cases may lead to some displacement of traditionally skilled craftsmen by lower-price women trained to operate the new technology (Cockburn, 1985).

STRATEGIES OF EUROPEAN MULTINATIONALS

Some of the European multinationals have set up garment factories in developing countries to produce for export. The case of Triumph International was mentioned earlier. The French garment firm Bidermann, which manufactures clothes under internationally known designer labels such as Yves St. Laurent, also has an agreement with the government of Viet Nam to set up a shirt factory near Hanoi employing 400 people and producing 500 000 shirts a year — half the total shirt production of the firm (ILO, 1980, p. 15).

Another example is Baird Textiles,[8] a division of William Baird Ltd, a company whose main activities are in engineering. Baird Textiles in 1978 purchased 80 per cent of the Intercontinental Garments Manufacturing Co. (IGMC), sited in the Bataan Export Processing Zone in the Philippines.[9] The IGMC factory produces garments (mainly raincoats and lightweight jackets) to designs sent from the UK with machines supplied from Japan and material — cloth, zippers, buttons, and even thread — from Hong Kong. All of the output is exported; some to Australia and Europe, but most to Britain, where garments are checked, pressed, and packaged for delivery to major department stores, such as Debenhams, Littlewoods and C & A. The IGMC employs about 1300 workers, 90 per cent of them young women between the ages of 16 and 25. Their basic weekly wage in 1984 was about £7.00. Over a quarter of the labour force are probationers, who receive only 75 per cent of the basic wage. Contrary to some popular myths about the docility of Asian women workers, the workers at IGMC are well organised in a trade union. They played a leading role in the Zone-wide stoppage of workers in 1982 (*International Labour Report*, no. 10, July-August, 1985).

But although some cases can be found which fit the 'relocate factories in areas of cheap female labour' model, this is too simple an explanation for the strategies of the larger European integrated textiles to clothing multinationals. It is true that the largest of these, Courtaulds, has set up factories in Portugal, Morocco and Tunisia.[10] The Portuguese factory produces knitwear; in Morocco there is a stitching unit and an underwear factory (Courtaulds, 1984). So the advantages of using cheap female labour have played some part in Courtaulds' reckoning. But the overall strategy is more complex, with considerable emphasis being placed on diversification out of traditional textiles and into non-woven textiles, plastics, surface coatings (including specialised paints) and packaging materials. Courtaulds employment in the UK declined massively — from 124 000 in 1975 to 56 300 in 1984. But overseas employment also declined, from 31 000 in 1975 to 13 700 in 1984, leaving the proportions of home and overseas employment much the same (ITGLWF, 1984, p. 10).

Some companies have radically changed the proportions of home and overseas employment. Dollfus-Mieg had 78 per cent of its workforce in France in 1974 and 22 per cent abroad. By 1980 the proportions were 59 per cent in France and 41 per cent abroad (ILO,

1984, p. 15). Even greater is the redistribution which occurred in the workforce of Tootal between 1975 and 1981. The company Annual Report for 1981 states that in 1975 Tootal's workforce was 57 per cent in the UK and 43 per cent overseas; in 1981 only 30 per cent of Tootal's workforce was in the UK and 70 per cent of it was abroad. This redistribution involved an absolute fall in Tootal UK employment between 1975 and 1981 of about 4900 and an absolute rise of total overseas employment, that is, including associates as well as subsidiaries, of about 14 700. This looks like a massive transfer of jobs out of the UK. What factors account for this?

THE INTERNATIONALISATION OF TOOTAL,[11] 1973–84

In 1973 Tootal had factories in Australia, Canada, West Germany, Hong Kong, the Philippines, India, Indonesia, South Africa, the USA and Zaire; either wholly-owned subsidiaries, or, as in India and Indonesia, associated firms which were under the overall control of Tootal, though Tootal did not own a majority of the shares. The overseas factories were concentrated in thread production. They were geared to supplying local markets, not to exports. It was production in the UK which was geared to exports, as well as supplying the UK. There was no 'global sourcing' of thread: each factory had its own, largely local, market to supply. The overseas operations were organised in separate overseas divisions, rather than an integration of UK and overseas operations with divisional organisation along product lines.

The example of the Philippines factory shows how overseas operations were organised.[12] The Allied Thread Company was established as a wholly-owned subsidiary in the Philippines in September 1953, as a way of getting over the trade barriers erected by the Philippines against imported thread. It was a classic example of foreign investment to safeguard a market, induced by a policy of import substitution industrialisation in the host country. The Allied Thread Company is now the largest thread manufacturer in the Philippines, producing cotton, spun polyester and covespun threads for domestic and industrial users. Direct exports of thread remain small; most output is sold to the big industrial users in the Philippines — such as the US multinational jeans manufacturer, Levi Strauss, and the German multinational underwear manufacturer, Triumph International. The basic materials are imported by the company — cotton

TABLE 5.8   *Tootal's employment, 1973–84*

Year[1]	UK	Average Number of Employees per Week	
		Overseas including associates[2]	Overseas excluding associates
1973/74	20 001	n.a.	9 243
1975/76	19 507	14 600[3]	8 795
1977/78	20 397	n.a.	9 224
1978/79	20 213	n.a.	9 239
1979/80	17 578	21 822	9 162
1980/81	14 580	29 374	8 804
1981/82	10 995	30 460	6 874
1982/83	8 878	25 580	6 887
1983/84	8 595	13 721	6 334
1984/85	7 966	n.a.	5 935

1. The Tootal financial year finishes at the end of April.
2. Associate companies are companies where Tootal has a controlling interest but usually owns no more than 50 per cent of the shares.
3. This figure is the average for 1975 and is derived from the Annual Report for 1980/81.
SOURCE   Company Annual Reports.

from the USA and synthetic fibre from Japan. In 1978 the company employed 1600 people, of which 53 per cent were men, and 47 per cent women.

In 1973 the majority of Tootal employees were in the UK, but only 48 per cent of profits for the financial year 1973–74 came from the UK; 52 per cent came from overseas, the bulk of it from the USA and Australia, though a growing share was from Southeast Asia. As can be seen from Table 5.8, in the period up to the beginning of 1979 there was no dramatic run down in UK employment in total. However, investment was concentrated abroad in the period 1973–79. According to the Chairman of Tootal, 'our expansion was geared to remaining in markets in newly emerging countries by setting up production units there' (*Financial Times*, 11 June 1984). Existing factories in Asia were modernised and a new subsidiary was opened in 1975 in Malaysia to make thread for the Malaysian market. This investment was motivated, not by a search for cheap labour, but by the rapid expansion of the market for thread in Southeast Asia, as a result of the growth of the garment industry, coupled with the desire of governments in Southeast Asia for local production, rather than imports, of thread. This investment did little to expand Tootal's overseas employment. Expansion due to the opening of new factories seems to have been offset by redundancy due to re-equipment in others. The annual report for 1979–80 records a 25 per cent reduction in employment in the Philippines plant, due to modernisation.

But although there was not much overseas job *creation* by Tootal, there was a dramatic increase in overseas jobs *controlled* by Tootal. In 1978 Tootal acquired a 40 per cent controlling interest in Bradmill Industries in Australia, making it the largest textile presence in the country. This acquisition is responsible for the dramatic increase, shown in Table 5.8, in the number of overseas employees including those of associates, between 1975–76 and 1979–80. Two years later, in 1980, Tootal acquired a 50 per cent controlling interest in Da Gama, the largest domestic textile group in South Africa. This took overseas employment including associates up to over 29 000 in 1980–81. These two acquisitions meant that Tootal had gained control over more than 14 000 jobs overseas — but it had contributed little to job creation. By the time the acquisitions were completed, the UK economy was in serious recession, and the UK textile industry was in deep trouble. 1979 and 1980 were years of disaster for the UK textile industry. In a depressed domestic market, UK production was exposed to severe competition from imports — though what Tootal complained of was not low cost imports from Asia, but unfair subsidised competition from America, and also from Comecon countries making up garments for West German firms. In Tootal they were years of redundancies, rationalisation and reorganisation which left the company internationalised in a much more profound way than before. In 1980 three spinning mills, several fabric factories, including both weaving and printing, and various clothing factories were closed. Spinning in the UK was concentrated on two modern mills located outside the traditional base in North West England, one being at Belper in Derbyshire and one at Lisnaskea in Northern Ireland. £5 million was spent on new equipment housed in purpose-built single-storey premises, so that a much smaller labour force could produce more thread.

At the same time the management structure of the company was reorganised. Four divisions were created: Thread, Textiles, Clothing and Non-Wovens. Organised around product lines, they spanned national boundaries. This clearly facilitated the comparison of costs and productivity around the world, so it is not surprising that 1980 also saw the beginning of global sourcing of thread within the company.[13] It was reported that a large order from Morocco would be supplied from Tootal's plants in the USA and Malaysia as well as the UK, whereas before overseas plants tended to supply only their own domestic markets. Tootal plans to supply standard yarn around the world, with marketing and sourcing co-ordinated from the headquarters of the Thread Division (*Financial Times*, 30 September 1980). By 1984 Tootal was sourcing two million kilos of spun polyester yarn for Tootal Thread in Hong Kong and Southeast Asia from the People's Republic of China. In 1985 Tootal signed a joint-venture agreement to set up a new thread mill in Canton. A third of the output will be sold in China, and the rest exported to other Tootal companies, especially those in Southeast Asia where Tootal does not have enough capacity to meet rapidly growing demand. The company has stated that it is confident the new joint-venture will enable it to produce spun polyester thread significantly cheaper than at present. However, global sourcing does not mean an end to new investment in the UK. Construction of a new computerised, automated thread dye-house was begun in 1984 near Glasgow. This will enable the rapid production of non-standard colours for the specialised, fragmented European market, but it will not create many jobs.

The internationalisation of the company has not, however, resulted in the relocating of any of its clothing factories abroad. Unlike some of the companies discussed earlier, Tootal does not own any clothing factories in developing countries. It does not design and cut out clothing in the UK, send it abroad for making up, and reimport it for sale in the UK. Instead of setting up new factories abroad, Tootal has pursued a two-pronged strategy of commercial subcontracting, both internationally and within the UK; and of investment in new technology, often in new factories, for its own in-house production in the UK.

Commercial subcontracting, in which smaller independently owned firms are contracted to produce to the design and specification of a larger firm which then markets the product as its own, is common in the clothing industry. The French Federation of Textile and Allied Workers suggests that the French multinational Dollfus-Mieg normally produces about 70–80 per cent of its output in-house, while the remaining 20–30 per cent is produced by subcontractors. This enables the multinational to stabilise its employment and production in the face of demand fluctuations, and to complete its product range in fashion wear. It is the subcontractors and their employees which bear the brunt of fluctuations (ILO, 1984).

Tootal has substantial subcontracting activities within the UK. Its subsidiary, Raysil Gowns Ltd, is one of the major middlemen in the London clothing industry. Raysil Gowns supplies fashion dresses and separates for the cheaper end of the market, selling both under its own brand name, and also supplying garments for sale under their own labels to major retailers, including C & A, Woolworth, Tesco, British Home Stores, Mothercare, and mail order firms like Great Universal. However, the actual production is subcontracted to about 20 small firms in London, which are supplied with designs and cloth and merely 'cut, make and trim' (Chisholm, Kabeer, Mitter and Howard, 1986). Working conditions and wages in small London 'cut, make and trim' firms are substantially worse than those of employees of larger firms in London and the rest of the UK which do not work on subcontract to wholesalers (Greater London Council, Industry and Employment Branch, 1985). There is considerable employment of women from ethnic minority communities living in the immediate vicinity of the factories (Cypriot, Turkish, Bangladeshi, Vietnamese). Machining is often further subcontracted from the small factories to women working in their own homes, on very low rates of pay. Commercial subcontracting within the UK enables multinationals to tap sources of cheap female Third World labour without any necessity to set up factories abroad (Phizacklea, 1984; Mitter, 1985).

International commercial subcontracting also obviates the necessity to set up factories abroad. Tootal Lebel, based in Hong Kong, sources ranges of garments for the UK, Australia and New Zealand from locally-owned Far Eastern firms.

Tootal's in-house clothing production has remained in the UK. The lynchpin of the strategy here is the Slimma subsidiary supplying the more up-market British retailer, Marks and Spencer, with own-label men's and women's wear. This is the fastest growing and most successful of the garment operations; by 1984 it accounted for one-third of Tootal clothing sales and employed over 2000 people (about a quarter of Tootal UK employment). Marks and Spencer, which purchases around 20 per cent of UK clothing output, has operated, up to now, a 'Buy British' policy. The reasons are not those of patriotism, but rather of quality control. The firm sets very exacting quality standards and works very closely with its suppliers in planning production. Exact specifications are set out for an acceptable item — number of stitches to an inch, number of inches in a hem, and so on. Marks and Spencer inspectors expect to have a free run of the factory. As a woman supervisor in a knitwear factory put it:

Marks and Spencer are coming in to look around so you have to get the place tidied up and the floors polished. Its not so bad if its Tesco. We might just throw the rubbish away and that's it. But with quality, you know if its good enough for M & S, its good enough for anyone. (Davidson, Keating, Richardson and Truman, 1986)

The enormous purchasing power of Marks and Spencer enables it to drive a hard bargain over prices. To make profits out of supplying Marks and Spencer requires very fast, highly accurate work.[14] Tootal has chosen to make substantial investment in new micro-electronic technology for production planning, designing, patternmaking and cutting, in order to secure this. The search for cheaper labour is not the only strategy that makes sense in clothing production.

Thus the overall contraction in Tootal's UK labour force, and the internationalisation of the company's internal organisation mask a variety of tendencies[15]: expansion of thread production in developing countries, but primarily motivated by the growth of the market for thread in Southeast Asia; expansion of some clothing production (Slimma), contraction of others (men's shirts, for instance), and recourse to commercial subcontracting both in the UK and overseas for the cheaper end of the market, but no relocation of factories to developing countries.

Redundancies and rationalisation were not confined to the UK. Following the major contraction in the UK workforce (a reduction of over 9000 between 1978–79 and 1981–82, came a contraction in the total overseas workforce (a reduction of nearly 5000 between 1981–82 and 1982–83). The American subsidiary, the American Thread Company, was re-equipped and the workforce reduced from 3500 to 2800. The Australian Bradmill and the South African Da Gama operations were rationalised, the workforce at Da Gama being cut by 40 per cent in two years. Having acquired control over thousands of jobs in Australia and South Africa, Tootal was busy eliminating many of them. A further fall in overseas employment occurred when Tootal decided it could not rationalise the Bradmill operations enough to generate the profits it required, and sold out its share to an Australian firm. So by 1983–84 total overseas employment was in absolute terms reduced below its level in 1975 — but since UK employment also continued to fall, 70 per cent of Tootal total employment remained overseas.

The sale of Bradmill set the seal on Tootal's transformation from a production oriented company to one with a marketing-finance orientation. The Chairman in the 1970s was a textiles specialist who had been with the company for 32 years; the Chairman in the early 1980s was the former finance director, who recruited young managers into the company who are not textile specialists but have experience in international marketing and finance (*Financial Times*, 6 February 1985).

To some extent the Tootal strategy has sought to take advantage of cheaper sources of labour; for instance, through commercial subcontracting in both the Far East and London; and expanding its thread production capacity in the Far East and Southeast Asia. But in the case of thread, it is the *local* markets in the Far East and Southeast Asia which have been the primary pull. In its clothing strategy, investment in new technology in the UK and the development of close relations with a major UK retailer has been even more important than a search for cheap labour.

The restructuring of Tootal was accomplished without any major disputes with the UK labour force. Tootal's directly employed workforce in the UK was, and remains, unionised. But there was no reaction to closures comparable to that of the Lee Jeans workers. This may be connected with the fact that whereas Lee Jeans was known by its workforce to be a growing and profitable company, Tootal in 1979–81, when most of the closures took place, was faced with a sharp decline in profitability, and was perceived as being hit by external forces (the recession, cheap imports) over which it had no control.

A NEW TYPE OF MULTINATIONAL: THE CASE OF BENETTON

Benetton has grown from a small Italian family business in 1965 to Europe's largest clothing producer. It produces knitwear, trousers, shirts, blouses and skirts. It has eight factories in the north of Italy; one in France and one in Scotland. But much more important to its operations is the network of small Italian workshops to which it 'puts out' production. It is estimated that in 1981 Benetton directly employed 1600 people in northern Italy; but through subcontracting arrangements with 250 small factories and workshops, indirectly employed more than 10 000 (ITGLWF, 1984, p. 103).

Benetton's output is sold without the involvement of any inter-mediaries through the worldwide network of 3200 Benetton shops in 57 countries. Benetton owns directly about 200 shops in Italy and another 20 in the UK and France. The others, including shops in Japan and the USA, are operated under franchises.

Micro-electronics technology is vital to the Benetton operation — but in marketing, distribution, designing, pattern laying and cutting, rather than assembly operations. At the Italian headquarters is a computer that is linked to an electronic cash register in every Bene-tton shop; those which are far away, like Tokyo and Washington are linked via satellite. Every outlet transmits detailed information on sales daily, and production is continuously and flexibly adjusted to meet the preferences revealed in the market. Benetton produces entirely to the orders received from the shops. An automated ware-house has been constructed which is operated by two technicians, each of whom, aided by 13 robots, is capable of unloading and loading a juggernaut in 30 minutes (Mitter, 1985).

Benetton's enormous success is based on a combination of control and flexibility: control over distribution and retailing and design, and flexibility in production. By using a network of subcontractors and franchises, Benetton is able to hold down overheads, avoid the problems of managing a large labour force, and enjoy the lower costs and greater flexibility of small firms and workshops. It can control *without* owning because of its possession of the information vital for both successful production and successful retailing. It can be a 'good employer', paying higher wages and benefits to its small number of direct employees, while avoiding responsibility for the lower wages and poorer benefits of its outworkers. The International Textile, Garment and Leather Workers Federation sees Benetton as 'prob-ably a model example of the apparel manufacturer of the future'. Benetton's success shows that it is possible for European clothing multinationals to prosper without locating factories in developing countries, or subcontracting to producers in the Far East or Eastern Europe. But is such success dependent on locating new sources of cheap labour within the EEC itself? It would be interesting to know a lot more about the wages and conditions of work of the women working for Benetton's subcontractors.

CONCLUSIONS

The strategies of multinationals in the textile and clothing industry of the EEC cannot simply be reduced to a movement of production overseas in search of cheap female labour. The evidence discussed here shows a much more complex picture; for some types of firm and some types of activity, relocation in search of cheaper labour outside the EEC does play a role, but for the major multinationals access to markets is an important factor in location of plant, not just labour costs. The introduction of new technology in production, and the reorganisation of the links between production and consumption, on the basis of the new information technology, are also significant. Increasingly, multinationals are defining their function not in terms of the *production* of yarns, or fabrics, or clothing, but in terms of the *co-ordination* of decentralised, frequently subcontracted, production, with a much greater emphasis on marketing and finance. Joint ventures, minority holdings, licensing agreements, subcontracting and outwork all seem to be of increasing significance, though it is impossible to be definitive because of the reluctance of companies to make sufficient information public.

Where does this leave women working for multinationals in the EEC textile and garment industry? Most women directly employed by multinationals appear to be members of trade unions, though some of the US-owned textile and clothing multinationals have a reputation for being anti-trade union (ITGLWF, 1984). A recent ILO report concluded, on the basis of very fragmentary evidence, that multinationals in the sector are generally in line with national standards established as a result of collective bargaining or labour legislation (ILO, 1984, p. 151). The earnings of women in the textile and garment industry are generally less than those of men, but there is no evidence to suggest that the earnings gap is any different in multinational firms compared to uninational firms.

There is nothing to suggest that multinationals are worse employers than uninational firms in the textile and clothing industry; indeed they may well offer higher pay and better working conditions to their direct employees. But they are, after all, generally more powerful than uninational firms, with greater resources at their disposal. With greater power and greater resources, must surely go greater social responsibility. Women working for textile and garment multinationals often feel like pawns in some global strategy as plants are closed here and opened there; bought here and sold there; by corporate decision-makers who are remote from the workplace and who operate according to a strategic logic which often has little to do with the productivity of individual plants.

The rights of workers, not just the rights of shareholders, should be recognised as multinationals reorganise their activities in response to the changing competitive pressures they face. There are three things that could be done to give greater recognition to the rights of workers. The first is full disclosure of relevant information: the Lee Jeans women felt very bitter about the failure of the company to keep them informed. Many felt they had been deliberately misled; when they had raised questions about the implications of the company's Northern Ireland operations for its commitment to Greenock, they had been told that there was no threat to their jobs. When management informed the women, in January 1981, that the plant was to close, they were stunned.

The second is safeguarding the rights of the workforce when factories are acquired by other companies through sales or take-over bids. Change of ownership frequently results in changes in conditions of work, and numbers of jobs. Acquisitions and mergers play a much more important role in multinationals' foreign investment than opening new factories. As the *Financial Times* has pointed out, most employees have a deeper commitment to the company that employs them than do most shareholders who can switch their funds elsewhere (*Financial Times*, 2 September 1986). Yet frequently employees are bought and sold as assets of the company that employs them. Former Tootal garment workers in Bury, Lancashire, are a case in point. The Tootal factory in which they worked was sold and they were, in their view, sold with it, on the understanding that they would be doing similar work for the new owners, and continue to enjoy trade union representation. According to them, neither condition was met. The new owner reputedly said, 'I don't know what you have been told but I will have no dealings with unions'. In The Netherlands, employees at least have a statutory right to be consulted before the ownership of the company for which they work changes hands.

The third is requiring multinationals to take some responsibility for the rights of workers employed by their subcontractors, subsidiaries and associates. The pattern seems to be for multinationals in the textile and garment industry to employ fewer and fewer workers directly, but to have a determining influence through marketing and licensing over the fortunes of many workers employed by subcontractors and subsidiaries and associates. Companies should not be able to wash their hands of any responsibility for the rights and conditions of work of those they 'indirectly' employ. The same codes of conduct that govern their dealings with their direct employees should be insisted on for subcontractors and subsidiaries and associates. Without this there is bound to be suspicion (cf. ITGLWF, 1984, p. 51) that textile and clothing multinationals pose as good employers with a concern for the jobs of their direct employees while getting their 'dirty work' done by formally independent associates and subcontractors.

It seems highly unlikely that textile and garment multinationals will move all their production 'offshore' (Hoffman, 1985; Zeitlin, 1985). The EEC will continue to have a textile and garment industry employing large numbers of women. The danger is that the balance between 'primary sector' or 'core' jobs (those which offer a reasonable wage, some stability of employment, and a full range of rights and welfare benefits) and 'secondary sector' or 'peripheral' jobs (those which offer low wages, little stability, few rights and welfare benefits) will deteriorate. A growing proportion of women may be in the 'secondary sector'. Multinationals in the industry insist that they do not discriminate against women in their employ (ILO, 1984). Judging by the criterion of equal pay for men and women doing the same job, there is no reason to doubt this. But multinationals should also be aware of the indirect discrimination which occurs when worse pay and conditions are attached to jobs which the unequal burden of domestic responsibilities means are more likely to be done by women than men — in particular to jobs in small neighbourhood workshops and to part-time work and outwork of various kinds. If the model for the future is the combination of centralisation of planning and marketing and decentralisation of production, embodied in Benetton, care must be taken that decentralisation to small associate units does not mean indirect discrimination against thousands of women, who while they are employed in the geographic 'core' of Europe, are nevertheless at the 'periphery' of the labour force.

NOTES

1. I should like to thank the following for information and comments which have helped me in the preparation of this chapter: Peter Lloyd, John Shutt, Harvey Ramsey, Annie Phizacklea, Joan Keating, Colin Kirkpatrick, Ian Steedman and Lyndon Moore.

2. The statistics presented here have been calculated from Eurostat, 1986, Tables II/7, II/9 and III/5, for the Europe of the Nine.
3. Wages here includes *all* payments made to employees, including basic wages, bonuses, cost of living allowances, holiday pay, sick pay, and payments in kind; and tax and social insurance contributions deducted from employees' pay. It does not include employers' tax and social insurance contributions.
4. UNIDO, 1983, p. 235, reports a tendency for the wage gap to be largest in sectors where wage rates are lower than the average for the manufacturing sector.
5. Ghertmann and Allen, 1984, p. 52, suggest that only 2.5 per cent of workers in the UK textile and clothing industry are employed by multinationals, but a comparison of their figures with those given by Stopford, 1979, p. 40, suggests they are counting only foreign multinationals and omitting UK multinationals. Stopford distinguishes UK national firms, UK multinational firms and foreign-owned firms. The percentages in Table 5.6 have been calculated on the basis of his figures.
6. For a vivid account of the lives of women workers in Mexico's export-oriented electronics and garment factories, see Fernandez-Kelly, 1983.
7. This account of the women's struggle is based on Bradley, 1983, and Counter Information Services and War on Want, 1981.
8. This account is based on information collected by Stuart Howard and Dave Spooner of the Manchester based bi-monthly. *International Labour Reports*.
9. For an extended discussion of conditions in export processing zones, see Maex, 1983.
10. No detailed information is available about these operations, but for a general overview of women's position in the export clothing industry in Morocco, see Joekes, 1982.
11. The information on which this section is based is largely taken from company annual reports, and the financial and trade press.
12. For information on Tootal in the Philippines, I am indebted to Barry Rawlinson.
13. For an account of the global sourcing of thread by one of Tootal's main competitors, Coats Patons, see Sinclair, 1982.
14. For a discussion of Marks and Spencer and the UK clothing industry, see Rainnie, 1984. Rainnie, however, focuses on the relation between Marks and Spencer and *small* clothing firms. This is probably the reason for his conclusion that the chances of Marks and Spencer suppliers using the most modern and efficient techniques of production and quality control, and taking advantage of the latest technology, are limited.
15. There is no space to discuss developments in Fabrics and Non-Wovens in any detail. In Fabrics, Tootal withdrew from non-specialised lines, and concentrated on home furnishings, and producing batiks and voiles for export to Africa and the Middle East. In Non-Wovens, which employs only a small fraction of the total workforce, the emphasis has been on developing and licensing new products.

REFERENCES

M. Bradley, 'Blue Jeans Blues', in W. Chapkis and C. Enloe (eds) *Of Common Cloth: Women in the Global Textile Industry* (Washington DC: Transnational Institute, 1983).

V. Cable and B. Baker, *World Textile Trade and Production Trends*, Special Report no. 152 (London: Economist Intelligence Unit, 1983).

W. Chapkis, 'Using Sex and Satan to Bust the Union', in W. Chapkis and C. Enloe, op. cit.

N. Chisholm, N. Kabeer, S. Mitter and S. Howard, *Linked by the Same Thread* (London: Tower Hamlets International Solidarity, 1986).

C. Cockburn, 'A Wave of Women: New Technology and the Sexual Division of Labour in Clothing Manufacture', *mimeo.*, 1985.

Counter Information Services and War on Want, *For a Few Dollars More* (London: War on Want Campaigns, 1981).

Courtaulds, *Annual Report and Accounts* (London: 1984).

M. Davidson, J. Keating, H. Richardson and C. Truman, *Stress and Job Design in the Clothing Industry: A Report of a Pilot Study* (Manchester: Women at Work Unit, University of Manchester Institute of Science and Technology, 1986).

G. Edgren, *Spearheads of Industrialisation of Sweatshops in the Sun. A Critical Appraisal of Labour Conditions in Asian Export Processing Zones* (Bangkok: ARTEP-ILO, 1982).

C. Enloe, 'Women Textile Workers and the Militarization of Southeast Asia', in J. Nash and M. P. Fernandez-Kelly (eds) *Women, Men and the International Division of Labor* (Ithaca: State University of New York Press, 1983).

Eurostat, *Employment and Unemployment, 1986* (Luxembourg: Statistical Office of the European Communities, 1986).

M. P. Fernandez-Kelly, *For We Are Sold, I and My People: Women and Industry in Mexico's Frontier* (Ithaca: State University of New York Press, 1983).

Financial Times, London, various issues.

F. Fröbel, J. Heinrichs and O. Kreye, *The New International Division of Labour* (Cambridge University Press, 1981).

M. Ghertmann and M. Allen, *An Introduction to the Multinationals* (London: Macmillan, 1984).

Greater London Council, Industry and Employment Branch, *The London Industrial Strategy* (London: GLC, 1985).

Greater London Council, Industry and Employment Branch, *Textiles and Clothing: Sunset Industries?* (London: GLC, 1986).

K. Hoffman, 'Clothing, Chips and Competitive Advantage: The Impact of Microelectronics on Trade and Production in the Garment Industry', *World Development*, vol. 13 (1985) no. 3.

International Labour Organisation, *Contract Labour in the Clothing Industry* (Geneva: ILO, 1980).

International Labour Organisation, *Employment Effects of Multinational Enterprises in Industrialised Countries* (Geneva: ILO, 1981).

International Labour Organisation, *Social and Labour Practices of Multinational Enterprises in the Textiles, Clothing and Footwear Industries* (Geneva: ILO, 1984).

International Labour Reports, July-August 1985.

International Textile, Garment and Leather Workers Federation (ITGLWF), *Multinational Companies in the Textile, Garment and Leather Industries* (Brussels: 1984).

S. Joekes, *Women's Jobs in Third World Export Manufacturing: The Clothing Industry in Morocco*, Research Report, Institute of Development Studies, University of Sussex, 1982.

P. E. Lloyd and J. Shutt, *Industrial Change in the Greater Manchester Textiles and Clothing Complex: Perspectives on Recent Events*, Northwest Industry Research Unit, Draft Report, School of Geography, University of Manchester, 1983.

R. Maex, *Employment and Multinationals in Asian Export Processing Zones*, Multinational Enterprises Programme Working Paper no. 26 (Geneva: ILO, 1983).

S. Mitter, 'Industrial Restructuring and Manufacturing Homework: Immigrant Women in the UK Clothing Industry', *Capital and Class*, no. 27, 1985.

OECD, *Textile and Clothing Industries: Structural Problems and Policies in OECD Countries* (Paris: OECD, 1983).

A. Phizacklea, 'Jobs for the Girls: The Production of Women's Outerwear in the UK', paper presented to Joint Meeting of Work Organisation Research Centre and Development Studies Association Study Group, Aston University, 1984.

A. F. Rainnie, 'Combined and Uneven Development in the Clothing Industry: The Effects of Competition on Accumulation', *Capital and Class*, no. 22, 1984.

E. Rhodes, D. Wield and N. Heyzer, *Clothing the World: First World Markets, Third World Labour*, Third World Studies, Case Study 7 (Milton Keynes: Open University Press, 1983).

A. Robert, 'The Effects of the International Division of Labour on Female Workers in the Textile and Clothing Industries', *Development and Change*, vol. 14 (1983) no. 1.

H. Rush and L. Soete, 'Clothing', in K. Guy (ed.) *Technological Trends and Employment: Basic Consumer Goods* (Aldershot: Gower, 1984).

H. Safa, 'Runaway Shops and Female Employment: The Search for Cheap Labour', *Signs*, vol. 7 (1981) no. 2.

A. Sinclair, *Sewing it Up: Coats Patons Multinational Practices* (Edinburgh: Scottish Action and Education for Development, 1982).

J. M. Stopford, *Employment Effects of Multinational Enterprises in the United Kingdom*, Working Paper no. 5, Project on Employment Effects of Multinational Enterprises in Home and Host Countries (Geneva: ILO, 1979).

J. M. Stopford and J. Dunning, *Multinationals: Company Performances and Global Trends* (London: Macmillan, 1983).

Tootal, *Annual Report and Accounts*, 1973–85.

United Nations Industrial Development Organisation (UNIDO), *Industry in a Changing World* (New York: UN, 1983).

J. Zeitlin, *Markets, Technology and Collective Services: A Strategy for Local Government Intervention in the London Clothing Industry* (London: Industry and Employment Branch, GLC, 1985).

6 Silicon Glen: Women and Semiconductor Multinationals
Nance Goldstein

The Central Valley of Scotland now has the largest concentration of semiconductor production in Europe, amounting to 80 per cent of UK production and more than 20 per cent of European production. In hopeful analogy with California's 'Silicon Valley', reference is now made to Scotland's 'Silicon Glen'. Six of the leading multinational companies in the semiconductor industry have plants in Silicon Glen. The Scottish Development Agency estimates employment in semiconductor production in 1985 at 4600, a considerable increase from 1800 in 1978.

The expansion of employment is very welcome in a region that has suffered a high level of job losses in the last decade, but concern has been expressed in some quarters about a 'female bias' in employment creation (Hood and Young, 1982, p. 20). When National Semiconductor announced a £100 million expansion plan that would create 1000 jobs in Greenock on the Clyde (*Guardian*, 6 March 1984) there was some disappointment that 60 per cent of the jobs would be for women rather than for men made redundant from the shipyards.[1]

This chapter explores the reasons for the location of semiconductor production in Scotland.[2] How far is the availability of cheap female labour a key factor, or are there other reasons for multinationals coming to Scotland? How stable is the employment created for women in the semiconductor industry? Scotland has already experienced an expansion followed by a decline in jobs in plant owned by foreign multinationals. Between 1976 and 1981 a number of foreign-owned factories closed which at their maximum had provided nearly 45 000 jobs (Hood and Young, 1982). In the electrical engineering industry many women were made redundant as multinationals like NCR, Burroughs and Honeywell changed from electro-mechanical to electronic components. Do the new investments seem likely to provide more secure employment? Or will it be merely a temporary boom?

THE SEMICONDUCTOR INDUSTRY

A semiconductor is a one centimetre square or 'chip' of solid silicon etched with a microscopic maze of channels along which electrical current flows. The chip is bonded or wired to external electrodes, and sealed to protect it from impurities. Chips can be mass-produced; or they can be custom-produced in small batches to precise specifications of a particular user. Chips can also be semi-custom, that is, a largely standardised circuit pattern can be modified for particular uses at the last stage in production. Chips can be produced to differing levels of reliability according to customer requirements. Over the past 20 years there have been successive reductions in the size of circuits on a piece of silicon, making the maze increasingly denser. In the early 1960s a chip had less than 100 transistors (switches) on it; now 256K devices with more than 250 000 transistors on one chip are going into production.

Semiconductor production involves several processes: design, mask-making, wafer fabrication, wafer test, assembly and final test. Electronics design engineers and computer experts design the complex of circuits at a computer-aided work station, specifying the functional characteristics of the device, doing the layout and testing the design's capabilities. Then masks, or patterns, are made to allow the transfer of the design to thin wafers of silicon in the fabrication process. The circuits are etched on to the wafers, layer by layer, using the masks in a photolithographic-chemical process.

Wafers are then sent to a computerised wafer probe machine that tests a sample of chips on each wafer and marks the defects. The wafers are then broken into individual chips, each of which must then be bonded to a carrier and wired. The device is then sealed and tested. Final test includes both careful visual inspection for structural faults and exhaustive testing of the conductive properties under a variety of extreme conditions (such as cold, heat, physical stress), simulated with sophisticated computerised equipment.

The design stage can take place in an office anywhere, miles and sometimes continents away from the production site. Fabrication requires stringent environmental control and has to be located in specially built 'clean rooms'. Assembly and packaging has until recently usually been done manually and has not required such stringent environmental control. Since the early 1960s US companies have been sending chips to plants in the Far East for assembly and packaging (NACLA, 1977; Grossman, 1979; O'Connor, 1983). Final testing has usually been located near major markets.

Each of the phases has different labour requirements. Design requires electronics engineering and computer programming skills. The sensitive, complex steps in fabrication require machine operators to load and unload cassettes of wafers; technicians to oversee machines and reset them between batches; and engineers (chemical, mechanical and electronic) to specify and reorganise processes and production flows. Wafer fabrication in California in the late 1970s and early 1980s typically required one technician for every two or three semi-skilled workers (Saxenian, 1981). Assembly and packaging requires manual dexterity, good eyesight, patience and concentration, but no technical qualifications. Testers, without much training, can do the preliminary checking of finished chips by inspecting them under a microscope. Technicians oversee running the chips through the panoply of tests in the electronic testing equipment, programming the microprocessor-controlled machinery, loading the batches, making sure defects are rejected, and resetting the equipment. Electronics engineers must write the test programmes, which change as the specification of the chip changes, to test each of its specific capabilities.

Jobs in the industry are segregated according to gender. In Silicon Valley a study carried out in 1978 showed that 77 per cent of the production operators were women, while only about 24 per cent of the technicians were women. Most of the engineers were men (Green, 1983). The 'offshore' sites for assembly and test in the Far East tend to have an even more skewed gender distribution: more than 90 per cent of the production workers are women (Siegel, 1981). Women are regarded as having 'nimble fingers' and a natural aptitude for repetitive, monotonous work (Grossman, 1979; Elson and Pearson, 1982; Wong, 1983).

The semiconductor industry is dominated by the 15 firms[3] shown in Table 6.1. Six of these firms are American-owned; seven are Japanese-owned; and only two, Philips and Siemens, are European-owned. The firms fall into two categories: the merchant producers, firms specialising in the production of semiconductors for sale to other firms; and the vertically integrated captive-merchant producers, which produce semiconductors partly for 'in-house' use in a wide range of electronic equipment and partly for sale to other firms. The leading merchant firms are all American — Texas Instruments,

TABLE 6.1 *Leading firms in the semiconductor industry*

Firm	Country of ownership	Sales of semiconductor in 1983 (US$m)
Texas Instruments	US	1 638
Motorola	US	1 547
Nippon Electric (NEC)	Japan	1 413
Hitachi	Japan	1 181
Toshiba	Japan	983
Philips	Netherlands	917
National Semiconductor	US	875
Intel	US	775
Fujitsu	Japan	688
Matsushita	Japan	600
Advanced Micro Devices	US	505
Fairchild[1]	US/France	500
Mitsubishi	Japan	440
Siemens	West Germany	333
Sanyo	Japan	329

1. Fairchild was bought by the French firm Schlumberger in 1979.
SOURCE *Financial Times*, 22 November 1984.

Motorola and Intel. The leading Japanese and European semicon ductor firms are mainly vertically integrated captive-merchant pro ducers.

Many of these firms have located assembly operations in develop ing countries, especially in the Far East, to take advantage of chea female labour. But most of their investment is located in develope countries. There is a great deal of cross-investment between the US and Europe, often involving takeovers and mergers; and since the mid-1970s Japanese firms have begun to set up production facilities i both the US and Europe. Table 6.2 shows the overseas locations o some of the major US and Japanese semiconductor firms in 1980 The dominant motive of overseas production in Europe is marke access, both to avoid the EEC tariff which adds 17 per cent to the price of a chip; and to meet conditions for eligibility for contracts to supply European governments, especially with military equipment.

Whereas most of the factories in developing countries are limite to test and final assembly, the factories in Europe include wafe fabrication facilities. However, very few semiconductor firms set up substantial design or mask production facilities outside their home country.

TABLE 6.2 *Overseas locations of fabrication and assembly of some major semiconductor producers, 1980*

Firm	Developed Countries	Developing Countries
Texas Instruments	England (F) Italy (F) France (F) Portugal (F) Japan (F)	Singapore (F) five others (A)
Motorola	Scotland (A, F) Germany (A) France (A, F)	Mexico (A) Malaysia (A) South Korea (A) Hong Kong (A)
NEC	Scotland (A) Ireland (A)	n.a.
Hitachi	US (F, A)	n.a.
Toshiba	None	Mexico (A) Malaysia (A)
National Semiconductor	Scotland (A, F) France (A, F)	n.a.
Intel	None	Puerto Rico (A)
Advanced Micro Devices	None	Philippines (A) South Korea (A)
Fairchild	England (A) Germany (A) Japan (A)	Philippines (A) Brazil (A) Hongkong (A) Mexico (A) Indonesia (A)

(A) Assembly and Final Test; (F) Wafer Fabrication
SOURCE Based on Dicken, 1986, p. 344; updated from interview sources.

THE SEMICONDUCTOR INDUSTRY IN SCOTLAND

This study focuses on six multinationals (see Table 6.3) which in 1984 employed approximately 3900 people in the production of semiconductors, a sharp rise from 1800 in 1978.[4] At the time this study was conducted, these firms all had expansion plans and expected to employ about 7000 people by 1989. Three of these corporations, Motorola, National Semiconductor and NEC, are in the top 15 producers listed in Table 6.1. The fourth is General Instrument Microelectronics, not quite as large, but in the top 25. The other two multinationals in the study are Hughes Microelectronics and Burr-Brown, both subsidiaries of US companies. These two companies

TABLE 6.3   *Leading semiconductor multinationals in Scotland*

Firm	Location	Date of establishment	Activity
Hughes Microelectronics	Glenrothes (New Town)	1951	Design and fabrication of customised hybrid circuits
General Instrument Microelectronics	Glenrothes (New Town)	1968	Fabrication; some fabrication on subcontract for other firms
National Semiconductor	Greenock	1969	Fabrication; some assembly and final test
Motorola	East Kilbride (New Town)	1969	Fabrication; assembly and final test
NEC	Livingston (New Town)	1982	Assembly and test; fabrication may be added
Burr-Brown	Livingston (New Town)	1983	Design, assembly and final test of customised hybrid circuits. Fabrication may be added

SOURCE   Interviews, 1983–84.

specialise in custom products: semiconductors incorporated into hybrid circuits and subsystems for military and telecommunications uses.

The employment of these six firms in Scotland is a growing proportion of the region's employment in the wider electrical and electronics industry. Though this industry has been seen by many as the only hope for Scotland's economic revival, employment in it declined considerably in the 1970s, and has only recently been restored to earlier levels, as is shown in Table 6.4. The decline has been due to the change over from electro-mechanical to electronic components, and the recessions of 1974 and 1979 (Hood and Young, 1982; Young, 1983).

Hughes Microelectronics has operated in Scotland since 1951, predating the commercial production of semiconductors; the firm produced components for the military market and began chip fabrication in the early 1960s. It also established a design capacity for

TABLE 6.4 *Employment in the Scottish electrical and electronics industry*

1970	43 258
1975	36 700
1978	34 300
1981	37 628
1983	41 500
1984	42 500
1985	45 800

SOURCES SDA, 1979; McCrone, 1983; Young, 1983; *Financial Times*, 14 June 1986.

hybrid circuits. The other semiconductor multinationals now in Scotland set up production in two phases, in the late 1960s and in the period 1982–84. General Instruments Microelectronics, National Semiconductor and Motorola opened plants in Scotland in 1968 and 1969. The Scottish plants did final test on chips sent from the Far East and established fabrication capacity soon after opening. These early investors in Scotland all expanded their production capacity in the period 1982–84, some of them doubling existing capacity. The first Japanese entrant, NEC Semiconductors, opened in 1982, followed by Burr-Brown Ltd in 1983, both starting with assembly and testing. The Burr-Brown plant also established a design capacity for hybrid circuits.

Among the latest developments, too recent to be included in this study, is the decision by the Digital Equipment Corporation to convert its computer assembly plant, set up in Ayr in 1976, to the production of chips; and the opening of a plant to supply the industry with silicon by the Japanese firm Shin Etsu Handotai. The Scottish Development Agency (SDA) announced that Indy Electronics will open an assembly and packaging plant to work on subcontract for the many regional fabrication plants (*FT*, 17 November 1984). This facility could replace current corporate arrangements for assembly in the Far East.

One of the main reasons for locating in Scotland is the financial incentives offered by the SDA. However, these incentives alone cannot explain the current surge of activity: development agencies in Wales, Ireland and in some other European countries offer packages that are highly competitive with those of the SDA. There are two factors specific to Scotland: a suitable infrastructure and a good supply of technically qualified labour. Particularly important is the

availability of design and engineering consultants and building con
tractors skilled in building high-tech factories, including 'clean
rooms'; and the availability of graduates and technicians with qualifi
cations in electronics specialisms.

Scotland offers the unique combination of extensive investmen
incentives in the same location as a good supply of inexpensive
technical labour. Some European regions that are possible sites fo
investment may offer multinationals substantial financial incentives
but they are far removed from existing pools of technical labour. Fo
example, a firm locating in Italy's Mezzogiorno would have to impor
technical personnel from the industrialised north, which would add
substantially to labour costs.

Interviews revealed another reason why multinationals decided to
expand in Scotland: the belief that labour turnover would be low. In
contrast to Silicon Valley, where labour turnover is high, Silicon
Glen is considered to offer a more stable labour force. This belief
seems correct. In the interviews management estimated labour turn
over at between 3 and 4 per cent per annum on average, in contras
with up to 40 per cent in Silicon Valley.

New technological developments and expansion plans

The technology of the current investment phase contrasts sharply
with that of many of the earlier investments. Many of the companie
will be producing new and complex products with technologies tha
are relatively untried. At least two of the firms will be producing
256K memories and very advanced microprocessors, the coming
generation of silicon chips. One company is installing equipment to
produce six-inch wafers, a scale of wafers new to the corporation
Managers and industry experts implied that in the past, equipmen
installed in Scotland had previously been used extensively in US
plants. But now things have changed: each new production invest
ment must be a step ahead of the technologies used in the past
because of the intensifying competition between American and Ja
panese firms (Ernst, 1983).

There is also pressure to join together the formerly separate
different processes involved in chip production, to improve quality
and yield and to speed up the turnaround time. Some managers
claimed that there is no longer any justification for sending wafers to
the Far East for assembly and packaging. The technical necessity to
keep chips extremely clean and to prevent breakage, and the pres-

sure to deliver chips as quickly as possible, has led managers to consider setting up the full range of production in Scotland. One of the long-established firms is setting up a *fully automated assembly and packaging facility*.

The assembly equipment other corporations are now installing is highly automated. One manager said his firm would train operators in manual wire bonding so they are capable of repairing defective chips: otherwise the operations will all be done inside the new machines. An assembler becomes a minder, loading two, three or several machines and monitoring the movement of batches. A technician will be close at hand to reset machines between batches and to repair any equipment fault. The ratio of operators to technicians in a new, fully-automated assembly facility is approximately one to five (interview data). One personnel manager explained the change:

> [Before] a girl had a lot of different parts to do. Now she puts it [the cassette of chips] on the machine and watches to make sure that nothing goes wrong.

Handling has been a major portion of the operator's job within fabrication but the process engineers are trying to reduce manual handling of wafers and chips in order to cut inventory costs and reduce the chances of defects in chips.

Most installations currently have a semi-automated system: a machine automatically unloads a cassette of wafers or chips, puts them through the process and automatically reloads them into cassettes at the end. Operators place the cassettes in the machines, and remove them when the process is completed. However, managers talked about having transport completely automated on site by computer-controlled carts, conveyor belts or robots within the next few years.

Using larger wafers (five-inch and six-inch) reduces handling and hence the need for operators. A three-inch wafer, the standard up to 1980, held about 250 chips; a six-inch wafer will carry nearly 1000 (*Guardian*, 6 March 1984). Larger wafers allow the processing of many more circuits with no increase in handling labour.

Computers have already substantially automated the test stage. In one case a computer with four linked microcomputers feeds chips into four different testing stations and monitors four different testing activities. Three or four years ago one computer was only able to handle two testing stations simultaneously. This change limits technicians to programming and monitoring fewer machines and reduces the need for operators for loading and unloading. Most managers commented that a more completely computerised, if not entirely interactive production system, was the most crucial next step in quality control and faster turnaround.

WOMEN'S WORK IN THE SCOTTISH SEMICONDUCTOR INDUSTRY

In 1984 approximately 2200 women were employed in production by the six corporations in the study. This is about 56 per cent of total employment in these firms. The figure includes women engineers, technicians and supervisors. But most of the women — about 95 per cent — are semi-skilled production operators. In five out of the six firms the job of semi-skilled operator is almost entirely done by women. But in one company men make up 53 per cent of the workforce in the assembly and test facility. This distinctly different gender composition may be explained by the fact that in this firm the job of operator has a much wider content. Operators in other companies are limited in their responsibilities to loading the machine and monitoring the procedure. But in this company each operator is expected to take on wider technical responsibilities including, for example, machine maintenance. This firm has the most advanced production process in Silicon Glen.

The drive to automate production stems from the competitive imperative for further miniaturisation and fewer defective chips, not corporate dissatisfaction with the performance of the industry's women workers (Ernst, 1983). Managers praised the low absenteeism, low turnover and high motivation and commitment of the workforce.[5] One manager emphasised the contribution of his female workforce thus:

> One of the things that is always commented on [by visitors to the plant] is the girls. They're always at it [work], beavering away, heads down. Our girls are very good here.

Recruitment and industrial relations

Recruitment procedures are aimed at hiring women who are careful, self-disciplined and neat. Firms want workers who will rigorously follow the rules of working in a clean room, the highly controlled environment for fabrication and test designed to reduce possible causes of defects. Clean rooms require special overalls and anti-static devices. In many clean rooms workers cannot wear make-up or jewellery, use certain shampoos, or drink, smoke or eat while at work. One firm uses temporary contracts as an effective screening procedure, and to protect those on permanent contracts from redundancy during downturns in the market.

Several companies prefer hiring young women, publicly stating their commitment to easing the problems of youth unemployment; but 50 per cent of the women employed in one large company are somewhat older and married to skilled men who work (or worked) in the Scott Lithgow shipyards. In the view of one manager, overdependence on *very* young workers can be disastrous. His company no longer exclusively hires school-leavers when starting up a new production activity because 16-year-olds lack the concentration and sense of responsibility of older women. Two companies have now decided to recruit women who are at least 18 years old. Another takes care to place the school-leavers among older, experienced women workers.

Managers are keen to create an atmosphere of 'team spirit' and loyalty to the company among employees. One way of promoting this is through 'single status' employment which usually means the company provides one cafeteria for all employees and equal access to the car park.

The recruitment of operators from a restricted geographical region, and often from family and friendship networks of the existing workforce, seems to help management create a team spirit. One manager referred to the importance of the community for the operation of his factory which is located in a town in the east of Scotland with a substantial electronics industry, including two of the six corporations in this study. He said that the absence of migration in or out of the town has generated a close friendship network among employees. Community spirit is readily translated into team spirit inside the plant. Employees feel responsible for one another, helping to cover the work of anyone absent and criticising workers who are thought to be slacking. It is noteworthy that all of the multinationals have located in close-knit communities.

The teamwork approach means that women are trained on a number of machines and processes and do not necessarily know when they will be working where. When a woman's machine is down, she is expected to do another job elsewhere in the factory. In addition,

TABLE 6.5   *Women's wages in selected industries in Scotland and Great Britain, early 1980s*

Industry	Average Hourly Rate (£)	
	Scotland	Great Britain
Production operators in semiconductor industry	2.33	n.a.
Manual workers in footwear and clothing	2.01	1.98
Manual workers in textiles	2.11	2.00
Manual workers in hotel and catering	1.84	1.88
Non-manual workers in insurance, business services and finance	2.68	3.10

SOURCES   Semiconductor industry, interview data from Scottish Development Agency; other industries, Department of Employment, 1983, Tables 120 and 122.

many companies arrange for teams to meet periodically to talk about productivity and production problems and to plan and implement solutions. The women I spoke to liked this feature of the work situation: they liked the variety of changing tasks and appreciated their views about the production process being sought.

The arrangements for determining pay break with this team approach. There is no collective bargaining. A woman's hourly wage is determined by a periodic written assessment by her supervisor followed by an interview with a manager. The assessment periods vary. Most companies have twice yearly or annual ranking; one company insists that all operators be recertified at their job each month. Absenteeism, productivity, flexibility and cooperativeness are all evaluated to determine eligibility for a merit increase. Even the rate of increase usually varies by individual. Across the industry, operators' and assemblers' pay has exceeded on average that of manual women workers in a number of other industries both in Scotland and in Great Britain (see Table 6.5).

The industry is known to pay well: in some cases even teachers and office workers are attracted because the pay is better. The industry has remained un-unionised since its beginnings in Scotland, and management intends to keep it that way.

The declining female share of employment

The proportion of women workers in the semiconductor labour force has been declining in Silicon Valley and other US locations for some years (Weiss, 1983). In 1965 production workers, the vast majority of whom were women, accounted for 72 per cent of all semiconductor employees in the US. By 1977 that share had fallen to 55 per cent, and by 1980 to 44 per cent. During that period the entire semiconductor workforce in the US had more than tripled (O'Connor, 1983). However, the decline from the mid-1960s to the mid-1970s can be largely explained by the shift of substantial assembly and test activity to locations in the Far East. Since the late 1970s the main reason has been technical change in wafer fabrication, assembly and testing.

The same process is at work in Scotland and the female share of employment in the semiconductor industry will decline in the next few years. The Scottish industry's focus on high quality and customised output requires an increasing proportion of engineers and technicians. For example, one corporation planning to design and produce custom chips in Scotland is expected to employ 1000 people eventually. According to one industry expert, 50 per cent of those jobs will be for degree-level design and process engineers. That does not include the technician-level employment that will also be necessary.

Table 6.6 summarises current and projected employment in five of the multinationals studied. Currently the overwhelming majority of

TABLE 6.6 *Ratio of operators and assemblers to technicians and engineers in semiconductor production in Scotland*

	1979 (%)	1984 (%)	Projections for 1989 (%)
Company A	553	295	112
Company B	237	236	262
Company C	424	320	138
Company D	n.a.	395	222
Company E	n.a.	156	149

NOTE The calculations in this table are derived from information given in interviews with corporate management. The projections for 1989 can only be very approximate, given the rapid fluctuations which the semiconductor industry experiences.

operators and assemblers are women, on average 87 per cent, and the technicians and engineers are male (on average 94 per cent and 96 per cent respectively). In four out of the five corporations the ratio of operators and assemblers to technicians and engineers is expected to decrease; in one case (Company E) the decrease is slight; in three cases (A, C, D) the decrease is substantial. Of course, if women were to move into technical and engineering occupations, the ratio of women to men would not decline at the same rate. But all the indications are that jobs requiring technical qualifications will remain overwhelmingly male.

Company B does not fit this pattern because it is not producing standardised chips. The company makes hybrid circuits and custom-ised electronics systems. These are produced in small batches and require some manual assembly because of the small volumes and the differing sizes and combination of components.

The figures for Company D fit into the general pattern for the industry. But there is one important difference: assembly and oper-ator jobs in this firm are not 'women's work' — 53 per cent of the plant's operators are currently men. So, for this firm, there is no direct correlation between the ratio of operators and assemblers to technicians and engineers and the ratio of women to men. As ex-plained earlier, in this firm assemblers and operators perform a wider range of tasks, overlapping with the tasks technicians do in other firms. In this firm, which is the most technically advanced, men have already displaced women to a considerable extent.

If the firms go ahead with their expansion as planned, there will be some absolute increase in operator and assembler jobs for women, but there will be a marked decline in women's share of employment in the industry, unless the sex-typing of occupations can be changed.

The gender segregation of jobs

Women are very much a minority among technicians, as Table 6.7 shows. But the fact that two firms had some women technicians while three apparently had none suggests that management practices do play a part in opening up these jobs to women. As was indicated earlier, a study of Silicon Valley in 1978 revealed about 24 per cent of technicians were women.

Management conceptions of who should fill which production roles are often surprisingly rigid and can be a major barrier in opening up training opportunities for women workers. The same managers will-

TABLE 6.7 *Women in technician level employment, 1984*

Firm	Women technicians as percentage of all technicians
Company A	0
Company B	21
Company C	11
Company D	0
Company E	n.a.
Company F	0

NOTE Most firms identified technicians as those who have received a Higher Certificate or Higher Diploma qualification from an acknowledged technical institution. However, there is some variation in the way the term is used. The data in this table refer to any employees managers called technicians, even if no formal qualifications had been required.

SOURCE Interviews.

ing to devise radically new methods of work organisation and re-cruiting in an industry that thrives on change, regularly referred to technicians as 'guys' and operators as 'girls'. One manager referred to manual dexterity as a quality still desired in operators in spite of the fact that technical change has eliminated almost all manual manipu-lations except pushing buttons and adjusting controls.

The argument management put forward is that a woman pro-duction worker would need both off-the-job education in electronics and process theory and extensive on-the-job training and supervision to move into a fully qualified technician's job. Managers estimated that this would require at least two years. That contrasts with the two or three weeks necessary to gain initial competence in many of the fabrication process tasks. It was argued to be too expensive to provide such a long period of 'training up'. The few 'training up' opportunities for women that exist are confined to a few individuals, and do not lead very far. Most frequently women in production are trained to be engineer's aides, production materials schedulers and lower level technicians and supervisors. This retraining requires little company investment (that is, two to six months on-the-job training supplemented by in-house seminars). The jobs involve tasks like collecting production data, keeping the equipment supplied with chemicals and scheduling the movement of work-in-progress. Some firms have created a new job, production materials manager, as part of the drive to reduce the costs of stocks and work-in-progress.

Women who are mothers are considered best suited to this job, according to an industry expert, 'because they have experience of organising'.

Male school-leavers recruited without any technical experience have been given both on-the-job training and day release to gain technician qualifications (usually a Higher Certificate or Higher Diploma) at nearby technical colleges. However, management usually focuses recruitment efforts on those already taking technical and science courses in schools and colleges. Young women are still sadly under-represented in both school and college technical and science courses (EOC, 1982; EOC, 1983; Hodges, 1982; interview data), so are excluded from the pool of suitable labour. Men are likely to continue to dominate technicians' jobs until more women are encouraged and financed to take these courses. This would require a major long-term initiative from both industry and schools and colleges.

CONCLUSIONS

The availability of cheap female labour is not the main concern of semiconductor multinationals locating in Scotland. Besides access to the European market, and the investment incentives offered by the SDA, the availability of technically qualified labour is the crucial factor. As all stages of production, assembly and packaging as well as fabrication and test, become more automated, the proportion of women in the labour force will decline. The current expansion of jobs for women cannot be projected into the long-term. The commitment and loyalty that the semiconductor multinationals demand from their women workers is unlikely to be matched by an equal commitment and loyalty from the multinationals to the women of Scotland.

NOTES

1. Less than a year after this announcement, National Semiconductor announced it was delaying the expansion as demand for semiconductors slumped.
2. This chapter draws on interviews with corporate management, and industry experts in California, London and Scotland; on interviews with trade union officials and Scottish women working in the industry; and on official publications, such as reports of the Scottish Development Agency. The interviews were carried out in autumn 1983 and summer 1984.

3. This is based on a definition of the industry which excludes 'captive' production, that is, production solely for internal use in other products made by the firm. IBM produces semiconductors on the same scale as the top five firms in Table 6.1, but it is not included in the table because none of this output is sold; rather it is used 'in-house' to make IBM computers and business machines. Other computer manufacturers, such as Hewlett-Packard and Digital Equipment Corporation, are also major producers of semiconductors for 'in-house' use.

4. The Scottish Development Agency estimate of 4600 employed in the semiconductor industry in Scotland in 1985 seems an over-estimate, probably based on optimistic projections made by firms in earlier years.

5. The same praise can be found in a recent glossy brochure used to advertise the benefits of investing in Scotland (Scottish Development Agency, 1982).

REFERENCES

Department of Employment, *New Earnings Survey* (London: HMSO, 1983).

P. Dicken, *Global Shift* (London: Harper & Row, 1986).

D. Elson and R. Pearson, 'The Subordination of Women and the Internationalisation of Factory Production', in K. Young, C. Wolkowitz and R. McCullagh (eds) *Of Marriage and the Market* (London: CSE Books, 1982).

D. Ernst, *The Global Race in Microelectronics* (Frankfurt: Campus Verlag, 1983).

Equal Opportunities Commission (EOC), 'Gender and the Secondary Curriculum', *Research Bulletin*, no. 6 (1982).

EOC, *Equal Opportunities in Craft, Design and Technology* (Manchester: EOC, 1983).

S. Green, 'Silicon Valley's Women Workers: A Theoretical Analysis of Sex Segregation in the Electronics Industry Labor Market', in J. Nash and M. P. Fernandez-Kelly (eds) *Women, Men and the International Division of Labor* (Ithaca: State University of New York Press, 1983).

R. Grossman, 'Women's Place in the Integrated Circuit', *Southeast Asia Chronicle*, no. 66 (1979).

L. Hodges, 'Computer Studies fail to lure girl pupils', *The Times*, 16 August (1982).

N. Hood and S. Young, *Multinationals in Retreat — The Scottish Experience* Edinburgh University Press, 1982).

A. McCrone, 'Electronics only bright spot in depressed economy', *The Glasgow Herald*, 19 December (1983).

NACLA, 'Electronics — The Global Industry', *Latin America and Empire Report*, vol. 11 (1977) no. 4.

D. O'Connor, *Transnational Corporations in the International Semiconductor Industry* (New York: UN Centre on Transnational Corporations, 1983).

A. Saxenian, 'The Urban Contradictions of Silicon Valley' (*mimeo*: 1981).

Scottish Development Agency (SDA), *The Electronics Industry in Scotland*, Report by Booz, Allen and Hamilton (Edinburgh: SDA, 1979).

SDA, *Labour Performance of US Plants in Scotland* (Edinburgh: SDA, 1982).

L. Siegel, 'Delicate Bonds: The Global Semiconductor Industry', *Pacific Research*, vol. 11 (1981) no. 1.

M. Weiss, 'High Technology Industries and the Future of Employment', *Built Environment*, vol. 9 (1983) no. 1.

Y. L. Wong, *'Oriental Female', 'Nimble-fingered Lassie', 'Women with Patience' — The Ghettoisation of Women Workers* (University of Sussex: M.Phil. Dissertation, 1983).

A. Young, 'The myth of Silicon Glen under scrutiny', *The Glasgow Herald*, 29 November (1983).

7 Production Relocation: An Electronics Multinational in France and Brazil
Helena Hirata

The internationalisation of production has, from the point of view of multinationals, been determined by economic factors: profitability, costs, differences in productivity (Michalet, 1979). But from the point of view of trade unions, the social consequences are a matter of concern. Trade unions have frequently connected the creation of employment at the periphery with the decline in employment at the centre. However, the relation between the two is not a mechanical one. In order to understand the forces at work one must study separately the change in employment in the two locations at the level of the plant, in the context of the technology and personnel management strategies in use.

This chapter examines the electrical and electronics industry in France and Brazil, with particular emphasis on the reasons why women are employed. A detailed comparison based on fieldwork undertaken in 1982–84 is made between two plants, both belonging to a French multinational, one situated in France and the other in Brazil.[1]

WOMEN WORKERS IN THE ELECTRICAL AND ELECTRONICS INDUSTRY IN FRANCE AND BRAZIL

The electrical and electronics industry employs a significant number of women in both countries. In Brazil in December 1981 31 per cent of the workforce in this sector were women, comprising 79 200 women out of a total of 258 388. In France in the same year women's share of employment in this sector was slightly higher at 34.6 per cent.

These overall figures for the industry conceal considerable heterogeneity. In the production of capital goods, or goods in small batches, the majority of the workforce are men with technical qualifications; while in the production of long runs of consumption goods, large numbers of women, classified as 'unskilled', are used (Azouvi, 1979). In this latter type of production, men are employed as supervisors and managers; maintenance engineers and technicians. Women's share of employment can reach as high as 60–70 per cent. This is true of the plants considered in this chapter: in both the French plant and the Brazilian one, women constitute more than 70 per cent of production workers.

REASONS FOR THE EMPLOYMENT OF WOMEN IN THE ELECTRICAL AND ELECTRONICS INDUSTRY

Some studies emphasise work organisation, arguing that 'taylorised' production in long runs, with assembly lines and subdivided tasks, generally uses a female workforce (for example, Eymard-Duverney, 1981). But this does not explain why women should be particularly suitable for such production.

Attempts to provide such an explanation were initiated in France by Madeleine Guilbert's research on women's work in the metal industry (Guilbert, 1966). More recent empirical studies of women in the electrical and electronics industry, such as Elson and Pearson, 1981; Kergoat, 1982; Milkman, 1983; and Hirata and Humphrey, 1985, have tried to analyse the reasons for the particular suitability of women.

Kergoat puts forward an explanation based on the interconnection of the spheres of production and reproduction. She argues that the skills that make women suitable for such jobs are not acquired through the channels used by men — the vocational diploma, apprenticeships, 'on the job' experience of industrial work; but are gained before they enter the world of paid work, through training in housework, sewing and other 'domestic arts'.

The fact that this training is not explicitly recognised by firms does not undermine Kergoat's contention that 'women are well trained by reproductive work'. The established structures of skill categorisation used by firms cannot take account of unmeasured skills, acquired informally, outside the system of production.

The reasons put forward by management for the employment of

women in the two plants described in this chapter emphasise particular qualities that they consider specific to women; no explicit mention
was made of relative wage costs. These reasons included:
(a) physical characteristics
    'A man's fingers cannot hold what a woman's fingers can' (a
    Brazilian manager).
    'It seems that women have thinner fingers, smaller hands, a better
    sense of touch in their fingers' (another Brazilian manager);
(b) endurance
    Women were regarded as having greater endurance, and the
    ability to do tasks which were 'painful for a man';
(c) patience and concentration
    'Men don't have the patience to look and choose' and so are
    unsuitable for a job that requires visual inspection of small discs.
    The Brazilian technical manager explained that women were
    employed for this job by saying 'Women pay more attention';
(d) speed
    Each woman was able to check 125 000 discs a day. Having tried
    employing men on the night shift, both Brazilian and French
    managers had a clear idea of the superiority of women.
    'The men's productivity was ten times lower' (a Brazilian man-
    ager).
    'Their work speed was lower by 20 per cent, even with somebody
    who tried to do his best' (a French manager).
   The plant managers did not mention women's apprenticeship
served in domestic work for the family. They also remained silent
about the various forms of control and constraint that women are
subject to. They did not mention 'submissiveness' or 'docility' of
women workers. However, several studies have shown that this is an
important factor in the employment of women in manufacturing:
studies on France (Molinié and Volkoff, 1980 and 1981); on a
Brazilian electrical goods factory (Hirata and Humphrey, 1985); and
on export-oriented factories in the Third World (Elson and Pearson,
1981).

A FRENCH MULTINATIONAL[2] IN FRANCE AND BRAZIL

French investment in Brazil goes back to the beginning of this
century but it was only during the years of the Brazilian 'boom'
(1969–73) that French investment became significant. In 1976 France

was the seventh largest investor in Brazil, after the USA, Federal Republic of Germany, Japan, Switzerland, Canada and the UK (Hirata, 1981). Most of the French investment in Brazil (65 per cent in 1980) is in the manufacturing sector[3]; in chemicals, textiles, engineering, cement, food processing and cosmetics, as well as electrical and electronic goods.

The particular French multinational studied here employs more than 100 000 people, of whom nearly 20 000 are outside France. According to a report on the firm produced by the Centre for Research on International Industrial Economics for the Ministry of External Relations, 50 per cent of the firm's turnover is produced outside France, 'with only 15 per cent of its workforce'. The two plants considered here are part of the division which makes 'passive' electronics components.[4] This division employs 15 000 people in 35 plants in France and abroad. Its most important overseas plants are in the USA, Spain, Southeast Asia, and Brazil. A breakdown of the company's employment by gender is not available, but the company certainly employs a considerable number of women. In the two plants studied, about 70 per cent of employees were women.

The French plant was set up in 1958 as a result of a government policy of decentralisation. It was engaged in a very diversified range of activities, many of which have now been transferred to plant in other regions. Beginning in 1976, its production was restructured, involving a reduction of the workforce from 2600 in 1975 to 860 in 1982. During the same period the company's total employment expanded: in a study of 15 large French industrial companies, it was mentioned as one of only four of the 15 which increased its total employment between 1974 and 1978. According to the study, the company increased its overall employment by 11.7 per cent (Soulages, 1980, p. 411). Despite the large cut in the workforce in the plant under consideration, it was able to double its turnover due to rationalisation and automation: 'We did a bit better with only one-third of our previous workforce, through a reorganisation of the shop floor and comprehensive automation' (a French manager). The French plant continues to have a diversified product range, but this study is concerned only with production of a type of component which is also produced at the Brazilian plant. At the time of the fieldwork, this engaged about one-quarter of the workforce (212 out of the total of 860).

The Brazilian plant was established to produce this component in 1968, but the company's relations with Brazil date back to the beginning of the century. In the early 1980s the company had five subsidiaries in Brazil making a variety of electrical and electronics apparatus (Chambres de Commerce Françaises au Brésil). The Brazilian plant in the study employed a total of 370 people in 1982.

Some indication of the unskilled wage differential between France and Brazil can be obtained by comparing the official French minimum wage and the lowest wage rate in the metal-working industry in Sao Paulo, Brazil's largest industrial city. In January 1983 the hourly wage calculated on that basis came to 7.45 Francs in Brazil and 33.88 Francs in France (Paul, 1983). This suggests that for unskilled workers, Brazilian wages were about 20–25 per cent of French wages. There were also additional reasons for the move to Brazil: for example, an expanding internal market protected by high tariff barriers; better opportunities to raise finance; and the different social climate. French managers felt that in France, social legislation did not leave much room for flexibility: 'we can't get the profitability we want for social reasons' (a French manager).

The Brazilian plant has a strategic importance that goes beyond its present quantitative contribution to the corporation. According to management sources, in 1983 this plant employed 'not more than 3 per cent of the whole workforce of the company's worldwide components division'. But the possibility of sourcing from Brazil may provide a solution to the problems of profitability of the French plant. At the time of the study, the Brazilian plant exported about half its production. Most of the exports went to Europe, to Germany, Italy, Spain and the UK; a small proportion went to the USA. Exports from the Brazilian plant have partially replaced exports from the French plant. For instance, the company's Spanish subsidiary used to be supplied with semi-finished products by the French plant; but now it is supplied by the Brazilian plant. Sales of finished products to the West German market used to be made by the French plant; now they are made by the Brazilian plant. A similar process has occurred in France and the UK. The company was able to keep certain markets only because of the competitiveness of the Brazilian plant.

PERSONNEL MANAGEMENT IN FRANCE AND BRAZIL

Despite the fact that the two plants belonged to the same multinational, and manufactured the same product with quite similar machines and production techniques, they operated systems of payment, selection, recruitment, training and promotion that were quite different. The reasons for these differences seemed to lie in the different national contexts: in Brazil management was far less constrained by social legislation.

The process of making workers redundant is a good example. In Brazil a worker who had been employed for less than a year could be dismissed without any justification being given. There was no obligation on the employer to inform the trade union or the Ministry of Labour. If the worker had been employed for more than a year, the employer had to inform the trade union and the Ministry of Labour. The latter could not challenge the dismissal, but only check that the worker had received any redundancy payment to which they were entitled. There was no state-provided unemployment benefit in Brazil.

In France the situation was quite different. A distinction was introduced in 1969 between redundancies for economic reasons and dismissals for poor performance. The Labour Code stipulated that redundancies for economic reasons are subject to authorisation from the relevant administrative authority. Employers were not allowed to replace employees made redundant for economic reasons for a whole year; and any employer with more than ten employees must consult the employees' representatives, such as the shop steward or the works committee. In the case of individual dismissal for poor performance of an employee with more than one year's service, a complex process of warnings and notifications was required; and the dismissed individual had the right to appeal to a tribunal against unfair dismissal.

The French plant had had to abide by these procedures in reducing its workforce from 2600 to 860. The reduction was accomplished in three ways: non-replacement of employees who retired or voluntarily left; financial incentives to individuals to accept voluntary redundancy; negotiated enforced redundancy 'for economic reasons'.

In the Brazilian plant the managers could dismiss whoever they wanted, and use dismissal as a tool of 'flexible' management of the workforce. 1980–81 was a year of sharp recession in Brazilian industry, and the management of the Brazilian plant were able to reduce the workforce from 470 in 1980 to 300 in June 1981 by simply dismissing the least productive workers.

Brazilian managers also had a freer hand in determining the grades and wages of individual workers. Brazilian vocational education is under the control of individual employers and lacks a standardised diploma system; whereas French vocational education is regulated at national level and leads to the acquisition of national diplomas recognised in collective bargaining agreements, and leading to generally agreed grades and wages. The individual negotiation of grades and wages seems particularly to weaken the position of women who do not tend to acquire the seniority within a firm that men do (Hirata and Humphrey, 1985).

Workers' organisations were much weaker in Brazil than in France. In the Brazilian plant in 1982 there were only 12 trade union members out of 370 employees and there was no trade union branch or shop stewards as this was outlawed by the labour legislation then in force. In contrast, in the French plant there was intense trade union activity: the CFDT was the most influential union, with 65 per cent of the factory's trade unionists, followed by CGT with 25 per cent. As a French manager said: 'You can't compare it [with Brazil]. In France we are obliged to negotiate with the trade unions'.

The atmosphere on the shop floor reflected these differences. In Brazil workers were not allowed to talk in working time and supervisors watched them intently. Brazilian management claimed the right to search workers for stolen goods at will, whereas in France workers could only be searched under strict conditions. Brazilian management was free to demand overtime at will. The Personnel Department document setting out the rules of the Brazilian plant says: 'It is the duty of all employees to carry out tasks outside normal working hours each time it is deemed necessary and requested'. In the French plant the obligation to work overtime was regulated by the law and by collective agreements with the trade unions.

All in all, much greater respect was accorded to workers' rights in the French plant. The Personnel Department document setting out the rules of the French plant refers explicitly to workers' rights in the case of dismissal: there is no such reference in the Brazilian document. The French document refers explicitly to trade union rights: there is no such mention in the Brazilian document.

STRUCTURE OF THE WORKFORCE IN THE FRENCH AND BRAZILIAN PLANTS

Table 7.1 shows the gender and skill composition of the workforce engaged on producing the same component at the two plants. The

TABLE 7.1   *Distribution of production workers by gender and skill classification, 1981*

	French plant			Brazilian plant		
	Men	Women	Total	Men	Women	Total
Foreman, supervisor, technician	31	6	37	14	4	18
Skilled worker	30	12	42	34	2	36
Unskilled worker	1	132	133	24	180	204
Total	62	150	212	72	186	258

NOTE   This table includes only those French workers making the same product as those in the Brazilian plant, so as not to distort the comparison. Since the French plant produced other products, the figures cover about one-quarter of the total number of employees at the French plant.

SOURCE   Fieldwork.

overall gender composition of the two workforces is much the same: 29 per cent male and 71 per cent female in the French plant, and 30 per cent male and 70 per cent female in the Brazilian plant.

In both plants most workers are in the 'unskilled' category, but it is noteworthy that only one French man is in this category: in France this category is overwhelmingly female (99 per cent). However, some French women do make it to the higher grades as Table 7.2 shows; 8 per cent of them are skilled workers and 4 per cent of them in the 'foreman, supervisors and technicians' grade. Brazilian women are much more concentrated at the unskilled level; only 1 per cent of them are skilled workers and 2 per cent in the 'foremen, supervisors and technicians' grade.

The workforce was younger in Brazil and had been with the firm for fewer years. Whereas the average age of the unskilled workers in Brazil was 23, in France it was 40. In the Brazilian plant the unskilled women workers had on average worked there for two years and eight months; in France their counterparts had on average worked in the plant for 13 years and two months. This reflects general tendencies in the Brazilian and French economies. In Brazil more than half of women working in industry are unmarried and under 25; the participation rate of married women in waged employment in 1980 was only 20.2 per cent, and married women made up only 35.7 per cent of economically active women. In France the corresponding figures are

TABLE 7.2   *Percentage of men and women in each grade, 1981*

| | French plant | | Brazilian plant | |
	Men (%)	Women (%)	Men (%)	Women (%)
Foreman, supervisor, technician	50	4	19	2
Skilled worker	49	8	47	1
Unskilled worker	1	88	34	97
Total	100	100	100	100

SOURCE   Calculated from Table 7.1.

much higher: in 1982 the participation rate of married women was 47.5 per cent, and married women made up 63.6 per cent of economically active women. The management of the Brazilian plant preferred to hire younger women without family responsibilities.

Wage differentials within the factory were much greater in the Brazilian case than in the French case: the highest wage was 5.6 times the lowest wage in the French plant, but 22.6 times in the Brazilian plant. The differential between women's and men's earnings was also higher in the Brazilian case: on average men earned 2.2 times women's earnings in Brazil, and 1.4 times women's earnings in France. Obviously, as Table 7.3 shows, the level of wages was higher in France than in Brazil. But it is interesting to note that the gap differs for different categories of workers. It was largest for unskilled women workers: Brazilians in this category get only 25 per cent of French earnings. This is in line with the results of the comparison, reported earlier, between the lowest level of wages in the Brazilian metal-working industry and French minimum wages. But the gap narrows in higher skill categories, as Table 7.4 shows. For the highest skill category in Table 7.4 the Brazilians earned round about 60 per cent of their French counterparts, with the gap between Brazilian men and French men being about the same as the gap between Brazilian women and French women. Similar findings have been reported in a comparison of the Brazilian and British car industries (Humphrey, 1984). It is noteworthy that Brazilian unskilled men did better in relative terms than Brazilian unskilled women. The position of the Brazilian unskilled women exhibits the cumulative disadvantageous effects of the international division, the social division, and the gender division of labour.

TABLE 7.3   *Average monthly wages in the two plants, 1981 (in French Francs)*

| | French Plant | | Brazilian Plant | |
	Men	Women	Men	Women
Foreman, supervisor, technician	6 268	4 947	3 849	3 002
Skilled worker	4 437	4 098	2 161	1 676
Unskilled worker	3 675	3 724	1 101	946

NOTE   This table includes only those employees of the French plant making the same product as the Brazilian plant.

SOURCE   Fieldwork.

TABLE 7.4   *Wages in the Brazilian plant as a percentage of wages in the French plant*

	Men (%)	Women (%)
Foreman, supervisor, technician	61.4	60.7
Skilled worker	48.7	40.8
Unskilled worker	30.0	25.4

SOURCE   Calculated from Table 7.3.

LABOUR PROCESS, TECHNOLOGY AND PRODUCTIVITY IN THE FRENCH AND BRAZILIAN PLANTS

The two plants produced identical goods with a similar labour process, but there were differences in productivity and in level of automation. Productivity in a number of tasks seemed to be higher in Brazil, though the level of automation was somewhat lower in Brazil. The explanation is probably the higher intensity of work in Brazil, with less rest breaks and stricter control of the rhythms of work.

The first stage of production is mixing the raw materials to make the components. This was carried out by men in both Brazil and France. According to a foreman in the French plant, 'it is heavy work, incompatible with women'. The second stage is pressing the mixture into discs using rotating presses: in Brazil this was done exclusively by men, while in France 20 of the 26 people doing the job were women. After pressing, the discs must be loaded on to fireproof holders and then baked. Loading the discs on to the holders was done by women in both Brazil and France. Attempts had been made in both countries to substitute men for women on this task, because of restrictions on nightshift work for women. But in both cases men had been unable to match the productivity of the women.

The discs are baked in an electric oven. Three teams operated ovens in Brazil, but in France there were five teams, the fifth having been obtained as a result of strike action. After the discs have been removed from the oven they have to be visually inspected. Defective discs have to be located and removed. The discs are variable in size, sometimes less than a centimetre in diameter; sometimes more than two centimetres. The pieces move along on a belt in front of the worker and the sorting out is done with the help of a brush in the right hand, the defective pieces being removed either by hand (Brazil) or with tongs (France). This job was done exclusively by women. In Brazil six women did this task; in France, even though the level of output was lower, ten women were employed. Productivity is therefore definitely higher in Brazil; this can be explained by a higher intensity of work. Each Brazilian woman sorted about 125 000 discs a day.

In this job not only speed, but also concentration is required. Explaining why men did not do this job, a Brazilian manager said, 'women pay more attention'. There are difficulties in automating this job. To use a camera to inspect for defects, the discs would have to be distributed on the belt perfectly evenly whereas the human eye can scan rapidly over unevenly scattered discs.

The assembly section comprised 163 people in the Brazilian plant; in the French plant 160 people were employed on comparable jobs. The proportion of men in this section was slightly higher in France (21 per cent) than in Brazil (16 per cent). Women operated the machines, while men worked as supervisors and technicians. First the discs have to be silvered. This was done by women in Brazil and France; but in Brazil women only operated the machines, which were set and maintained by men, while in France women set their own machines, although they did not repair them. According to a Brazilian manager:

Before, when there were only men in this workshop, the operators carried out the setting themselves. In the last two years, we have had a system whereby the women operate the machines, and men are setters. The women are not allowed to touch the chines, because the less they are touched, the better it is.

But a French foreman saw things differently:

The women do the setting themselves; having more responsibi they take more interest in their work. They do it even faster t the men setters, because of their experience.

The assembly process itself is carried out by women in both Fra and Brazil; an automatic, continuous assembly process is availabl France, but the Brazilian plant used a non-continuous proc though there were plans to use the continuous process in future. (reason for lower automation in Brazil is lower labour costs, but th are also others. There were difficulties in obtaining technician: Brazil with the requisite training to maintain automatic equipm incorporating microprocessors. Moreover, the automated assem process produced a product only suitable for customers with auto: tic insertion equipment, and such equipment is still relatively rar Brazil. The automated process also required a higher quality product: if the edges of the pieces were uneven, the machines co not be fed automatically. Similar factors explain the lower leve automation in other branches of Brazilian industry (Hirata, 19 1984).

CONCLUSIONS

Firstly, what can we conclude about the consequences of the tran: of production for employment? The opening of the Brazilian p happened at the same time as a clear reduction in the level employment in the French plant. But the employment created Brazil has not matched the diminution of employment in Fran Whereas about 1500 jobs were lost in France between 1975 and 19 the total figure for employment in the Brazilian plant has ran; from 470 to 300. The Brazilian plant was able to improve producti due to technical improvements, and the ability to dismiss less prod tive workers. The jobs lost in France were mainly women's jobs the sections of the plant which made the kind of components prod ion of which was transferred to Brazil were precisely those in which women were concentrated.

However, these facts do not demonstrate that the opening of the Brazilian subsidiary was the direct *cause* of the decline in employment in France. According to the President-Directeur General of the Company, 'the decline of employment in France was the inevitable consequence of ceasing to make products which were very unprofitable: even without any Brazilian investment, this production would have stopped'.

A second conclusion is that despite considerable differences in conditions of work and employment between the two countries, women were used in both cases for jobs with a low technological level but high intensity of work. The jobs of loading the discs for baking, visually inspecting the discs and silvering the discs all required deep concentration, a long attention span, and visual acuteness; high manual dexterity; and patience and the ability to withstand monotony. Women were so indispensable for these jobs that the Brazilian management has decided to request authorisation for employment of women on the nightshift on certain jobs which are 'difficult for men' and 'painful for men'. Men's jobs were less intense, though they frequently required more physical strength. It is possible that the gender segregation of jobs may to some extent protect women's employment (for a critical discussion of the gender segregation issue, see Hirata and Humphrey, 1984).

It should be noted that a new programme of vocational training for women has been instituted for some women in the French plant. When 40 jobs were abolished at the beginning of 1984, affected by the transfer of production to Brazil, a new training programme was set up to allow 15 women workers to obtain further qualifications. This will enable them to move from 'unskilled' to 'skilled' jobs, and to supervise automatic machines. But in Brazil, nearly all the women remain 'unskilled' and do not have these training opportunities.

This is also relevant to the third conclusion: that the combined effects of the social, gender and international divisions of labour place the unskilled Brazilian woman at the greatest disadvantage. She is confined to the lowest grade of work; and suffers the greatest wage differential, in relation to French wages. Her disadvantage cannot be wholly accounted for by differences in age and seniority and is certainly not due to lesser ability in the work.

Finally, it is clear that a model of the internationalisation of production which put all the emphasis on wage differentials ('cheap labour') would miss many significant factors. The internationalisation of production involves a thoroughgoing restructuring of the conditions of work. What is coming under pressure is not just the number of jobs for women in Europe, but the rights that European women have enjoyed. At the time of the study, much greater recognition had to be given to workers' rights in the French plant than in the Brazilian plant; but following the defeat of the Socialist Government in France in the 1986 elections, French labour legislation is likely to be changed. The new government is proposing to introduce a system which is much closer to that in operation in Brazil.

NOTES

1. Part of the research on which this chapter is based was carried out in collaboration with Jean Jacques Paul, Institut de Recherche sur l'Economie de l'Education, CNRS. Some parts of the chapter draw on sections of an article written jointly with Jean Jacque Paul. I should like to thank him for his collaboration, and for permission to draw on this article. Thanks are also due to the following for comments on earlier drafts of this chapter: Diane Elson, Danièle Kergoat, Jean-Daniel Reynaud, John Humphrey, and the Groupe d'Etude sur la Division Sociale et Sexuelle du Travail, CNRS, Paris.
2. A condition of permission for the research was that the multinational would not be identified in any ensuing publications. The corporation produces a wide range of electrical and electronics products, including consumer goods, computers and telecommunications equipment. Fieldwork was carried out in France and Brazil in 1982–84 and thanks are due to management of the two plants who facilitated this.
3. Calculation made on the basis of the companies listed by the French Chamber of Commerce in Brazil in 1980.
4. 'Passive' components include resistors, capacitors, switches, wires and cables and connectors. They transfer electrical current but do not modify it, unlike semiconductors, which are 'active' components.

REFERENCES

A. Azouvi, 'L'emploi des femmes et l'emploi des etrangers — une etude de cas: les industries électriques et électroniques', *Revue d'Economie Industrielle*, no. 10 (1979).

D. Elson and R. Pearson, 'Nimble fingers make cheap workers: an analysis of women's employment in Third World export manufacturing', *Feminist Review*, no. 7 (1981).

F. Eymard-Duverney, 'Les secteurs de l'industrie et leurs ouvriers', *Economie et Statistique*, no. 138 (1981).

M. Guilbert, *Les fonctions des femmes dans l'industrie* (Paris: Mouton, 1966).

H. Hirata, 'Internationalisation du capital, techniques de production et division sociale du travail', *Critiques de l'Economie Politique*, no. 14 (1981).

H. Hirata, 'Division internationale de travail et taylorisme: Bresil, France et Japan', in M. de Montmollin et O. Pastré (eds) *Le Taylorisme* (Paris: La Découverte, 1984).

H. Hirata et J. Humphrey, 'Crise economique et emploi des femmes: une etude de cas dans l'industrie bresilienne', *Sociologie du Travail*, no. 3 (1984).

H. Hirata et J. Humphrey, 'Division sexuelle du travail dans l'industrie bresilienne: le cas d'une usine de construction electrique', in N. Aubert, E. Enriquez et V. de Gaulejac (eds) *Le sexe du pouvoir: femmes, hommes et pouvoir dans les organisations* (Paris: Editions EPI, 1985).

J. Humphrey, 'Car production in Britain and Brazil: a comparison', *mimeo* (1984).

D. Kergoat, *Les ouvrieres* (Paris: Editions Le Sycomore, 1982).

C. A. Michalet, 'Pourquoi les firmes multinationales?', *Les Multinationales, Cahiers Francais*, no. 190 (1979).

R. Milkman, 'Female factory labor and industrial structure: control and conflict over "woman's place" in auto and electrical manufacturing', *Politics and Society*, vol. 12 (1983) no. 2.

A. F. Molinié et S. Volkoff, 'Les conditions de travail des ouvriers et des ouvrières', *Economie et Statistique*, no. 118 (1980).

A. F. Molinié et S. Volkoff, 'Les contraintes de temps dans le travail', *Economie et Statistique*, no. 131 (1981).

J. J. Paul, Le système technologie, marché du travail et gestion de la main d'oeuvre: l'exemple de l'industrie électrique et électronique française au Brésil, Rapport de Recherche (Dijon: IREDU-CNRS, 1983).

B. Soulages, Stratégies industrielles et sociales des groupes français, Université de Grenoble, Doctorat d'État ès Sciences Economiques (1980).

8 Women's Response to Multinationals in County Mayo
Lorelei Harris

Discussion about the impact of multinationals on the consciousness and organisation of women workers in Ireland[1] tends to be characterised by three basic features. First, there is an implicit assumption of voluntarism: thus, for example, questions about women's motives in working for foreign-owned firms and comments about their political myopia presuppose a possibility of choice which may be absent from the women's actual situation. Second, insofar as a model of employment conditions in multinationals within Third World countries forms the basis for such discussions (see, for example, Barry and Jackson, 1984), there tends to be an automatic assumption of dissatisfaction on the part of women working for multinationals in semi-peripheral European countries such as Ireland. Finally, there is the optimistic assumption that women's entry into paid employment automatically leads to their radicalisation through their very presence outside the home (MacCurtain and Ó Corráin, 1978); and/or through some magical raising of collective consciousness of the wrongs against their sex and class (undifferentiated) (Sinn Féin The Workers' Party, 1977).

This chapter attempts to challenge these assumptions. Using case material from the northern part of County Mayo,[2] it examines the gaps between assumptions about women's employment in foreign firms and women's actual experience of such employment. It concentrates on the effects of previous local experience on women's consciousness and on the forms in which women organise themselves within the work place. In so doing, it argues against monocausal notions of personal change and locates the structural constraints which impede the raising of women's consciousness in relation to local preconditions for multinational investment in Ireland.

ECONOMIC DEVELOPMENT AND WOMEN'S WORK IN NORTH MAYO

The economic transformations which have occurred in north Mayo result primarily from the introduction into Ireland of large-scale factories owned by multinational corporations. Forming the second of two patterns of foreign investment that have emerged in the Republic since 1958, firms of this type have located there for a number of reasons. Ireland's membership of the European Economic Community provides a way through European tariff barriers. Its lack of effectively implemented environmental and health constraints on industry permits a certain leeway that is lacking elsewhere.[3] If these factors are not enough in themselves, there is also the lure of non-repayable grants of up to 60 per cent on fixed assets and a low rate corporation tax of ten per cent for manufacturing industries, introduced in 1978 to replace export profit tax relief (McAleese, 1977) and guaranteed until 2000 (IDA, 1972).

In the Industrial Development Authority's (IDA) 1973–77 *Regional Industrial Plans*, County Mayo became a 'designated area'. In other words, because of exceptionally high levels of population decline, unemployment and a sectoral imbalance in favour of agriculture, Mayo became an area in which greater incentives were offered to potential investors than elsewhere in the Republic. It also became a target for 'special remedial action' (IDA, 1972, pp. 28–37). In the northern part of the county, this consisted in four towns and their outlying rural areas being grouped together and placed under a planning target of 600 new manufacturing jobs (IDA, 1972, p. 20). Through both IDA and local initiatives, two multinational branch plants located in the area and already operative firms within the grouping were given grants.

By 1979 the multinationals in north Mayo had generated approximately 2100 jobs, of which approximately 1785 were held by local women.[4] The reasons for this large-scale entry of north Mayo women into manufacturing industry are straightforward. First, the new firms manufactured synthetic fibre and health care products by processes which entailed high levels of manual dexterity and an ability to work at speed: that is, work regarded by both factory management and local men as 'feminine'. Second, with the continuous production techniques used, a relatively malleable labour force was of importance. For example, both the management of the textile factory and local trade union officials agree that, because of the specific production processes and raw material involved, industrial disputes involving strike action by operatives would automatically result in a production standstill of minimally six months within the factory. Finally, as will be seen, the multinationals in north Mayo were able to recruit women for the simple reason that the range of local employment opportunities open to them outside of the factories was minimal.

WOMEN'S PERCEPTIONS OF EMPLOYMENT WITH THE MULTINATIONALS

Initially the Mayo women who began working in the new factories understood this dramatic transformation of their area largely as an occasion for rejoicing and thanksgiving.

Anne:
It brought a lot of people to the town. You know, workers from all over . . . Cork, Dublin, all over. And town was very busy then. Very, very busy. I thought it was great.

Ger:
I think it was harder for our parents, you know. They hadn't much money really. I don't know really. There was just no proper unions and things like that. They were stuck for jobs and just took the first one that came. . . . There were times when Mammy was afraid of losing me. . . . that I'd go to England like Bridie. She thought like, that I wouldn't wait with her. So when I went to the factory, I said I wouldn't leave her. So she was delighted then and I didn't want to leave her because I had a good life like, you know.

Industrial employment enabled them to stay in their home area with dignity and with the independence of a living wage in their hands each Friday:

I think the wage is good. You see, compared with what I was used to in the town. You know, working in the town, the wages was very bad. . . . working nights then. . . .

This is not to say that they did not have reservations about their new employment:

Assumpta:
People like myself are people who've been through the wars a bit and are disillusioned. . . . like they're fighting a losing battle. Like once you start talking to them, you have an idea of what management attitude is. Every single woman down there has it you know. . . . and when I go into a meeting on an issue that concerns the women and that, they'll sort of say to you before you go in: 'Take no shit. They're not going to give us the run around like they might do to their wives'.

Siobhan:
Work is alright. I think its alright. Like I'm used to it now. I like it sometimes. No, I tell you, you just get sick of work. Sometimes its murder. Oh, its okay but at times its very bad. Like the heating. You know what it was like. During the winter it's freezing.

Many also had dreams of moving on to other things:

Mary:
I'd say, though, that if an old people's home was put in Ballina tomorrow, I'd fly into it, no bother. Looking after old people. I loved it. I adored it. I could spend day after day talking to them. . . . I'd do anything for them, sitting down or helping them in any way I could. I loved them.

Carmel:
I want a secretarial job. I do, yes. I want an office job anyways. I'd like to go to Germany. I got friends there and they say it's not bad. I'd like to work there.

Attracta:
I'd like to become a nurse. Maybe combine nursing and travel. Maybe take up nursing for six months to a year in different countries. That is until I meet a man of my dreams. . . . my knight in shining armour and get married and live happily in a house with a garden. I will own it and it will have a garden.

WOMEN'S LIVES IN COUNTY MAYO PRIOR TO THE COMING OF THE MULTINATIONALS

To understand the perceptions of the Mayo women factory workers, we need to look at the material conditions of their existence prior to the advent of multinational branch plants in their area. Women's labour force participation rates in County Mayo lagged behind those for Ireland as a whole. In 1961 the rate for County Mayo was 23.2 per cent, whereas for Ireland as a whole it was 28.3 per cent. Mayo women were much more concentrated in agriculture than Irish women in general. In 1961 40.6 per cent of employed women in County Mayo were in agriculture, and only 8.3 per cent in industry, whereas for Ireland as a whole, 14.7 per cent were in agriculture and 18.2 per cent in industry.

The IDA *Regional Industrial Plans 1973–77* indicated that most industry in County Mayo prior to 1964 was oriented towards providing infrastructural facilities such as water, turf and electricity and, as a consequence, towards a predominantly male labour force (IDA, 1972, Pt. 2, pp. 8–10). There were a few attempts to create manufacturing employment that might have used more female labour but these were short-lived. The 1930s saw a single abortive attempt to bring a factory to Ballina, the main town in north Mayo. Similarly, a biscuit factory opened and closed during the 1950s (Chadwick *et al.*, 1972, p. 13). More recently, older women who now work in the new factories recall clocking out of a German-owned leisure wear factory for their Christmas break, only to find unexpectedly that the gates were permanently closed when they returned after the holiday season. An Irish-owned toy factory opened in 1964 and a Northern Irish-owned knitwear factory opened in 1968, but both have subsequently closed. In sum, there appears to have been virtually no stable manufacturing employment for women in north Mayo prior to the location of the two multinational firms that have been mentioned. Most women who worked for money did so in the agricultural sector, as farm labourers, frequently doubling as domestic helpers as well. Others worked in the few badly-paid, non-unionised service jobs that were available.

This said, we should not lose sight of the fact that the vast majority of women aged 14 and over were not in paid employment in Mayo during the period under consideration here. For them, there were four basic survival strategies.

First, women could enter religious orders which, until recently, operated on a two-tier system. Women who could afford to pay a dowry for the privilege of becoming brides of Christ entered as 'choir' nuns and generally tended to work in the lower echelons of the professional hierarchy as teachers, nurses and so on. Those who could not pay their way became 'lay' nuns and worked at servicing their wealthier sisters within the confines of the convent. Though this option may seem to be a somewhat drastic survival strategy to women today, many women in County Mayo viewed godliness and celibacy as a small price to pay for a lifetime's guaranteed high status housing, clothing and food. Vocations grew steadily from 1900 to 1966 when they peaked and have been in gradual decline ever since (Maynooth Research and Development Unit, personal communication).

Second, women could migrate from north Mayo to the cities and larger towns in search of employment. Many did, entering the Civil Service, the commercial banks, nursing, teaching, domestic service and so on. However, one of the main problems which had plagued the Irish economy in the decades following the introduction of economic protectionism during the 1930s, was the continual movement of labour from the land to the cities, where it failed to be totally absorbed. With rising unemployment in urban areas, the 1930s and 1940s saw concerted efforts by the Fianna Fail Government to redress the balance by creating employment in rural areas. Attempts to move agricultural production from livestock to tillage (Lee and Ó Tuathaigh, 1982, pp. 131–5), extensive building programmes (Brown, 1981, pp. 144–5), regressive legislation on female employment such as the 1936 Conditions of Employment Act (Ward, 1982, pp. 234–7), all of these failed dismally in generating stable long-term employment, which was in any case conceptualised largely as 'jobs for the boys'. Thus, while many women did find jobs in Ireland's cities and towns, many more were obliged to go further afield to the United Kingdom, North America and, even in some cases, to Australia, New Zealand and South Africa. Women from Mayo and Donegal also migrated on a seasonal basis, going to Scotland to work on the 'potato squads' or seeking summer farm work further south, returning home once again for the winter months.

While these first two options entailed women leaving their home county on a permanent or seasonal basis, there appear to have been at least two ways in which they could remain in their natal region, short of finding paid work.

The third alternative confronting women was to remain within the confines of their natal household helping with younger siblings, assisting on the family farm and so on. However, the exercise of this option would have been dependent on a number of factors: the availability of resources within the domestic unit to support an unwaged person past school-leaving age (if for that long); the life cyclical stage of the woman concerned in relation to that of her male relatives; marriage and inheritance decisions within the family; domestic ideologies of where a woman's place really was on the attainment of social adulthood. For whatever reason or combination of reasons, single adult women within conjugal/stem family domestic units appear to have been the exception rather than the norm.

Finally, women could remain in the north Mayo area through marriage to local men and, given the high percentage of adult women who were not in paid employment during the period under considera-tion here, a large number of them must have availed themselves of this option (cf. Hannan, 1979).

For women who married men from working class or small farm backgrounds, life was far from easy. The period after the famine of 1845–48 saw a dramatic transformation in the rural inheritance sys-tem and, as a consequence, in the 'traditional' pattern of marriage. From a situation of early and prolific marriages of choice between partners of a similar age, the second half of the 19th century witnessed the emergence of fewer, later and arranged marriages in which men were frequently considerably older than their wives. This situation continued well into the 20th century, with marriages being arranged on a more sporadic basis in certain areas up until the present day. Indeed, it was not until 1959 that the marriage rate showed a sustained upward trend, accelerating only after 1967.

For rural women this new 'traditional' marriage pattern had certain serious consequences. First, it meant that their chances of marriage were relatively low. Second, when they did marry, it was likely to be to men of their fathers' age group and at a relatively late stage of their childbearing years. Third, in combination with the Catholic prohibi-tion on all forms of fertility control, this marriage pattern meant that women bore the possibility of frequent later childbirth with all its attendant dangers. As Walsh's demographic study indicates, it was not until as late as the period 1964–70 that the number of sixth and later children born to women aged 40 and over dropped by approxi-mately one-third (Walsh, 1971–72, p. 255). Finally, marriage at a older age to even older men meant that many women faced the prospect of relatively early widowhood, with the possible complica-tion of a young family to rear single-handed.

Until the advent of the multinationals, County Mayo had one of the highest levels of emigration within Ireland. For married women this frequently meant the almost permanent absence of their hus-bands working on the lump[5] in the British construction industry or in the potato squads which have already been mentioned. Moreover while national unemployment and emigration figures declined steadily through the 1960s as the first effects of the much heralded economic recovery made themselves felt, the economic crisis of the 1950s lingered on into the 1960s in areas such as north Mayo. As their daughters' accounts reflect, the expression 'times were hard' has a special resonance in the hidden history of their mothers' social experience during this period.[6]

Living conditions in north Mayo during the 1950s and 1960s left much to be desired and intensified the women's work within the home. There was considerable overcrowding. Most of the houses, both in Ballina and in the country areas, lacked basic infrastructural facilities such as bathrooms, piped water and any effective form of heating.

Furthermore, most of the families could not afford basic modern household conveniences. Refrigerators, vacuum cleaners, washing machines and electric cookers remained unimaginable luxuries for many women until the early 1970s, by which time the number of earners in most of these families had increased significantly. While it could well be argued that the wives of migrant workers enjoyed a higher standard of living in Mayo than they would if they had joined their husbands in Britain, this in no way detracts from their experience of the 1950s and 1960s as 'hard times'. The following extract describes the daily routine of a woman with five children, no husband in the house, no piped water and no modern conveniences:

> She'd get up in the morning. She'd get our breakfast. We'd go to school then and she'd tidy up the house. Then she'd go up and make the beds. And then she'd go down to town and get the messages [do the shopping] for the dinner — the meat and things. Then she'd go back and cook the dinner.[7] So then she'd go out and wash the clothes. And then she'd sit down for a while but it'd nearly be time for us to come home and she had to get the tea ready. The only time she'd sit down really was for an hour or two in the evening. She went all the time. She never took a rest. Only on Sunday now, was the only day she'd take a rest. She's a very religious woman.

For her and for many women like her, 'times were hard' meant an interminable struggle to make ends meet against the odds. It meant taking all the important family decisions by herself; living housebound in a two-bedroomed house with five children and a total lack of privacy; making scant money stretch far enough to put food on the table and keep her children clothed and shod. It meant walking a mile to town for food each day and an endless round of fetching and boiling pots of water on the range for cooking and laundering.

The lot of women who lived on small farms was similar. However, in addition to the usual round of childbearing, childrearing and domestic labour, many of the farm women were expected to maintain the farm and livestock if their husbands were working away:

> Well, at that time when we had cattle and worked the land, she used to have to milk the cows and feed the calves and we used to keep chickens and hens and, you know, she used to have a lot of extra work to do. Apart from the washing for us and the cooking and the cleaning. . . . When I was young and times were hard there wasn't much money. . . . there was six of us and we wa small and my mother couldn't afford to buy all the lovely things she would like, you know. She always seemed to have to make end meet, kind of thing.

The wives of migrant workers occupied a curiously ambiguou social position. On the one hand, they took their primary definition of themselves from their children. In the absence of their husbands their role as mothers gained in importance and came increasingly to stand as their main reason for being. On the other, however, the minimal prerequisite for socially acceptable motherhood was a legall contracted marriage relationship. Bar widowhood, being a 'lon distance' wife was better than not being a wife at all. So it is hardl surprising that the wives of migrant workers did not define them selves as single parents, even though this was the day-to-day basis o which they operated. Rather, as the following quotation shows, the carefully fostered a strong ideology of the nuclear family for then selves and their children:

> Mammy used always to write to him and he'd put a letter in for u and she used to read it to us, so we always believed that our fathe would be home. Like, you know, we knew he wasn't a strange We knew he was our father and looked forward to him comin home, it was like Christmas, you know.

The position of women whose husbands lived permanently Ireland does not appear to have differed radically from that o migrant workers' wives in most areas relating to domestic labour. The extent of men's contribution to housework appears generally to have been confined to bringing turf into the house. However, there was a variation in women's role in relation to childrearing tasks, with husbands and wives sharing authority and responsibility for children more evenly.

It is against this background of widespread unemployment, poverty and a range of potentially unattractive alternatives that north Mayo women lived their lives and reared their daughters during the 1950s and 1960s. For many women of both generations, the foreign firms which have located in north Mayo since the early 1970s represented their first opportunity to enter paid employment in their home area, to control the course of their lives and to experience the indisputable social power conferred by an independently earned income. For other women who had previously worked locally, factory employment meant a living wage and properly regulated conditions of work for the first time in their experience of wage labour. Given this, it is hardly surprising that foreign investment as a means of national economic development is not the same anathema to them as it is to many of the critics of Irish economic policy in the decades since the late 1950s.

This is not to say that women factory workers in north Mayo are unaware of the political and economic issues involved. Indeed, from the late 1960s onwards, local newspapers and community organisations have ensured a fairly high level of continuing public debate about the regional industrialisation process and it would be rare to meet complete neutrality or ignorance about the subject. Nor, as will be seen, are women disinterested in ameliorating the conditions under which they work in the factories. Yet, while they will take up the cudgel both from within and outside the trade union movement on certain work-related issues, the bottom line remains underscored by gratitude, relief and an extremely strong memory of the recent past.

FORMS OF INDUSTRIAL ORGANISATION

Formal structures: the trade union movement

Before looking at the ways in which north Mayo women's experience informs the work situations around which they are prepared to organise, it is useful to outline the main formal and informal structures through which such organisation becomes channelled.

During the 1970s it was standard practice for multinational firms locating in Ireland to enter into closed shop agreements with particular trade unions. Most usually the Irish Transport and General Workers' Union (ITG&WU) was the beneficiary of such agreements, though, to a lesser extent, the Federated Workers' Union of Ireland also gained members in this manner. Indeed, the prevalence of the closed shop agreement and the fact that trade union agreements were frequently in place before factories had started up, would seem to suggest that it might have been an informal constituent of the IDA package to incoming firms. While this pattern of trade union recruitment has been weakened in more recent years, with a substantial minority of foreign-owned electronics firms pursuing non-union industrial relations policies more commonly found in their home countries than in Ireland (Murray and Wickham, 1982), the multinational firms which located in north Mayo during the early 1970s had what many workers in the area regard as 'sweetheart' agreements with trade unions.

All of the female operatives who work in the north Mayo factories are members of the ITG&WU. At job interviews agreement to join the union is a precondition for being seriously considered for employment. This does not mean that the women who go to work in the factories are militantly involved or even particularly interested in trade unionism. For the vast majority, trade union membership is merely another example of the extent to which the conditions of their existence have denied them the right to choose and their attitude to the union tends to be ambiguous. On the one hand, they see the ITG&WU as a monolithic institution which is completely outside them, docking dues off their weekly wages and doing very little for them. On the other hand, there is a recognition of the fact that the union has the ability to negotiate significantly better wages and conditions of work than might otherwise prevail. So, while for a variety of reasons women find it extremely difficult to participate actively in union affairs and are reluctant in putting themselves forward for union positions on the shop floor (Harris, 1983), they very rarely oppose union directives on specific issues.

The women's membership of the ITG&WU is coordinated through a single branch of the union, run by a paid male official. At a shop floor level, trade union organisation differs from factory to factory and appears to be constructed on a relatively *ad hoc* basis.

In one of the factories the original organising principle was to elect a female shop steward on each shift to represent women on the shift. In practice, this did not work out. While the women on one shift had the good fortune to have a militant feminist in their midst who was prepared and well able to take on the predominantly male shop stewards' committee, the women on the other shift did not fare so well. The main stumbling block was the extremely sexist joking type of relationship which the male shop stewards in the factory tended to set up against their female counterparts. In addition, there was also the common problem of how women with no background in trade unionism appropriate the necessary language with which to make themselves heard by their male colleagues. After a rapid succession of women had been elected to and resigned from the position of shop steward for women on the second shift, this approach was abandoned and the situation settled down to one in which there was a single female shop steward representing the interests of all the women in the factory.

By contrast, in another of the factories, the representation of women by women was not considered to be an issue. The same man had been shop steward for several years on an unchallenged basis. Here, though there was a union committee made up of the shop steward and representatives (mainly female) who were responsible to him, union meetings occurred infrequently and usually only in response to serious management-instigated crisis situations such as redundancies. In this particular factory the union was rarely called in to help settle contentious issues arising within the work place. Rather, women tended to bring the full pressure of peer group opinion to bear on specific issues and, perhaps because of this, were less frequently the victims of the shop floor sexism of their male trade union colleagues (Harris, ibid).

Informal structures: women's peer groups in the factory

Irrespective of the strength or weakness of union organisation, however, the key structure through which women organise themselves are the female peer groups which emerge within the factories in relation to a series of informal work practices (Harris, ibid). On a day-to-day basis, such groups have no more of an institutionalised existence than which women eat together in the canteens; take illicit breaks together in the toilets; cover up for one another to supervisory staff; gossip together; joke together, and so on. Certainly, the women themselves do not recognise the existence of an ongoing peer grouping process at work. Instead, they tend to conceptualise their own specific group and others in terms of their constituent elements: certain women are special friends, or are related. Yet the existence of such relationships is reproduced in a ritualised group form and is largely confined to the shop floor, with a minimum of group or individual contact outside of work (Harris, 1984). Perhaps because of this, the influence of this type of structure is immense.

The daily activities through which the peer groups are constituted fill in crucial gaps between formal union-management agreements and women's experience of industrial wage labour. At one level this consists in the creation of an exclusively female shop floor culture. While in many respects this takes the appearance of an extension of schoolgirl relationships into the factories through joking, confidences and gossip, it cannot be dismissed so lightly. In essence it is the primary way in which women organise to domesticate what for many of them is a frightening and alien world. The peer groups also generate a series of informal work practices which ameliorate women's working conditions in the factories on a daily basis. Some of these have already been mentioned: the illicit breaks and loyalties in the face of authority. Others include task swopping to ensure that pregnant women are allotted sit-down jobs; helping less dexterous women to meet hourly/daily quotas; arranging elaborate ceremonials, especially when one of the women is getting married. They represent a form in which women organise and create solidarity among themselves.

The women's peer groups are also critical to the formation of consensus in relation to specific issues and go some way towards determining whether or not these may be taken up on a union platform. For example, the north Mayo ITG&WU secretary in principle favoured the provision of daycare facilities for the children of female factory workers. However, in practice he was not prepared to initiate action in this connection since he felt that the women themselves would not approve. His view was correct. Despite variations in age, social class and marital status, the majority of women who worked in the factories would not have supported the establishment of pre-school care at their work places. Their opposition to it undoubtedly stemmed from the ambiguities they themselves experienced about the relation between maternity and paid employment and, also, from the social pressures imposed by their kin and friendship networks outside of work. In the factories their opposition became focused through their peer groups and through the range of sanctions such groups have the power to wield. It was not unusual for pregnant women or new mothers to be forced out of their jobs through the combined pressure of disapproval at home and at work. While fellow workers would not intervene directly, distances and silences usually achieve the same effect in the context of the cultural code in operation.

ACTION VERSUS INACTION: PEER GROUPS AND THE INFLUENCE OF PERSONAL HISTORIES

In this and other ways, the peer groups may be seen as a filter through which women constantly reinterpret their social experience in a mode appropriate to their work situation. In turn, the common histories with which women enter the factories determine how the information disseminated through the peer groups is interpreted by the women involved and what action, if any, they are prepared to take.

Thus, for example, women in a north Mayo factory manufacturing synthetic fibre fought a highly vocal and successful struggle during the late 1970s for the introduction of equal pay. The impetus came from a woman shop steward:

I just walked into this meeting and. . . . I looked at this board which had all these coloured kind of little squares on it. Anyway, the lowest sort of colour was yellow and it was at the bottom all the time. And anyway, every women's job was yellow. Every single one of them and it was pretty bad. So then we went down through each individual job. . . . and I interjected into every one of them, because there was nothing else you could do like. It was so obvious. So anyway, it was in the meeting that I decided we should claim for equal pay.

However, while the woman shop steward quoted above initiated action for equal pay, it was really the female peer groups within the factory who decided that it was an issue worth pursuing:

Oh yeh. It was THE big issue, you know. I mean, the girls were really prepared to dig their heels in.

Yet while the women in this factory were prepared to take up the equal pay cause without hesitation, they avoided health and safety issues like the plague.

The reason for this anomaly is straightforward. In the atmosphere which prevailed throughout Ireland after the implementation of anti-discriminatory legislation at the end of 1975, it was highly unlikely that a multinational corporation which espoused an ideology of 'community integration', and for which labour costs were not the primary consideration, would consider a campaign for equal pay as a cause for relocating. Moreover, the women understood their relative strength against precisely such a background:

> They wouldn't have had a chance if they'd objected to it. It would have gone to the Labour Court and I think, well, there's one personnel officer down there. . . . was kind of embarrassed by the whole thing. . . .

When it came to health and safety issues, things were different. The firm's Irish operation revolved exclusively around the use of a raw material which has been banned elsewhere for its purported carcinogenic properties. In this connection it fell squarely into the second pattern of industrialisation that has been mentioned: that is, firms that have been attracted to Ireland in some measure precisely because of incompetent local implementation of health and environmental legislation.

Inhabitants of north Mayo were well aware of the issues involved. The location of this factory in the region entailed rail and road transportation of the raw material through their residential areas and, also, the potential ruination of one of the finest salmon fishing grounds by the factory's waste. Public debate and private assurances were the order of the day long before the question of workers' safety even surfaced. By the time the factory started its operation, a consensual frame of reference existed among workers and general public alike. A campaign for better health and safety conditions in the context of a firm using hazardous raw materials was seen as a potential threat to the firm's future in the area and, consequently, as endangering jobs. The message was broadcast loudly in pubs, shops and the local media: any jobs are better than no jobs, so people should 'shut up and put up' both inside and outside of the factory.

This consensus was reproduced primarily through local community ideologies (Harris, 1984). In the factory itself it was further reinforced and personalised as an individual responsibility through the female peer groups. When a local journalist decided to write a series of articles about the effects of this raw material both inside the factory and in the area at large, she met with a predictably negative response from her advertising-conscious editor. She had not, however, expected a uniform refusal to talk on the part of the women who worked in the factory. From the women's point of view, however, silence was common sense. They regarded her intervention as vicarious curiosity, threatening both their jobs and their standing in 'the local community'. However, the women were well aware of the health risks involved in working with this raw material and more than prepared to 'give out' about them in private conversation:

I know nothing about 'X' except it's banned in America. And if America bans something, there must be something wrong with it because they'd get the last buck out of anything. There's supposed to be things like skin irritation. . . . your skin gets very dry. You know, you're always pulling and scratching at it and things like that. It's irritating, very irritating . . . You know, the flax and that, get caught in your lungs and that. Yeh, it's everywhere. You know, you're pulling it out of your eyes and that. And say, if you ate a sweet, it'd be covered with dust. . . . And it affects, though people aren't talking about it much, it really affects your periods. : . . completely irregular. Some people, okay, it might not affect them in that way but it really kills you when you have it. I find it does, plus there's no way I know when I'm getting it. Like you know, you get pains and you feel weak, really painful. . . . I've never seen a place like it for complaints about periods. . . . You feel half doped half the time. As if you were after waking up from an overdose of valium. That kind of thing. Headaches. And if you smoke, well you know you notice it when you go in there in the morning. You feel you'll pass out. Can't breathe. Those kinds of things. You know, when you really look at it, it does affect you.

The new women factory workers in north Mayo are compelled by necessity to swallow the multiple ambiguities they experience about the ways in which their lives have been affected by the introduction of export-oriented industry to Ireland. The possibility of relatively dignified conditions of work and relatively good pay lends a magnetism to the multinationals which is difficult to withstand in the absence of viable alternatives.

This is nowhere more clearly documented than in the long job waiting lists held by the foreign firms' personnel officers. It is also demonstrated by the clientelistic negotiations for work: the use of relationships with management, local politicians and other influential contacts to acquire the crucial job for sisters, daughters, other relatives and friends. Finally, it is witnessed by the response to announcements of interviews by the companies. An advertisement is placed in the local newspapers announcing a day on which interviews for a new intake of operatives will be held in one of the local hotels. On the day the venue is invariably crowded with job seekers. Resembling the traditional hiring fairs of days gone by, this method of interviewing struck many women as arbitrary and irrational. From the firms' viewpoint, it represented an invaluable time-saving device and enabled them to build up reserve labour forces which could be called on at short notice.

Apart from indicating the extent to which women in north Mayo are propelled into employment with the multinationals by the paucity of jobs open to them locally, the seemingly unending scramble for jobs in the foreign firms also serves as an index of the conditions under which women work in domestic manufacturing industry and in the service sector. This unfavourable comparison is more clearly illustrated by the attitudes which emerged among working women during the course of a local industrial dispute.

In July 1979 the ITG&WU signed a new agreement with a foreign-owned pharmaceutical firm located further south in County Mayo. At the time, it was regarded as a major coup in both local and national trade union circles. It was expected to provide a new model for pay, holiday and sick leave conditions in multinational companies throughout the west of Ireland.

In north Mayo news of this agreement created a wave of discontent among women workers within the multinationals. In the firm manufacturing health care products, women on the day shift promptly staged a go-slow in favour of immediate parity with their counterparts in south Mayo. From the outset, their action was in breach of the prevailing trade union agreement which gave the factory management full control over production decisions and laid down a detailed procedure for dealing with grievances. Because of this, the union refused to back the women, leaving them out on a somewhat precarious limb. Added to this, with a week to go to their annual holiday period, the timing of the go-slow could not have been worse. The factory management simply suspended the entire shift staff five days early and left them without pay until after the break. The issue fizzled out as quickly as it had begun.

Local reaction to this dispute was mixed. While women working in the textile multinational were sympathetic to the other women's cause, the general feeling was that the situation could have been avoided through the simple expedient of following the correct negotiating procedures.

By contrast, women who worked in the one Irish-owned firm which employed a large female labour force were completely mystified by the dispute. While they felt sorry for the women who faced a holiday period without any money, they also regarded the latter's conditions of work as highly desirable and as an inappropriate catalyst for industrial action. This puzzlement is hardly surprising when we consider that women workers in this Irish-owned firm endured an abysmal physical work environment in which they were at the mercy of a somewhat unpredictable management style and worked for relatively low wages based largely on piece rates.

The response of women working in the service sector as hotel maids, shop assistants and the like was even more ambiguous. Though drawn from the same class backgrounds as women who worked in the factories, many of them chose to work in the largely non-unionised service sector precisely because they were virulently opposed to the labour movement[8] and refused to submit to the closed shop system in the factories, regarding compulsory trade union membership as an infringement of their personal liberty. At the same time, however, they evinced deep hostility and resentment to the idea of women entering an industrial dispute over conditions of work which were already immeasurably better than those which prevailed in the local shops, hotels and bars.

CONCLUSION

Using case material from north Mayo, I have been arguing that women workers' perceptions of the local industrialisation process are partly a product of their and their mothers' experience during the 1950s and 1960s. Their attitudes are further determined by the conditions under which they live today. With a choice between no jobs, bad jobs in the domestic manufacturing and service sectors or jobs in the multinationals, the latter present the most attractive alternative. In a world in which jobs grew on trees and fell off for the asking, many of them would choose other kinds of work. However, this notion of choice is irrelevant to their situation. Indeed, the majority of north Mayo women do not even conceptualise the world in terms of a range of choices, free for the making. Their histories and their social universe have been and continue to be bound by harsh necessity.

This argument suggests that the social and political implications of internationalisation of production by multinationals cannot be understood without examining the regional social contexts in which it occurs. Until such an approach becomes an integral part of political and theoretical analyses of the activities of multinationals, discussing strategies for social transformation is much like counting the number of angels on the head of a pin.

NOTES

1. 'Ireland' is used here to refer exclusively to the Republic of Ireland.
2. Much of the material used in this paper comes from a 14-month fieldwork project which I did in north Mayo between 1979 and 1980, during which time I lived in the area and worked in one of the local factories. As ever, I remain indebted to the women I interviewed and with whom I worked for their time, tolerance and kindness.
3. This is not to imply that Ireland has no environmental or industrial safety legislation. However, the costs of implementing such legislation are high and, in many rural areas, inspectors are linked into kin and friendship networks which conflict with their official position.
4. The sources for these figures were local trade union books and interviews with personnel managers and trade union officials. The figures include estimates of female employment in a third multinational firm located further south in Mayo (approximately 700 workers). They are approximate because of discrepancies between the sources and because high turnover levels could alter calculations dramatically in a very short period. Moreover, it is highly unlikely that as many women work in the north Mayo multinationals today as in the 1970s. As early as 1981 I received reports from female shop stewards in one of the branch plants to the effect that as women left, they were being replaced by young men rather than by other women. With the progress of the recession generally and the closure of a large Irish firm in particular, an acceleration in this trend has probably occurred.
5. 'The lump' refers to a form of employment in which the worker subcontracts her/his labour on a self-employed basis. Though not necessarily non-unionised, there is nevertheless a tendency in this direction, with many workers on the lump inhabiting the untaxed and uninsured world of the black economy.

6. All of the women interviewed held jobs in one or other of the local factories. The majority came from small farms and unskilled/semi-skilled working class backgrounds, though a few were drawn from local lower middle class families. Obviously, women from other class backgrounds would have a different experience of both the period under discussion here and of the subsequent rapid industrialisation which the area underwent. Indeed, even within the class spectrum being discussed here, one would hardly expect to find a rigid homogeneity of experience.
7. 'Dinner' usually refers to the midday meal. Unlike in Britain, it is the exception rather than the norm for Irish schools to provide food for pupils.
8. The question of how anti-union sentiments are generated and reproduced is complex. Until the post-1958 period trade unionism was largely alien to rural Ireland and regarded with deep suspicion in areas such as north Mayo. In recent years a combination of the Catholic Church's social teachings and anti-farmer rhetoric of the union-backed movement to reform the Pay-As-You-Earn taxation system, has done little to bolster support for the labour movement among inhabitants of rural Ireland. This said, however, the precise reasons for varying attitudes to trade unionism among women who share common class backgrounds and social experiences. remains open to question.

REFERENCES

U. Barry and P. Jackson, 'Women workers and the Rationalisation of Services', *Social Studies*, vol. 8 (1984) nos. 1–2.

T. Brown, *Ireland: A Social and Cultural History 1922–79* (Glasgow: Fontana Paperbacks, 1981).

J. W. Chadwick, J. B. Houston and J. R. W. Mason, *Ballina: A Local Study in Regional Economic Development* (Dublin: Institute of Public Administration, 1972).

D. F. Hannan, *Displacement and Development: Class, Kinship and Social Change in Irish Rural Communities* (Dublin: Economic and Social Research Institute, 1979).

L. Harris, 'Industrialisation, Women and Working Class Politics in the West of Ireland', *Capital and Class*, no. 19, Spring 1983.

L. Harris, 'Class, Community and Sexual Divisions in North Mayo', in C. Curtin, M. Kelly and L. O'Dowd (eds) *Culture and Ideology in Ireland* (Galway: Galway University Press, 1984).

Industrial Development Authority, *Regional Industrial Plans 1973–1977*, Parts 1 and 2 (Dublin: IDA, 1972).

J. Lee and G. Ó Tuathaigh, *The Age of De Valera* (Dublin: Ward River Press, 1982).

D. McAleese, *A Profile of Grant-Aided Industry in Ireland* (Dublin: IDA, 1977).

M. MacCurtain and D. Ó Corráin, *Women in Irish Society: The Historical Dimension* (Dublin: Arlen House, The Women's Press, 1978).

P. Murray and J. Wickham, 'Technocratic Ideology and the Reproduction of Inequality: The case of the electronics industry in the Republic of Ireland', in G. Day *et al.* (eds) *Diversity and Decomposition in the Labour Market* (Aldershot: Gower, 1982).

Sinn Féin The Workers' Party, *The Irish Industrial Revolution* (Dublin: Repsol, 1977).

M. Ward, *Unmanageable Revolutionaries* (London: Pluto Press, 1982).

B. M. Walsh, 'Ireland's Demographic Transformation, 1958–70', *Economic and Social Review*, 1971–72.

9 Fighting Plant Closure: Women In the Strike at Videocolor
Shahizer Aydin and Ilse Lenz

A process of international industrial restructuring combined with an on-going crisis is currently taking place in Western Europe. Industries like electrical instruments, electronics, steel and ship-building are strongly affected. In a number of cases large plants have been completely closed down, pointing to a possible industrial decline of whole regions. Multinational corporations, with their capacity to concentrate and allocate their production according to comprehensive inter-regional strategies, have been a major factor in this restructuring. The workforce of these plants and the population of their surrounding regions have been confronted with a new situation owing to the mobility of multinationals.

This is conditioned by specific regional industrial structures and history. One important trait in some regions is ethnic diversity in industry resulting from the employment of migrant labour. This has not generally been analysed in terms of its implications for the internationalisation of the employment structure of multinational corporations. Rather, the internationalisation of multinationals' employment structures has been discussed mainly in the context of offshore production in 'low wage' industrialising countries (Fröbel, Heinrichs, Kreye, 1977). Less attention has been given to the reverse process of a growing mobility of migrant workers from poor 'peripheral' regions to the 'centres' of the capitalist world economy which are also the home base of most of the multinationals. By the extension of the labour market to Mediterranean countries in the early 1960s, and later to Turkey, post-war economic development in Germany has led to a marked fragmentation of the working class according to ethnic group which relates to and sometimes affects the pre-existing differentiations.

In this chapter we consider the fragmentation of the workforce according to ethnic group and gender in a multinational operation in the electrical industry, Videocolor in Ulm, South Germany. We examine the consciousness and the actions of the fragmented workforce in a three-week-long strike, in January 1982, against the decision of the parent company to close down the plant as part of a strategy of international economic restructuring. For a short time, the German, Spanish, Italian and Turkish workers developed a provisional alliance and acted in unity. One remarkable feature of the strike was the formation of a women's group consisting of women workers and the wives of some male strike leaders, predominantly German, which actively supported the occupation on different levels. Our analysis will focus on the fragmentation of the workforce by ethnic group and gender, on resulting characteristics of the strike, especially the new relationship between the factory and the family during the occupation, and on the ambivalent achievement of the women's group.

Our information is, in part, derived from a research team of the Institute of Sociology, Münster University, which undertook a qualitative empirical study of this strike in 1983.[1] About 50 former employees were interviewed, paying special attention to the fragmentation of the workforce by ethnic group and gender and to its meaning for the workers' action. It became clear that an inter-ethnic research team was necessary to investigate these questions: Turkish workers related aspects of their experience of German racism openly to Turkish team members while they might understandably have been more reserved towards German researchers not close to their experience and culture. The gender composition of the research team was also important for an adequate investigation of the position of Turkish women workers: without a Turkish woman talking with them and sharing a common background of sexist and ethnocentric subordination we would not have heard their side of the case.[2]

THE VIDEOCOLOR OPERATION[3]

The Videocolor plants in Ulm primarily made colour tubes for televisions. Originally these plants belong to the German electrical multinational AEG. Although AEG had technical license agreements with the Dutch multinational Philips and the US multinational RCA, it had its own technical development department for tube technology. At one time it also had advanced production technology: its factory for colour television tubes in the outlying Ulm industrial estate was called the most modern production site for television tubes in the world at its opening in 1967 (IG Metall, pp. 9–10). In addition, AEG had an older factory, located within Ulm itself making tubes for televisions and for technical instruments. However, AEG was unable to keep up with Japanese competition, and for this and other reasons, got into serious difficulties.

In 1979, as part of the rationalisation of the declining AEG, its colour tube production operations were taken over by Videocolor, a company owned by the French multinational Thomson Brandt and the US multinational RCA.[4] Part of the deal was to close down the assembly lines which employed about 250–300 female workers, and to rely on offshore assembly in a low wage country, preferably Puerto Rico or Spain, probably by an RCA subsidiary. As a 'compensation' for the women's jobs endangered by this arrangement, the Ulm operations would become the European development centre of the Videocolor enterprise. This plan may have formed part of a strategy of the French multinational Thomson Brandt to develop a more independent European position lessening the dependency on RCA at the technical and decision-making level. From the perspective of the workers and the trade union, this rivalry between multinationals was experienced as a series of contradictory steps and policies which made it difficult to estimate future trends. While on the one hand during 1981 there were some periods of production cutbacks and short-time work, on the other hand, expensive investments were undertaken, even including advanced fully-automatic production lines technologically developed at Ulm.

In early 1981 the Videocolor manager who developed the strategy of a strong European independence was dismissed and a group of US engineers and management arrived to evaluate the plant. But the lack of concrete information, the reassuring statements of the management and especially the visible and material testimony of new machines and investment caused the larger part of the workforce to repress their misgivings. When in November 1981 the management, in direct contradiction to declarations made only a week before, announced the imminent closure of the Ulm factories in a general meeting, it came as a traumatic shock, a thunderbolt. As a Spanish worker put it: 'I was left without blood.'

Seen from the present perspective, the closure seems to be part of a strategy of concentration of tube production at the European level in very few production sites. It certainly indicates a more comprehensive and radical restructuring strategy than just the closing down of labour-intensive assembly lines, and relying on assembly with lower wage costs in Third World countries in other plants owned by the same multinational. In this case we are confronted with a rather more complex pattern of international competition and the 'social distance' of foreign multinationals which operate without sufficient checks and with no obligations to nationally bound trade unions.

THE STRUCTURE OF THE VIDEOCOLOR WORKFORCE IN 1981

The structure of the Videocolor workforce just before the strike is shown in Table 9.1. At the time of the closure the workforce on the production floor was predominantly male; the majority of workers were of foreign origin. They had come in the 1960s and 1970s from Italy, Spain, Portugal, Yugoslavia and Turkey; the Turkish workers, the latest arrivals, were the largest foreign group. A considerable number of workers were older than 45 years and therefore rather handicapped in looking for a new job.

The proportion of women workers in the Videocolor tube plants (about 10 per cent) was much lower than is usual in the German electrical industry where it is generally relatively high — about 36 per cent in 1980 (see chapter 4). This is primarily due to the dismantling of the assembly lines when Videocolor took over the plant in 1979. In the 1950s a female sector of unskilled or low-skilled assembly jobs, consisting of repetitive and monotonous activities with very limited possibilities of promotion, coexisted with a mainly male sector consisting of the technical department, the skilled repair and maintenance jobs, and the tube production floor. The jobs in tube production implied unskilled or semi-skilled work; in some parts — as in the pumproom — it was backbreaking physical labour on a three-shift

TABLE 9.1   *Structure of Videocolor workforce in Ulm, November 1981*

| | Manual workers | | White collar workers | | |
	Male	Female	Male	Female	Total
Total	1 222	133	214	61	1 630
Foreign origin	908	43	6	2	959
Older than 45 years	298	43	111	19	471

SOURCE   IG Metall, p. 44.

system. The various male labour market sectors thus had different profiles of qualifications, work conditions and earnings, whereas the female assembly jobs were not strongly differentiated in qualifications and working conditions, with the possible exception of the supervisors.

The German male workers — and to a much lesser degree the Spanish and Italian workers entering the firm after 1960 — had the possibility of advancement to foremen, mechanics and technicians through on-the-job training and further education promoted by AEG. As tube manufacture in the 1950s was a new industry, it did not yet rely on a distinct set of qualifications and work patterns as, for example, in the metal industry. Many of the men interviewed had previously worked or received training in other industries, mostly in electrical engineering, construction or in crafts. They acquired a specific qualification profile in the enterprise which was of limited use in the general labour market. In combination with the high wage level of the plant, this qualification structure may have contributed to the trend of long-term employment in the German group and the resulting high average age of the workforce. Many of those interviewed were beyond middle age and had been working for some ten or 20 years. Most of the German women interviewed had also been working in other industries or had some professional training, mostly in female occupations such as hairdressing or sewing. Their wages were lower than the average male wage but they were still higher than in their former jobs in small factories or shops. Many of them, however, were paid by piece-rate. Their upward mobility was limited to one stage up as a forewoman or supervisor in the assembly department.

In the period of rapid expansion from the early 1960s to about 1975 a new pattern of stratification was created by the large-scale entrance of workers from Mediterranean countries to the plants. In the male sectors of the tube production floor the new arrivals were integrated at the lowest layer of the job hierarchy, whereas on the female assembly line, the foreign women workers were apparently distributed randomly amongst their German colleagues.

The different skill and mobility structures in these sectors were reflected in different patterns of discrimination. With the mass arrival of foreign workers, the German workers in tube production, mostly men, moved upwards as a group to positions of foremen or technicians after they had received on-the-job training or special education. The unskilled positions on the production floor were first filled by Italian and Spanish workers. When some years later the enterprise began to recruit Turkish workers, they were directed to jobs at the bottom with unpleasant working conditions, for instance, to jobs in the pumproom, where mostly Turkish men worked three shifts around the clock in high temperatures. Then some Italian and Spanish workers could climb up one or two steps in the factory hierarchy by showing work discipline and technical understanding. The male Turkish latecomers could hardly follow suit, because the expansion of the enterprise had come to an end by 1976. We heard of only nine Turkish foremen, while most of the German male workers had advanced to this position. Around 1970 no German would have stayed on the shop floor considering the working conditions and the wage level. This ethnic hierarchy also appeared in the everyday relations between the groups. Whereas some German foremen had friendly relations with their foreign co-workers, others 'considered a foreigner to be like a coolie', as some trade union leaders put it.

On the assembly lines, staffed mostly by women, this stratification pattern with the last arrivals as the bottom layer was absent. This levelling influence of relatively homogeneous jobs was reinforced by women's domestic responsibilities. Irrespective of ethnic group, many women had opted for the late shift from 2 pm to 10 pm as a way to combine waged work and housework and childcare.

However, despite this relative equality between women, German women were 'more equal than the others'. We heard of no foreign forewomen. Whereas two Turkish and Yugoslavian women interviewed spoke of good relations in their assembly group, two other Turkish women complained of social isolation, hard work and being sent to do the dirty jobs.

However, following the dismantling of most of the assembly lines when Videocolor took over the Ulm plants, the proportion of women had gone down to about 10 per cent of the production workers. At the end of 1981, at the time of the closure announcement, and just before the strike, some women workers still remained on assembly work whereas others had been transferred, for instance to the quality control department.

THE CONSCIOUSNESS OF THE WOMEN WORKERS

In spite of the strenuous working conditions in the assembly sector, the German women workers expressed contentment. The women workers repeatedly mentioned the high wage level at Videocolor relative to the region, the possibility of combining family responsibilities and wage work by doing shift work, and relationships with fellow workers. They were committed to the firm and interested in continuity and stability of employment. They did not consider the firm to be simply some temporary employer which they would exchange for another. As one women said: 'When I went there I imagined that this would be my future. . . . for as long as I would have to go to work'. For them, this strong bond with the enterprise was intensified by the close social relationships in the assembly work groups. The women frequently described these groups in terms of the family: 'We were just like a little family, especially in the late or dark shift'. 'We were a wonderful group. . . . we were almost like a family.' One woman said that her close relationships with her work group was a reason for staying on after the take-over by Videocolor.

In view of the working conditions, and of occasional quarrels with colleagues, this intimacy may have played a compensatory role. However, it was limited to the work group. Information and communication concerning the whole workforce were different matters; in this context, the geographical separation between the assembly sector in the old factory in central Ulm and the tube production sector in the newer plant on the outskirts of Ulm constituted a communication barrier.

In spite of these close group relationships, the German women workers did not emphasise a common gender identity with their female colleagues. Rather, they tended to express contrasting definitions of identity, that is, they tended to define their own position in contrast to other women mainly along a dividing line drawn between unmarried mothers and married women. The unmarried mothers stressed that they had to work and to provide for the future — whereas in their view, the married ones could rely on their husbands. Some wives paid lip service to this assumption but pointed out that they needed their wage and the social contacts that went with the job. Their common experience of the triple workload — childcare, housework and wage work — was apparently simply taken for granted as part of 'women's role', and was not openly questioned.

The German women workers had an intermediate position in the trade union communication and representation network. Quite a few women served as the equivalent of shop stewards in the assembly department, but only one was a member of the factory committee. They received some basic information about company development, but they were not in strategic decision-making positions in the official or unofficial trade union structure. The negotiation of the closedown of the assembly department showed their relative weakness within the union (see next section).

The Turkish women moved between two cultures; they experienced sexist subordination in both and ethnic discrimination in the dominant German culture. This influenced their work attitude as well. On the one hand, they, like the Turkish men, often expressed themselves in terms of what could be called a 'defensive utilitarianism'. After all, they came to Germany to better themselves economically; some of them also to further their education and training. The wage level was an important consideration and some women told of their wish to save for a house or a business of their own, as a hairdresser, in Turkey. However, for some, their economic and personal expectations had not been fulfilled. '. . . .we are not developing forward, but backward. We live like bacteria, from work to home and from home to work. We don't even have the time to see the daily news or to watch T.V. The lack of time means that one works, eats, and sleeps. We could not do anything outside our everyday needs. . . . We have not had much out of it. We have given away so much of our life and our body. . . .'

The married Turkish women workers were also conscious of the triple workload of wage work, housework and childcare. In common with the German women, many tried to accommodate to these multiple duties by opting for the late shift. One woman describes her working day during employment as being continually out of breath and worrying about shortcomings: she did the housework till 1.30 pm and looked after her two children; when she arrived at her job at 2 pm she was breathless already and uneasy about the children who were at home alone. Another Turkish woman states: 'Till two o'clock I worked at home like crazy. Sometimes I felt quite dizzy because of all this housework. At one thirty I left the house and worked on the production line from two to ten o'clock. That was very straining. Because the parts were hot, they nearly burned our fingers. And they were very heavy. . . .'

They also felt keenly about the restrictions on them as women in the Turkish culture and some voiced open criticism about the attitude of Turkish men.

I think their behaviour towards Turkish women is worst. Many use their women only as an instrument or a means.

You know what it is like to be married to a Turkish man. You cannot look out on your own any more. Therefore I am not willing to marry, because I love my liberty. . . .

All this exerts a certain pressure. As a Turkish woman one is used to being reserved when men are present. I think I could engage more in many things if I would not have this reserve. . . .

Interestingly, in our small sample of interviews, there was no open antagonism between the one unmarried Turkish mother and the married Turkish women comparable to the tensions among the German women. It seems that their identity was perhaps defined rather by reference to common experience and that apparent contrast played a lesser role.

What mattered was the common experience of women of their own ethnic group. Ethnic discrimination, pride in their own cultural background and a certain everyday ethnic solidarity figure as the most prominent reasons for this. One woman who was rather passive during the strike tells how she used to interpret for countrymen when they were snubbed. She also relates that her German colleagues did not talk to her, but rather to Italians, and that Turkish men and women were sent to the dirtiest and hardest jobs. A woman who was working in an otherwise purely German group gives a different example of close friendship with her co-workers. But certainly ethnocentrism in a large part of the German workforce reinforced a certain 'communalism' in the attitude of the Turkish working women.[5]

One possible result of this double subordination was the psychological insecurity, the sometimes startling lack of information, and the isolation from communication with workers' representatives of the Turkish women. Rushing from housework to the assembly line and back they apparently had few trade union contacts and very minimal time to gather information about basic trade union mechanisms and the development of the company. Whereas there was a fairly broad representation of Turkish men in the shop stewards' body and a smaller one in the factory committee, Turkish women apparently were not represented in either organisation.

BARGAINING FOR WOMEN'S JOBS: THE CLOSEDOWN OF ASSEMBLY OPERATIONS

The transfer of the former AEG plants to Videocolor involved the closedown of the assembly lines in exchange for establishing a technological development centre. The bargaining about this trade-off should be examined in the broader context of the specific limitations of plant-level trade union leadership confronted with a foreign-owned multinational corporation.

In West Germany, the factory committee, which is elected by the workforce, must be consulted on all matters concerning recruitment and dismissals, and it has representatives on the company's board of trustees. Its members are legally restricted in giving information on company matters and in leading collective action, especially initiating strikes. Usually the appropriate general industrial trade union will be strongly represented on this factory committee. (German trade unions are organised as industrial and unitary unions and therefore an inter-union competition parallel to the situation in some British industries is practically non-existent.) In the Ulm Videocolor plants, 67 per cent of employees were trade union members (IG Metall, p. 18). Furthermore, a system of 'persons of trust' (*Vertrauensleute*), who in some respect resemble the British shop stewards, represents the union on the shop floor.

The transfer of colour tube production from AEG had entailed the formation of a new factory committee with a rather inexperienced leadership mainly from the outlying plant. The committee faced a difficult situation without much experience, and without a communication network with workers' representatives in Videocolor plants outside Germany. This difficulty was intensified by their lack of knowledge of French. Finally, they were confronted with what in retrospect can be called ambiguous, inadequate and inaccurate information from the firm, culminating in the promise to go on operating only one week before the announcement of the final closedown!

The closedown of the assembly lines was a precondition laid down by Thomson Brandt for the takeover of the Ulm colour tube operations. The French firm states as its basic reason, the lower production costs achieved by RCA from assembly at lower wages in Costa Rica. It also promised to upgrade the existing development centre to the European Centre for Videocolor which would contain a pilot assembly department with 50 jobs where some of the redundant workers could be employed. Whereas the factory committee at first wanted to resist, the promises of Thomson Brandt finally caused them to swallow the bitter pill and to agree. The reasoning is summed up by one committee member:

> We also knew if they are to take us over that a certain cut down is necessary. . . . We were also prepared to make sacrifices. . . .

Well o.k. we cannot help agreeing to the closedown of the assembly sector and we will get a development centre, as they said with fifty jobs. Maybe it will be twenty technicians, but we may still keep thirty women in. Down there we will get fifty people [in an expansion of parts manufacture] that makes about eighty jobs, two hundred we had before, so after all it would not be that bad. . . .

Some women workers resisted with protests and letters to the factory committee, to no avail. There has been some speculation as to whether the protest of men would have been taken more seriously. Certainly, the male skilled workers were dominant in the factory committee. However, it seems that the committee was following the then common line of thought, an inheritance of times of low unemployment, that redundancies should be agreed if they were compensated by other jobs or at least by redundancy payments. Still, some German women felt very bitter about it: 'we only realised that we had been shoved aside in a very mean way. . . . Yes, we women felt shoved aside . . .'. The company put some psychological pressure on women to resign, promising them termination benefits of about two months wages, or transferring some to the day shift where they could not take care of their children. The factory committee did not consent to the dismissals, but they could not prevent the individual arrangements of the management with the women leaving. They did participate, however, in the decision about the transfer of the women staying. Some Turkish women were sent to a men's department in the control section in the factory on the outskirts of Ulm and they remember vivid reactions:

We were transferred and men and women came together in one department. And you know our men, when they see women they become over-dominant. They approached us and of course we did not like that. . . . But you can see that the German as well as the Turkish men had bad thoughts. For years they were used only to work with men; then the women came and that of course confused them. . . .
When we came into the department, the men were really cross. They said they would become unemployed if we did the work. Especially Italians and Germans. They said, our wives are housewives, why are the Turkish women working?

The factory committee had followed the classical bargaining strategy of the 1960s and 1970s of conceding some cuts in the marginal workforce while trying to limit the negative consequences by negotiation for transfers and redundancy payments. This procedure had a certain superficial plausibility before the growth of unemployment when the workers concerned could find new jobs. In retrospect, some trade union leaders acknowledged the need to fundamentally review this policy.

THE STRIKE AGAINST CLOSURE IN 1982

The compromise could not save the colour tube operation; in November 1981 the management announced the closedown. The decision to strike for the conservation of the jobs was taken after one and a half months of negotiations rendered ineffectual by the tough stand of the management. After a market assessment by trade union experts had proclaimed a realistic chance of survival for the plant, the workforce occupied the outlying factory and went on strike for its conservation. As this strike was not covered by legal provisions, the regional trade union office and the factory committee did not appear as official organisers. Also the usual financial support of strikers by the trade union could not be given. The trade unions, especially the metal workers' union (IG Metall) supported the action by a huge campaign and public relations week all over Germany, and by providing expertise.

A strike committee which included foreign workers was constituted. It coordinated the occupation arranging for the guarding of the factory, and organising actions like a visit to the Federal Swabian Ministry of Economics or to the other Videocolor factory in Italy to inform the Italian workers. A German core group of skilled and semi-skilled workers and the foreign, particularly the Turkish workers, formed the backbone of the strike, whereas the foremen and office workers stood aside. Dramatic scenes ensued: the blocking of the gates to prevent the removal of products by the firm, the burning of the letter of dismissal by the leaders of the strike committee. There were some tensions between different groups of workers: but with the help of a Turkish trade union organiser from the central IG Metall office, both right-wing and left-wing Turkish workers co-operated in unity in the strike.

In the conservative town of Ulm the general public sympathised with the strike because of the shock of this uneconomic destruction of a highly modern plant, or in a more nationalistic vein, because of the damage done to a German firm by a foreign-based multinational. The Church organised a support group and the Social Democratic Party and the Green Party expressed their concern and sympathy. After three weeks of occupation, often in a tense atmosphere, the strike ended. The main goal of conserving the jobs could not be attained and the factory was closed after all; but the management conceded much higher redundancy pay, payment of the wages for the time of the strike and no legal or other prosecution of the participants, which was especially important for foreign workers whose residence permits would otherwise be threatened.

In this context, we can only summarise the basic features of this defensive strike: the workers' motivation came not from a cool economic calculation because the high risk of losing was generally acknowledged, but it originated from a deep-seated attitude of workers' resistance against an 'unjust' capitalist offensive; and from the high value they placed on work. This made the struggle for jobs a legitimate issue for collective action even if it was not legally sanctioned. As one trade union leader said: 'Who struggles, can lose, but who does not struggle, has lost already'.

In spite of the marked fragmentation by ethnic group and gender, the workforce acted in outstanding unity; from the crumbling of this unity after the strike we interpret the occupation as a temporary alliance between the different groups of workers who met in a common unified action against imminent redundancy.

The occupation as an 'untypical' form of struggle made new and high demands, especially on the strike leadership. After all, it implied a 24-hour effort inside the plant and the leadership was confronted with a previously unknown responsibility for the whole factory and for the negotiations. They had to redefine their situation and the usual tactics of strikes in several ways. They needed to develop a comprehensive knowledge of the strategy of Videocolor's owners on the international and national levels to find ways of survival for the plant as a whole, which went much beyond their former activities in the factory committee. They also had to find ways to create a stable unity in the fragmented workforce and to strengthen the provisional alliance. Last, but not at all least, the division between the family and the factory, the separation between production and reproduction, had to be overcome. In the conservative Swabian workers' culture, this division between factory and home had been firmly established. The relation between the two spheres is expressed in the proverbial Swabian pattern of 'work, save

and build a house' which was achieved in the post war prospe▮
phase by a large group of German workers. The sudden revolut▮
caused by the occupation in this established life rhythm betw▮
production and reproduction provoked a crisis with the wives ▮
children in some German strike leaders' families, leading to a pot▮
tially demobilising lack of solidarity.

THE ROLE OF THE WOMEN'S GROUP IN THE STRIKE

The necessity of a newly-defined relationship between product▮
and reproduction was the starting point of the women's group. ▮
group did not originate from the action of the trade unions or fr▮
the women in the plant, but from the reaction of Church sympat▮
ers to the domestic crisis of the leaders. One female Church educa▮
active in the organisation of the group, describes the process:

> The women's group originated from outside and not from wom▮
> in the workforce. . . . we had been approached because the n▮
> could not get along with their wives anymore. . . . In this situat▮
> one came to us and said 'Can't you talk things over with ▮
> wife?'. . . . Well, we just said, 'Tell your wives to come to ▮
> factory, we will meet there'. Then we met them for one hour, q▮
> relaxed in the factory and from then on the problem was solved▮
> was easy to solve but awfully important.

A core group formed which soon developed self-help activities▮
different levels: they organised a telephone chain to inform e▮
other about strike events, they helped each other doing the hou▮
hold jobs which the men had done, like shopping with the car, ▮
repairing the washing machine. The basic aim was to support ▮
struggle of men by developing self-reliant action. They held co▮
parties to meet, exchange information and involve more women ▮
brought collective organisation into the supposedly private dome▮
sphere. These activities related to the women's everyday culture ▮
were thus attractive to them. In a few days the women's group g▮
to about 30 with foreign, especially Turkish women among them▮
included women employed by Videocolor as well as wives of m▮
employees.

The women asked right away: how about the women in the fir▮
That meant that immediately after we had set up we asked

women working for the firm 'come and join us, we want to have you with us. . . . Maybe you have a problem, too. Your husbands are not coming home either'. After that the women employees were with us. . . . they wanted to participate in the coffee parties and they said, 'we also want to do some public action'.

The involvement — often for the first time — with the husbands' place of work and with the striking workers' organisation created strong support from the wives. Previously the wives could not really imagine what was happening in a strike but then they had the chance to see for themselves.

And then. . . . I went out to the firm for the first time and I realised what was going on. And one is really carried along, seeing how many people are there and how they hold together.

The women's group thus constituted a new coalition between wives of workers and women working at the plant. The ambivalent aspect of this achievement should not be overlooked: the aim was at first 'helping the husbands' and, for example, the needs of the unmarried mothers for help with their children during the strike were not discussed. But it formed a focus for women's discussions and actions, enabling a rapid growth of self-reliance and political consciousness. The most important action was to set up an information stall in the shopping area to gain publicity and sympathy for the strike. First, the women informed themselves about the whole background and the goals of the action in long sessions. Besides writing letters to the editors of different newspapers as a women's group, they then planned their public appearance in the shopping area which was covered widely by the press. They symbolised that the struggle against redundancies is not only a matter for trade unions, but also involves families, and thus extended sympathy for the fight beyond organised workers. Women publicly taking a stand and leaving their assigned role of political passivity provoked a lot of response from the media and the public in conservative Ulm. How this involvement changed the political consciousness and the self-assurance of the women can be seen in two incidents during this action: they argued with the head manager of Videocolor who happened to pass by; and they challenged a neo-fascist group campaigning in the shopping centre for foreigners to leave Germany. The women had created their own organisation in which they could inform themselves starting from their questions as women, and then make their voices heard in public. Whereas in some strikes the division between home and firm implies a contradictory element undermining solidarity, in this case, the struggle expanded by integrating women and some elder children. The 'family afternoons', during which the families and friends of the workers were invited to the occupied plant to enjoy a multi-ethnic cultural programme there, were very popular. Here, the presence of other women enabled some Turkish women to come along and get a direct understanding of the strike. A Turkish worker married to a German told of the arguments he had with his wife when he did not come home because he was occupying the factory:

> Two days before I had 'phoned home that I could not come. My wife told me that the child was weeping. I said: 'Can you put the child to bed and come here? Here are other women, too. Then we can be together and see what we can do'. Then my friends said: 'Is your wife coming? Well, then, my wife can come as well'. And the other ones said the same thing. When they saw our situation in the factory. . . . they said that they understand us and they supported us as far as they could.

The women's group had some limitations. It was not able to involve the majority of the women workers[6]: some did not know of it, and some younger, unmarried foreign women did not join as they considered it a wives' group. The political consciousness it generated was limited to the social and political causes of unemployment in refusal of the still dominant argument of individual failure. It was not transferred to general issues and especially not to a critical approach on the issue of women's subordination. Still, a visible women's group in the strike helped to promote the participation of women, especially foreign women workers and wives. Some interviews hinted at fears of women mingling with so many men, especially Turkish men, in the occupation. In the case of Turkish women, this fear or cultural reserve may have been counteracted by the visible presence of women. Even so, one Turkish woman living under her parents' control seems to have had problems in going to the factory as she usually would have done for the late shift, stating as her reason: 'There were many Turkish men, about one thousand, and to enter this group as a woman is a little difficult. I was somewhat reserved'. Other Turkish women participated in the women's group and thus overcame this problem.

However, after the settlement of the strike, the women's group shrunk to a few leader's wives and one former worker. Nevertheless, in autumn 1983, it was the only independent group — close to the trade unions, but forming no part of them — which carried out follow-up actions on unemployment after the strike. Demand from outside — letters, interviews — may have contributed to keeping them going. They continued to gather information about plants threatened by a closedown, to collect money for the workers' resistance there, to communicate their own experiences and send support letters. They are realistic about the limited impact of their activities, but point out that if many such groups were formed, the resistance against the employers would be greater.

An organisational core for the women thus proved to be important for sustaining the occupation. There is a long series of historical experiences of the importance of similar women's groups from the strikes in Chicago of the 1930s to the plant occupation at LIP, France and that at Erwitte, Germany during the 1970s. Still, the formation of a women's group for wives of male workers and for women workers does not form a central part of trade union strategies. Rather, it is left to supporting groups, such as the Churches, or even to chance.

The formation of a women's group and the generation of community support is not specific to the resistance of workers facing closure by multinational corporations. The critical factor in overcoming the division between production and reproduction is the objective scope of the problem — here the loss of all jobs — and the subjective economic and moral concern confronted with this overturn of established norms and procedures. However, in the case of a multinational corporation, the scope of resistance is limited by the multinational's superior information, high mobility and interregional strategy, developments which can hardly be countered by national trade union movements, even with community support.

NOTES

1. We want to thank the research team (N. Beckenback, R. Fluder, T. Karakurt, R. Kobler, M. Ravenstein, A. Salgado, J. Schmidt, C. Sigrist) for discussions. Of course, the responsibility for interpretations lies with the authors.
2. A common experience as women did not suffice to establish an open dialogue; ethnocentric subordination has to be considered as well.

    Surprisingly, the female interviewer stated that she considered there to be no barriers in her interviews with Turkish men.

3. The following summary of the history of the Videocolor operations in Ulm is based on the Interim Report, 1984 and Final Report, 1984 of the Project Group Videocolor, Institute of Sociology, University of Münster.

4. RCA had a majority of the shares.

5. We found that Turkish women workers had developed forceful arguments countering this ethnocentrism, as in the following statement about the custom of wearing scarfs, which provokes a lot of aggression among Germans: 'The Germans see the Turkish quite wrong. They think they are all backward and at first ask why the Turkish wear scarfs. Then I say why do the nuns wear black in your place? They are closed up as well Then they tell me that they do it from religious reasons. Well I say, we also do this from religious reasons. Our people are religious and therefore wear scarfs. Besides here people who live in the countryside are no modern either. In Turkey there are many modern people. You have to see that it is like that in every country, I will say then.'

6. One reason for this, and for non-participation of women workers in the strike, was the geographic distance between the occupied outlying plant and the women's workplace in central Ulm in the old factory.

REFERENCES

F. Fröbel, J. Heinrichs, O. Kreye, *Die neue internationale Arbeitsteilung* (Hamburg: Reinbek, 1977).

IG Metall, *Der Kampf um die Arbeitsplatze bei Videocolor* (Ulm: IGM Dokumentation, no date).

Project Group Videocolor, *Interim Report* (Münster: Institute of Sociology 1984).

Project Group Videocolor, *Final Report* (Münster: Institute of Sociology 1984).

10 Fighting Plant Closure — Women in the Plessey Occupation
Patricia Findlay

INTRODUCTION

The occupation of the Bathgate plant of Plessey Capacitors in 1982 provides an interesting example of collective action taken by a mainly female workforce against their multinational employer. This particular dispute has important implications both for the involvement of women in industrial action, and for the debate about the most effective strategies to counter the power of multinational corporations, particularly in the case of plant closure.

The material presented here is based on a series of interviews carried out in the period August to November 1983. Time constraints prevented interviewing the workforce on a large scale. However, attempts were made to interview one or more representatives of the various categories of workers involved in the dispute. Thus, the three most prominent shop stewards (two female and one male) were interviewed, as were 12 ordinary workers involved in the occupation. This group included workers who had been re-employed after the occupation, as well as workers who had been made redundant. One full-time union official closely involved in the occupation was interviewed, as were two members of a group which acted as a support to the Plessey workers. Attempts were made to interview a representative of the Plessey management and a representative of the Engineering Employers' Federation, of which Plessey is a member, but both refused to be interviewed.

The workers of the Plessey plant chose to occupy their factory in response to its proposed closure, rather than to negotiate with the company over the closure through official trade union channels. Why was such a tactic chosen? This can be considered in terms of three main conditions which the form of industrial action chosen had to satisfy. Firstly, the action had to generate the support and active involvement of the majority of workers threatened with redundancy.

Secondly, it had to take account of the rationale behind the operation of multinational corporations like Plessey, and therefore had to have the potential of challenging directly that rationale. Thirdly, the form of action chosen had to be able to overcome the usual limitations of official trade union action with respect to closure. The Plessey workers' assessment of the sit-in as a strategy which could fulfil these three conditions will be looked at in more detail. Some evaluation will be made of the potential gains for workers in choosing direct action rather than negotiation in response to the policies of multinational corporations, as well as any limitations in doing so. Before this, however, the dispute must be set in context by looking at the main activities of the Plessey Company worldwide, particularly at their changing corporate strategies in recent years, as well as the setting up of the Plessey plant in Bathgate, the characteristics of its workforce and its industrial relations.

THE PLESSEY COMPANY

Plessey began as a small jig and tool-making firm in East London in 1917. The company expanded steadily in the years up to World War II, and after the war a series of mergers diversified the company into such areas as machine tool control, hydraulics and consumer electricals. Further mergers took place in the 1960s, bringing Plessey into the areas of telecommunications, numerical control, radar and semiconductors. Today, Plessey's business activity is made up of three main divisions: telecommunications and office systems, electronics systems and engineering. The company operates in 130 countries, having research and development establishments in 13 countries. However, this does not put Plessey in the top league of multinational corporations by the standards of its international competitors like IBM. Plessey is the fourth largest UK electronics company (TURU Report, 1982), and ranks 27th in the league table of leading British manufacturing multinationals (Labour Research, 1978). Sales in the United Kingdom account for 51 per cent of Plessey's turnover, with its next largest market being the USA, with 14 per cent of sales. Continental Europe and Asia follow closely behind. The group also has sales and subsidiaries in Africa, including South Africa, Australia and Latin America.

Plessey's sales figures in the UK are largely made up of state contracts — such contracts provided Plessey with 76.4 per cent of its profits on 72.4 per cent of sales in 1981–82. These contracts had become increasingly important to the company since 1971 (excluding the years 1977–79, when cuts in Post Office expenditure detrimentally affected Plessey's sales to the state). Government departments and British Telecom (formerly the Post Office) are Plessey's primary customers of electronic systems and equipment and telecommunications respectively. Many of the state's purchases from the Plessey Company are defence-related.

In 1975 Plessey employed approximately 55 180 workers in the UK. By 1981 the Plessey workforce had fallen to 39 922, a fall of around 35 per cent. The reasons behind such a massive fall in employment levels will be looked at in some depth later.

PLESSEY CAPACITORS, BATHGATE

Bathgate, with its population of 14 000, lies in West Lothian, some 18 miles from Edinburgh. The town has undergone some major changes in recent years. From being a lively, prosperous town in the 1960s and early 1970s, it has become one of the major casualties of the recession in Scotland, with its present unemployment rate approaching 30 per cent.

The early post-war period from 1947–57 was a boom time for Bathgate in employment terms: its shale oil, coal, iron, steel and paper industries were prospering. Added to this, in 1947, the Telegraph Condenser Company set up in the town to manufacture condensers for electrical and electronic machinery. The company was the first major employer in the area not dependent on the exploitation of natural resources. Further, its establishment linked the local economy to one of the post-war boom industries, and brought increased employment opportunities for women, an important factor in an area dominated by traditional industries, where employment was almost wholly a male preserve. This was followed by the setting up of the British Motor Company (now British Leyland) in Bathgate in 1961, with a target labour force of 5600.

In 1965, however, TCC was taken over by Plessey Capacitors, a wholly-owned subsidiary of Plessey Ltd, in a spate of amalgamations within the British telecommunications industry. The takeover incorporated the Bathgate plant and its workforce into a major international manufacturing operation in the increasingly competitive electronics industry. Employment at the plant rose from 1400 in 1965 to around 2400 by 1973. Around 75 per cent of the employees at the plant were women involved in the production of capacitors. A capacitor is an electric or electronic device which stores an electric charge, and which is incorporated into all kinds of electric and electronic equipment, such as transistor radios, washing machines, electricity sub-stations and on high-speed electric trains. The Bathgate factory consisted of four plants producing four lines of capacitors and some related products.

In the years before the occupation, Plessey was considered by many of its workers at Bathgate to be a relatively good employer in terms of wages and conditions, comparing favourably with other plants in the area. In contrast to many of the electronics plants in Scotland, trade unions were accepted by the Plessey management at Bathgate, and the workforce was heavily unionised. The majority of assembly workers were members of the Amalgamated Union of Engineering Workers, while the staff employees were represented by TASS, the white collar associate of AUEW. A small number of workers were represented by the Electrical, Telecommunications and Plumbing Union and the Association of Professional, Executive, Clerical and Computer Staff.

A distinction must be made here between official trade union representatives and shop stewards. Shop stewards in British industrial relations are generally elected representatives of a workgroup, who deal with union and work matters at a workplace level. These are unpaid representatives, who, in the AUEW, constitute the intermediate level between full-time, paid officials of the union, and the union's rank and file members. Many trade unions rely to a considerable extent on shop stewards, and have arrangements for granting them credentials. At Plessey, the 20 female and six male shop stewards at the plant prior to the occupation were granted full recognition and facilities by the company. In the remainder of this case study, shop steward refers to unpaid workplace representatives while trade union officials refers to the full-time, paid officers of the union. The term 'convenor', which will be used later on, refers to the senior steward in a plant where a number of stewards exist.

In the late 1970s and early 1980s the Bathgate plant became the victim of Plessey's changing corporate strategies. In the post-war period Plessey followed a policy of mergers, expansion and diversification, such that between 1962 and 1971, the company's turnover grew fivefold. Nevertheless, Plessey's profitability record was poor with earnings per share in 1971 the same as they had been in 1963. In response to this, Plessey began to pursue a policy of consolidation and 'strategic divestment' in the early 1970s, which involved the elimination of all those businesses considered to be outside the mainstream activities of the company, such as turntables, hydraulics, sheet metals and capacitors, in order to release resources for more lucrative areas of production, such as office systems and defence equipment. It was not considered important that in some cases these items were being produced profitably — as Elder (1982) points out, on the basis of an interview with a senior Plessey executive, the issue had to be looked at from a corporate standpoint, where the key issue was total corporate profit position, not individual plant profitability. Thus, the company appear to have based their decision to move into other areas of production on the expectation that a higher rate of profit for the company as a whole could be secured.[1]

As pointed out earlier, the employment consequences of the strategic divestment policy were immense, with UK employment falling by 35 per cent. The Bathgate plant did not escape rationalisation, and through both voluntary and compulsory redundancy, employment levels fell steadily from 1973, when 2400 workers were employed, until 1981, when only 330 workers were left at the plant. This was the size of the workforce at the time of the occupation.

There was little worker reaction against the redundancies, although many of the stewards argued that redundancies should be resisted. As one of the women interviewed told me:

There were big rows because we couldn't stop people volunteering for redundancy. The shop stewards wanted them to fight, and not sell their jobs, but they didn't take any notice. . . . people could get jobs in Edinburgh then. . . . it's different now.

It is interesting to speculate on why no worker action was taken in response to previous job losses. The women themselves argued that at the time of these redundancies, the surrounding labour market was less depressed, and thus the effects of redundancies may not have been so severe. Further, some of the women indicated that the closure announcement destroyed any hopes held previously that cutbacks in production and job losses could be reversed at a later date when the effects of world recession had lessened. It may also have been the case that the example of the Lee Jeans sit-in influenced the decision to resist closure.[2]

In December 1981 Plessey announced that the Bathgate capacitor division would close in March 1982: on the grounds that the capacitor market was flooded; that the plant itself was technologically obsolete; and that the factory was making losses of £0.5m per annum, despite a significant investment programme in recent years. This announcement set in motion an occupation by over 220 workers. The occupation lasted eight weeks, and ended with a takeover by Wedge International Holdings BV, the company to whom the entire capacitor division of Plessey, both in the UK and abroad, was sold. The takeover retained 62 jobs at the plant, while the rest of the workforce were made redundant.

The occupation is described in detail in Findlay (1984). What will be considered here is the rationale behind the decision to occupy the factory, and the way in which the strategy was put into operation. An assessment will also be made of the gains made by the women during their struggle, both in terms of job retention and in terms of the development of their own attitudes and beliefs.

THE DECISION TO OCCUPY

Some worker action to resist the closure was inevitable, given the strength of feeling amongst the Plessey workforce at the time of the closure announcement. The continual decline of Bathgate's traditional industries and its major manufacturing establishments, such as British Leyland, had led to a situation in 1981 in which 3350 men and 1635 women were unemployed in the Bathgate area. Taking Bathgate and the nearby towns of Broxburn and Livingston together, male unemployment stood at 21.2 per cent, while official female unemployment stood at 19.0 per cent. Unemployment was a likely prospect for many of the workers:

> I was only forty-five, and I was thinking, where will I get another job at my age, with so many unemployed?

Bathgate and its surrounding areas are made up of relatively small, tightly knit communities, and concern for the future of those communities, particularly their youth, pervaded the views of all the women interviewed:

> We had watched the place go down through the years and there wasn't any other employment in the area. . . . this was the major

employer for women in the area. . . . so the women had said, enough is enough.

We all thought the same — where are our kids going to work?

This concern was especially strong among the older women, many of whom were approaching retirement age, having worked in the plant for more than 30 years. For these women, it would have been in their own self-interest to have taken their redundancy payments, but they decided to support the sit-in for the sake of maintaining employment in the area, thus risking the loss of their redundancy entitlement.

However, the reason put forward most strongly by the Plessey workforce to justify resisting plant closure was a belief in their own profitability. The workers were very scathing of Plessey's claims of heavy losses and technologically obsolete equipment, and were backed up in their assessment by a report on plant profitability by the Trade Union Research Unit of Glasgow College of Technology (TURU,1982). The report pointed out that while there were two other capacitor manufacturing operations in Scotland (Hughes Microelectronics in Glenrothes and Sprague Electrical in Galashiels, both foreign-owned), their product ranges were narrower than Bathgate's, and their combined sales only half of Bathgate's. Plessey Bathgate was therefore Scotland's major manufacturer of capacitors. The Report agreed with the workers' assessment that the machinery at Bathgate was not technologically obsolete. It was felt that the manufacturing equipment installed at Bathgate was comparable, in terms of efficiency, with that used by other manufacturers. Indeed, £200 000 worth of new machinery had been installed at Bathgate as recently as September 1981. The Report argued that Plessey's strategy of trying to build up defence contracts and communications systems and software, while at the same time phasing out its manufacture of microelectronics and components, including capacitors, was extremely risky. It also argued that to sell out the major British-owned capacitor operation into foreign control or cut back or close Bathgate, the major manufacturing base of that operation, made no sense for the electronics components industry or for the Scottish or UK economy.

At the time of the closure announcement the order books of the Bathgate plant were full and growing. The annual accounts of Plessey Capacitors, Bathgate, show sales in 1981 of £6 575 000 — an increase of £128 000 on the 1980 sales figures. The annual profit and loss statements for Plessey Capacitors do in fact show losses on sales for

all three years that accounts exist (that is, 1979, 1980, 1981). How
ever, the accompanying notes to the accounts suggest that these wer
paper losses produced by the way the accounting was done. Fo
instance: in 1979, the Bathgate firm made provision for 'produc
rationalisation, including redundancy and evacuation of buildin
costs' which effectively converted a profit on trade for that year into
substantial loss. To the workers, this indicated that the company wa
deliberately engineering the apparent lack of profitability of th
plant.

The workers also argued that the annual accounts would not give ₐ
true picture of the profitability of the Bathgate plant because the
believed that Bathgate's capacitors were being 'sold' to other Plesse
plants at transfer prices which were set at levels detrimental t
Bathgate, so that some of Bathgate's actual profits were being trans
ferred to other plants. Furthermore, they felt that the company wa
deliberately diverting orders to other plants to the detriment of th
Bathgate plant. Certain long-standing orders had ceased to be place
at Bathgate:

> This didn't ring true in the capacitor world. In the capacito
> industry you have to keep ahead with new designs, but old design
> keep on going — they trickle out — they don't dry up at once.
> just didn't believe them — there was a lot of our work going dow
> to England, and Plessey were deliberately diverting orders.

An evaluation of the annual accounts was made by members of the
Edinburgh group of the Conference of Socialist Economists, takin
into account possible transfer pricing. This suggests that a modes
profit was actually being made at the Bathgate plant, even during ₐ
period of severe recession.

The Plessey workers totally disbelieved the reasons for closure
given by the company, and this was a major contribution to the
strength of feeling that the decision should be resisted. The worker
believed, and were eventually proved right, that Plessey's aim was t
move out of capacitor manufacture altogether. For the Plessey workers.
then, it can be argued that a belief in their own profitability and
efficiency played a greater part in bringing about resistance than did
any conceptions of a natural right to employment.

One identifiable group of workers, however, was not convinced by
the reasons put forward for resisting the closure of the plant. Out of ₐ
group of 80 skilled and semi-skilled men employed in the plant, only

12 agreed to stay and fight with the women workers. Two alternative views were put forward on why this should be the case. One steward argued that the skilled men at Plessey had 'a track record of weakness and lack of political clarity with respect to their situation. . . . with very little trade union principles'; another explained the refusal of the skilled men to support their action as being a response to previous hostilities which had existed between the toolmakers and particular stewards: 'skilled men are very petty, they always have been. They won't be dictated to by semi-skilled people'. Other workers argued that the skilled men thought it unlikely that their action would achieve any measure of success, and they may have believed that having a skill made it more likely that they would obtain alternative employment. Whatever their reasons, the failure of the male workers as a whole, skilled or semi-skilled, to support their fellow workers, indicates the traditional problems of trying to build solidarity where internal divisions exist, based on skill, sex or some other factor, among the workforce.

The workers realised that some extraordinary action was needed if Plessey was to be forced to reconsider its decision. They considered that the factory's machinery and stocks were still valuable assets for Plessey though the building itself belonged to the Scottish Development Agency. They decided that occupying the factory provided the best method of keeping control over the machinery and stocks. It was felt that to try to negotiate with Plessey through traditional trade union channels, or to try to block the removal of equipment and stocks from outside the plant would have proved ineffective: 'We couldn't go on a strike and we couldn't go on a go slow — what was the point?' Further, the idea of a sit-in had become popular due to the action taken by the women at Lee Jeans in 1981 — 'the idea was just there. . . . sit-ins seemed the natural thing to do'. Once the decision to occupy was made, the workers were encouraged by stewards to produce as much output as possible in the period between the closure announcement and the occupation, to boost their negotiating position. This enabled them to earn increased bonus payments, thus helping to ease the financial difficulties likely to occur when wages ceased to be paid. Also, by holding back work in the dispatch stage, the workers were increasing the value of the assets which they would control.

The decision on what action to take against Plessey was influenced by the workers' assessment of the most potentially effective ways of fighting multinational companies like Plessey. However, the decision was also conditioned by a belief on the part of some of the workers that conventional trade union tactics were of little use in dealing with multinational corporations. These issues have been dealt with elsewhere (Baldry *et al.*, 1980). Such a choice may be more attractive to women workers, many of whom do not feel themselves to be wholly integrated into conventional trade union practices and forms of struggle.

THE ORGANISATION OF THE SIT-IN

One of the first tasks facing the 220 Plessey workers who occupied the plant was to overcome the practical difficulties involved in taking over a factory and maintaining it to a standard adequate for large numbers of people to live in for a lengthy period of time, while at the same time trying to carry on an industrial dispute, and gain support from other sections of the community. As may have been expected, most workers described the first few days of the sit-in as extremely chaotic:

> We had to cover the factory 24 hours a day, and we needed someone on the factory gates at all times. We also had to find transport and organise cooking and cleaning. But the effort put in by the workers was absolutely tremendous. . . . people were willing to do shifts for the sit-in, but they never would have worked shifts for Plessey.

Since there were many tasks to be done, committees were set up to take charge of the workforce's finance; to establish contact with other workers and other trade unions; to speak at meetings in the surrounding communities; to cope with the large amount of correspondence which came in; and to collect funds from other organisations.

> Each member of the working committee took charge of a specific task. There had to be people to share responsibility with the stewards — that's where a lot of things fall, with big shots trying to do everything themselves, instead of drawing all the people together.

Inevitably, it took a few days for any order to be arrived at, but most of those involved give the impression that the organisation of the sit-in was very effective. Serious attempts were made to involve the whole workforce in decision-making: mass meetings were held regularly and all of the major decisions were taken when the entire occupying force was present; no matter what shift was in progress when a meeting was held, the workers from all other shifts were called to the factory to attend. Further, in the views of the workers interviewed, most people were keen to make their opinions known, both during mass meetings and in the day-to-day conduct of the occupation, and were keen to become involved in the actual running of the sit-in, in the various areas specified earlier:

> Everybody got their say. But the stewards did a good job and we were quite happy to follow their leadership.

The Plessey workers retained a high level of morale and a great feeling of solidarity and collective consciousness: workers dedicated a far greater proportion of their lives to the sit-in than would have been devoted to work, in most cases completely uprooting their domestic life in the process. Women, many of whom had never been involved in industrial action in their lives, were encouraged to go out and address public meetings, to visit other plants and ask for the support, both moral and financial, of other workers. Thus, there were many positive aspects of the Plessey occupation, no matter what its eventual material outcome. This involvement was important for many of the women:

> We all got really involved as we got to understand more. . . . we were happy to get involved when we realised the degree of support we had, and we knew we were not fighting alone. I know the sit-in was successful in getting people involved. There was a definite feeling of everybody working together.

It is paradoxical that women are willing to undertake a form of industrial struggle which, more than other forms of action, disrupts their domestic life. Sit-ins require a great deal of workers' time and commitment. Since many women have a double burden, wage work and unpaid domestic labour, one might expect them to be less attracted to forms of action which make extra demands on their time. Participation in the Plessey occupation did involve added burdens for many women. These were twofold. Firstly, working shift rotas in the sit-in and looking after children proved to be particularly difficult.

Efforts were made to exclude women with children from the night shifts, since this may have led to problems of child-care. There is, however, no indication that any collective child-care was organised. Secondly, for some women, the attitudes of their husband's proved to be a source of anxiety:

> A few women left as it [the sit-in] was causing family problems. . . . it was difficult to cope with families without a wage. Some got a lot of stick from their husbands and had to leave the sit-in to prevent domestic troubles. But there were many glowing examples of husbands' changing their attitudes.

However, although the women workers did believe that their domestic situation made participation in the sit-in more difficult, many of them also believed that women in general possess greater determination and stamina than men when faced with an adverse situation:

> If women put their teeth into anything, and are really determined enough, they will exceed men at any time. . . . women are more determined than men will ever be, and they'll take more knocks than men.

Informal discussions with a group of women involved in the occupation indicated that the solidarity they felt may well have been engendered by a sense of common interest as women: the belief that they shared a common work and life situation. The awareness of women workers of the similar situation of other women workers, most of whom share similar domestic responsibilities, may foster attitudes of co-operation and mutual assistance. This can obviously be a great advantage during industrial disputes. Whatever the explanation of the fact that recent prominent sit-ins in Scotland have been carried out by women workers, the women of Lee Jeans, Plessey and many others, have clearly smashed the notion of women as passive workers. As one woman pointed out:

> One of the achievements was that women were able to speak up for themselves, women that I would never have dreamt would have made a contribution at a union meeting, all had an opinion to give. . . . it puts a backbone into people.

SOLIDARITY FROM OTHER SECTIONS OF THE LABOUR MOVEMENT

Most of the occupations which have taken place in the UK in recent years have attracted considerable support for occupying workers from other sections of the labour movement. The Plessey occupation was no exception. Stewards from other Plessey plants in Britain were asked to elicit the support of their members for the workers' struggle at Bathgate. According to the Bathgate stewards, the response was heartening: regular financial contributions were made to the Bathgate strike fund, and representatives of the other workers were often present at the Bathgate plant to offer their moral support:

> The other Plessey workers gave us a tremendous amount of support. . . . they showed great interest and levied their members to give us finance.

On another level, the workers at other Plessey plants in Britain took part in a one hour stoppage, then in a half-day stoppage to show their support for their fellow workers at Bathgate, as well as demonstrating outside Plessey headquarters in London. The Bathgate stewards believed that these actions alarmed the Plessey management: before the half-day stoppage, management at the English plants printed and distributed thousands of leaflets to their own workers, telling them that they should not support the Bathgate struggle. The Bathgate workers felt that this was an indication that the management were feeling pressurised:

> In a way, the company must have realised that if we were getting support from other places, they might have the same problem on their hands later on.

Some of the workers had hoped that the company's employees outside Bathgate would call a full stoppage to support them. Others seemed more aware of the difficulties involved in such a course of action:

> Some of the Bathgate plant was being transferred down south, so it meant jobs for them. . . . they weren't going to strike to put themselves out of a job.

The dispute shows the contradictions involved in any attempt to co-ordinate protest between employees of the same company in different plants in different parts of the country, or across countries. While it may be in the workers' long-term interest to try to prevent policies which involve mass redundancies from being carried out, in the short term the increased job security which the closure of one plant may mean for another plant can be a source of division among workers (Haworth and Ramsay, 1984).

Despite the fact that the support of other Plessey workers was qualified, the Bathgate stewards argue that it was significant:

It was the first time Plessey factories had ever helped each other, and it hasn't happened since. There have been other redundancies and closures, but none of them even fought.

However, the workers involved in the occupation and subsequently re-employed in the Plessey plant do now show a great deal of solidarity with other workers' struggles, in the form of financial contributions to other strike funds and the offering of help and advice to other groups of workers. This appears to be in marked contrast with their behaviour prior to the occupation. It can be argued that for some of the Plessey workers at least, experience of collective struggle did enhance their belief in the need for labour solidarity to fight multinational corporations, and their consciousness of the resources which workers possess, although it may also have increased their awareness of the contradictions involved in attempts to extend solidarity among workers.

An attempt was made to co-ordinate pressure on Plessey internationally, by making contacts with the Plessey plant at Arco in Italy, a sister plant to the one in Bathgate. The Bathgate workers encountered difficulties in getting information on the Bathgate struggle to the Italian workforce, not least because the Italian management had provided their workforce with entirely misleading information on the dispute. Finally, the Bathgate workers sent a representative to Italy to inform the Italian workers directly of the occupation.

Since the occupation ended shortly after the contact was made, it was impossible to test whether the Italian workers would have taken direct action in support of their Bathgate colleagues. Many of the workers and shop stewards at Bathgate believed that a basis was there for extending the struggle to an international level, with the Italian workers refusing to accept machinery and stocks from the

Bathgate plant, and perhaps pressurising the Plessey management through stoppages. This hope appears to have been based on a verbal commitment from the Italian workers to take some action on Bathgate's behalf.

Had the dispute continued, the hopes of the Bathgate workers might have been disappointed. The divisions which exist among workers at one plant can have a detrimental effect on solidarity, and this is compounded by divisions which exist between workers at different plants, even where these workers are employed by the same company. Such difficulties are magnified when attempts are made at international solidarity (Haworth and Ramsay, 1984). This is not to say that international labour solidarity is unachievable. However, such solidarity cannot be assumed to exist automatically.

Support in the United Kingdom for the Plessey women was not confined to Plessey employees. According to one worker: 'We caught the imagination of the trade union and labour movement in Scotland'. This certainly appears to be true. The Plessey workers received massive financial contributions: the ship workers, miners and others paid a levy from their wages each week into a strike fund, while many other workplaces carried out collections at regular intervals. Towards the end of the sit-in, the workers were receiving between £5000 and £6000 per week. Clearly, this was a crucial component in the ability of the workforce to continue with the sit-in. More importantly, however, the Plessey workers emphasised that support from other workers, mobilised in the main through informal shop steward networks, provided a tremendous boost to their morale:

> This is what gave the women the will to fight on. . . . they felt that to stop fighting wasn't only letting themselves down, it was letting down that whole labour movement as well. If we'd been left on our own, I don't know if we would have lasted eight weeks.

The dispute does show that the labour movement can elicit significant reserves of solidarity and support. However, there are constraints on such support: it will be forthcoming so long as other workers do not feel they are putting their jobs in jeopardy by offering support. Financial contributions and participation in demonstrations are unlikely to jeopardise jobs. However, strikes by other Plessey employees may indeed have threatened their jobs, and this may explain why such action was not taken.

COMMUNITY-BASED SUPPORT

The sit-in not only won the support of workers in other areas, but it also won the commitment of the Bathgate community. The realisation of the dire prospects facing the town contributed to the support which the townspeople showed the Plessey workers. Donations came from all sources to the plant: from local shopkeepers, families, pensioners, in the form of finance and provisions, and from the few factories which still existed in the area, particularly from British Leyland. The workers were also supported by their local regional and district councils, and by their Member of Parliament, Tam Dalyell. The workers argued that the townspeople had realised the impact that the closure would have on the community, and on their children's prospects.

> People could see the community going down and down. The British Leyland dispute was going on and everyone was worried there wasn't going to be any work left. It let the workers know that the people outside did care about them, and were appreciating the fight the workers were putting up.

It may be the case that the domestic roles of many women workers, such as shopping, involvement in local schools, youth and community organisations, and also in informal neighbourhood groups and kin groups, provide the foundation on which community support can be built, more so than is the case for male workers. Many women spend time and energy constituting these kinds of networks, and these may be of great significance in an industrial dispute, particularly where a dispute affects many members of the same community, as was the case at Bathgate.

THE ROLE OF FORMAL TRADE UNION STRUCTURES

In accordance with previously laid down procedures, the trade union officers were informed of the Plessey closure decision at around the same time as the workers. According to the AUEW Glasgow Divisional Officer, they were stunned at the news, and apprehensive about Bathgate's employment prospects in the future. Many of the leading members of the unions involved encouraged the workers to fight to save their jobs. However, this was before any specific form of industrial action had been decided on. Such a supportive position did not continue throughout the dispute.

Formally, the full-time trade union officials were not informed of the intended occupation until it took place, and thus were not party to the decision. However, it seems likely that certain officers of the union, with whom the workers had good relations, were told informally of the workers' intentions.

The main assistance given by the official trade union structure took the form of paying strike pay (although this was not paid until four weeks after the occupation began); helping to collect funds; commissioning a study on the reasons behind the plant's closure, and of the state of the capacitor industry in general; and attempting to provide legal advice for the workers (although in some cases this advice proved to be wrong). As far as the Glasgow Divisional Officer of the AUEW was concerned:

> Whatever assistance was sought by the workforce, if it was physically possible to provide that assistance, whether it be financial, moral, legal or whatever, then it was given. That is what the trade union is for.

Some stewards and ordinary workers at Plessey disagreed with this view, as these comments indicate:

> I thought the officials could have done a lot more. . . . they left an awful lot in the hands of the officials [stewards] here.

> They could have given us more support. We didn't see them doing anything. We always got the feeling they were too busy.

> I'm quite sure they could have done more. They should have played an active part in what was going on.

> As far as I'm concerned they wanted the dispute tidied up and wrapped in a bow and then they would have been quite happy.

It is worth quoting at length the comments of one trade union official when confronted with the views of the Plessey workers:

> We live in a democracy and everybody is entitled to their opinion. Bearing in mind the conflict and confrontation people were faced

with, in a situation like an occupation, or any form of industrial action. . . . you look at that kind of situation as you want to see it, irrespective of whether that may be the true position affecting everybody. The simple matter is that if indeed the membership were dissatisfied with the officials who were directly involved at a local level, or even at a national level for that matter, they have the opportunity at a future date to ensure that that official is no longer a representative of the union.

However, while trade union members may have the periodic opportunity to vote against any official with whose conduct they are dissatisfied, this can hardly be said to compensate for the lack of active support during a dispute, when such support is most necessary. Trade unions cannot afford to be complacent with regard to the feelings of sections of their membership if they are to retain support in the future.

PLESSEY'S TACTICS

The Plessey company used various tactics to put pressure on the workers occupying the factory, in attempts to end the occupation. At an early stage in the occupation, the *Glasgow Herald* newspaper reported the workers' fears that Plessey might organise a raid on the plant to snatch £650 000 worth of components for electronic circuits. These fears were fuelled by the appearance, on several occasions, of a Plessey helicopter circling above the plant. In their defence, the workers had piled up barrels and wooden palettes in readiness for scattering to prevent any helicopter landing.

On 12 February Plessey management left dismissal notices at the gatehouse of the factory for all of the workers involved in the occupation, informing them that they had been dismissed without any entitlement to redundancy payments. At the same time the company instructed telephone engineers to cut off all telephone lines at the factory, leaving the workers with only the payphone at their social club. Despite these mounting pressures, and even after the company had announced the dismissals on radio, and had intimated that the sit-in had cost the workers their redundancy payments, the workers unanimously reaffirmed their intention to continue the occupation.

It can be argued, however, that all these pressures had a far smaller effect on the workers than had the court action taken by Plessey against the occupying workers. For ordinary working people, the courts are an arena in which they have very little experience, and about which they appear to have great apprehension. The complex debate on the legal situation surrounding the Plessey occupation cannot be discussed here (for a detailed discussion, see Findlay, 1984). The attempts by Plessey to use the courts to evict the occupying workers, although ultimately unsuccessful, were significant in indicating that the owners of capital will resort to the power of the state to defend their property rights against perceived challenges by workers.

THE NEGOTIATIONS

Negotiations between the unions with members involved in the Plessey occupation and the Plessey management began on 5 February 1982. The first real hint of any breakthrough came much later, however, on 8 March, when the union negotiating team attended talks at the London offices of the Arbitration and Conciliation Advisory Service on the invitation of the company. The talks were arranged to consider a proposed management buy-out plan, and also to discuss a possible takeover by Wedge International Holdings BV. At the end of these discussions a plan was outlined in which Arcotronics, a subsidiary of Wedge Holdings, proposed to take over part of the plant and employ around 80 workers on the condition that the occupation be terminated immediately.

However, at a mass meeting, the workers at Bathgate voted overwhelmingly to reject the Arcotronics takeover bid on the recommendation of their stewards. They were dissatisfied with the number of jobs on offer; they were not convinced that the takeover would prevent an asset-stripping operation by Plessey; and they did not believe that they had enough information on Arcotronics to warrant accepting its offer — as one shop steward pointed out, 'It was like asking you to take a house with no roof'. Only seven days later, however, the Plessey workforce voted two to one to accept the Arcotronics takeover bid. The proposal had changed little since it had been on offer the previous week, except that Plessey had agreed to guarantee that the jobs would remain in existence for one year, by placing sufficient orders with Arcotronics. In the first bid the guarantee had been for three months only.

Some of the Plessey workers have very strong views on why the takeover was finally accepted so soon after being overwhelmingly rejected. The Convenor at the plant believed that in the week separating the two offers, the trade union officials worked to undermine the sit-in. According to this steward, the officials were talking privately to key shop stewards, and winning them over to their position, 'They were really saying, "That's all you're going to get; reject this and you'll lose everything"'. Other rank and file workers argued that the unions, along with management, 'had an almost common objective to bring the occupation to a halt as quickly as possible'.

> We felt they [the union officials] could have got more jobs than 80, but they said it was over. They weren't for us, they were for the firm. . . . more on the management side than on our side.

> They wanted to get us off their back really — they were paying us strike pay and unions don't like to pay strike pay.

> They [the union officials] said they did their best, but you've just got their word for that.

For these workers the sit-in was still going strong: the interim interdict and order for eviction against the workers had been recalled; the Italian factory had indicated some willingness to refuse to allow any of the Bathgate machinery into their plant; and financial contributions were flowing in at a rate of £6000–£7000 per week.

However, many of the occupying workers held opposing views to these, as indicated by the outcome of the vote. Many workers accepted the interpretation of the situation given by the union officials:

> They had taken us to the end of the road, and there was nowhere else they could take us.

> The unions were persuading us to accept the takeover — I listened to them and thought '80 jobs are better than none'.

As the sit-in had progressed into its later stages, divisions had appeared between the workers. Some were becoming increasingly disaffected with the struggle, and were increasingly more vulnerable to mounting external pressures. To them the sit-in was falling apart and the workers were becoming depressed and anxious over the possible loss of redundancy payments. As one woman pointed out:

> You can fight as long as you have your troops, but when people want out, irrespective of what the union thinks, or what the people who have led that fight think, they're not going to stay and fight, and the majority of people in that hall had had enough.

It is difficult to assess which view of the sit-in was more realistic. On the one hand, the offer involved only 80 jobs, which meant that only one-third of those workers who occupied would remain in employment; the offer included a management right to appoint the workers they wanted; and a wage freeze imposed for one year. Further, workers were to sign an agreement saying that they would not oppose the movement of any machinery out of the plant, in direct opposition to the aims of the sit-in. However, on the other hand, there is little concrete evidence to indicate that a more acceptable settlement could have been obtained. Moreover, there were obvious difficulties in sustaining the momentum of the industrial action over a long period, and the appearance of divisions among the occupying force augured badly for the continuance of the sit-in.

For those workers who had disagreed with the decision to accept the takeover bid and end the occupation, the general feeling at the end of the sit-in was one of bitterness and disappointment.

> There was no victory feeling — just a lot of bitterness.

> Much, much more could have been achieved if others had had the confidence to keep going.

However, amongst those workers interviewed, there was complete agreement that the sit-in had been a worthwhile experience, and most expressed satisfaction at having taken part:

> When you consider how things were stacked against people, the occupation was remarkable, courageous and solidaristic.

> The sit-in definitely brought people together. There was a great feeling of being together and of camaraderie during the fight.

> The sit-in was a success as everybody pulled together — the majority took their turn at doing what needed to be done.

These workers argued that they would recommend the sit-in to other workers facing closure, where they felt that there was some possibility of either reversing the closure decision or attracting new capital. The general feeling was that the sit-in was an effective tactic against redundancy: in many ways it was seen as the only action workers could take which had any hopes of success. They did point out, however, that workers who were considering occupying their factories should be fully aware of the difficulties involved in occupations, and should take into consideration the sacrifices of home life and social life which have to be made: 'Yes, I would recommend it to other workers, but everybody has to want to do it'.

CONCLUSION

Examination of the Plessey occupation enables us to take a close look at the potential significance of direct action against multinational companies — at the rationale behind such action, as well as the gains to be made by workers who choose to use it. Forms of direct action such as occupations are responses to the absolute power of capital with respect to plant closure. Multinational corporations are particularly powerful in this respect, due to their ability to relocate investment and production in various parts of the world. This has rarely been successfully challenged by the labour movement. Trade unions work from the basis of a continuing bargaining relationship with the employer. Where such a bargaining relationship ceases, as in the case of closure, conventional trade union actions such as strikes and go-slows are unlikely to have much effect on employers' policy decisions. Many workers have come to realise these limitations on trade union actions with respect to closure, and have been forced, therefore, to resort to the other methods of protest.

It would be difficult to argue that the Bathgate plant would have remained open at all (albeit with vastly reduced employment levels), without the direct intervention of the workforce. Thus, in this respect, this form of action paid off for the Plessey workers. However, it also brought other gains — as outlined earlier, the occupation stimulated high levels of solidarity, involvement and collective identification amongst the Plessey workers, as well as extensive support from the labour and trade union movement.

The involvement of a large number of women in this dispute was also a significant factor. There is no evidence to suggest that the decision to close the plant or the tactics used against the occupying workers were affected by the fact that the workforce was mainly female, and thus the importance of the workers being female was not in terms of its effect on the company's policies. Rather, in this particular dispute, there is some basis for suggesting that the importance of the workers being women was in terms of their attitudes to struggle and solidarity, and their particular experience as women workers. The questions surrounding the particular nature of women workers' involvement in, and attitudes towards, industrial action, need to be further investigated, however, before any definitive conclusions on the specific role of women in industrial action can be drawn.

NOTES

1. Baldry *et al.*, 1980, came to similar conclusions on the strategy of the Massey-Ferguson company in the run up to the closure of the company's Kilmarnock plant.
2. The workers of the Lee Jeans factory in nearby Greenock had occupied their factory in February 1981, in protest at the decision of their employers, the American VF Corporation, to close the plant. See chapter 5.

REFERENCES

C. Baldry, N. Haworth and H. Ramsay, 'Confronting Multinationals: The Case of Massey Ferguson, Kilmarnock', Paper to British Sociological Association Conference, Aberdeen, March 1980.

A. Elder, 'Plessey: A Multinational in the Eighties', Junior Honours Dissertation, University of Edinburgh, 1982.

P. Findlay, 'Worker Reaction to Closure: A Case Study of the Occupation at Plessey, Bathgate', Honours Dissertation, University of Strathclyde, Glasgow, 1984.

N. Haworth and H. Ramsey, 'Grasping the Nettle: Problems in the Theory of International Labour Solidarity', in P. Waterman (ed.) *For a New Labour Internationalism* (The Hague: International Labour Education, Research and Information Foundation, 1984).

Labour Research Bulletin, 'Leading British Multinationals', *Labour Research Bulletin*, October 1978.

R. MacPherson, 'Bathgate — Frontline Town' (Edinburgh: Conference of Socialist Economists, 1982).

Trade Union Research Unit, *The Proposed Closure of Plessey Capacitors Ltd., Bathgate: A Trade Union Report* (Glasgow College of Technology, 1982).

11 Restructuring Women's Employment in British Petroleum
Marilyn Davidson

An Equal Opportunities Audit in BP (UK) aimed at analysing women's current position in the company in order to identify any reasons for job segregation and blocks to career progression is described in this chapter. Based on the findings of this study, recommendations for a programme of positive action are presented (some of which have already been initiated by BP).

The project was sponsored by the UK Equal Opportunities Commission, and was carried out by the author over a six month period from May to October 1983. There were two major phases to the study: firstly, examination of company policies and practices with particular focus on the Engineering and Oil Supply and Trading Departments, in order to identify any *structural* barriers to recruitment, training and promotion of women; and secondly, interviewing of representatives of the workforce (male and female), relevant staff organisations, and management in order to identify any *attitudinal* barriers to the recruitment, training and promotion of women.

WOMEN IN THE OIL INDUSTRY

Research into the problems experienced by women at work has revealed that women face most problems when entering and working in organisations where men have traditionally held professional and managerial positions (Davidson and Cooper, 1983a, b, 1984). The oil industry is a prime example of this. Women have always been concentrated in secretarial and clerical jobs and even with an increase in the intake of female graduates, women are still not breaking into the middle and senior management grades. This is not solely explained by the fact that some women leave before they could qualify by service for the higher grades.

About 18 per cent of employees of the UK oil industry are women.

TABLE 11.1   *Women's share of employment in the UK Oil Industry*

Occupation	Female Share (%)
Managers	1.6
Supervisors	9.0
Technologists	2.5
Sales representatives	0.5
Computer staff	39.6
Professional and administrative staff	16.3
Technicians	8.1
Craftsmen	0
Production operators	3.7
Other operators	1.6
Drivers	0
Office support	61.1
Others	22.8

SOURCE   Adapted from McCormack (1981), p.4.

Table 11.1 shows the percentage for each occupational group. As McCormack (1981) points out, the table clearly illustrates that the majority of women are found in office support and computing; few are employed as technologists, craftsmen, technicians or supervisors and managers. She believes the reason today's managers fail to take the career aspirations of women seriously is due to the fact that before the development of North Sea oil there were very few opportunities for women professionals in exploration and development (especially in the Middle East). Indeed, unlike the Norwegians and Americans, British oil companies are only just beginning to allow women to work and stay on the offshore oil rigs.

The supply of technically qualified women is expanding. In the universities and polytechnics there has been a gradual increase in the numbers of women studying engineering and technology from 4 per cent in 1975 to 6.9 per cent in 1980. Over 32 per cent of science undergraduates are now female and the Industrial Society estimated that in 1986 women scientists would account for one in seven of the total scientific population; in 1979 it was one in four. Local government and the other public authorities are the major destinations for female graduates. Even so, women graduate entrants to industry and commerce have almost doubled over the last ten years to one in four.

Trends in women's employment as engineers have been mixed. While there has been a decrease in the percentage of female instrument and electrical engineers since 1975, there have been slight increases in the percentage of women in other engineering specialities. In 1982 15.3 per cent of mechanical engineers and 8.2 per cent of shipbuilding and marine engineers in industry were women — an increase since 1975 of 0.2 per cent and 2 per cent respectively. However, the percentage of women in instrument engineering declined from 38.6 per cent in 1975 to 32.6 per cent in 1982; and in electrical engineering from 36.2 per cent to 31.9 per cent.

Female membership of professional engineering institutes is still very low; in 1982 women constituted 2.3 per cent of the membership of the Institution of Chemical Engineers, 0.5 per cent of the Institution of Mechanical Engineers, and 0.4 per cent of the Institution of Production Engineers.

THE POSITION OF WOMEN IN BP

The BP Group is an energy and natural resources company. It is one of the largest industrial concerns in Britain; the second biggest in Western Europe; and amongst the top half-dozen or so companies in the non-communist world. BP's total operation comprises some 1900 subsidiary and related companies which between them are active in more than 70 countries on six continents. Over 130 000 people work directly for BP around the world, some 33 000 of those in the UK alone.

The Group's Head Office and main businesses are based in London, but there are offices in major towns and cities throughout the UK and the rest of the world. The principle business remains that of exploring for, producing, transporting, refining and marketing oil. However, the Group also has major investments in chemicals, minerals, coal and gas, as well as interests in nutrition, detergents and a whole range of other activities.

The job grading system in BP ranges from the lowest grade of 2 to the most senior director level of 20. Non-professional grades range from 2 to 6; professional grades from 7 upwards with graduate intake starting at grade 7. Grade 12 signifies Line Management level and grades 13 and 14 Branch Management.

At the time of the study, over 80 per cent of women employed by BP in the UK were in the non-professional grades, whereas about 75 per cent of the men were in the management and professional ranks.

Recruitment of female graduates in BP

In 1983 women accounted for one in every four applications received. But by the time the second interview stage was reached the proportion of women had fallen. The reduced proportion of women at the second interview stage might at first suggest that discrimination was operating. However, a breakdown of the female applicants by degree discipline indicated that this reduction was probably being caused by the disproportionately large number of women who apply for the relatively few vacancies for jobs in areas such as Accounting, Computing, Planning and Personnel. For example, in 1982 only 7 per cent of female applicants had engineering degrees compared with just over 30 per cent of male applicants, yet the engineering functions accounted for 38 per cent of the jobs on offer.

In the later stages of the recruitment process women do as well as, if not slightly better than, men. For instance, in 1982 women represented 16 per cent of the second interview population yet accounted for 17 per cent of offers and nearly 17 per cent of acceptances.

Examination of the intake by employing function showed that whilst the proportion of female graduates recruited had remained constant over the previous three years, the proportion of females entering the technical functions had increased from just under 11 per cent in 1980 to 17 per cent in 1982. During the same period, the proportion of females entering the engineering functions had decreased from 12 per cent in 1980 to just under 9 per cent in 1982. BP seems to be similar to the rest of the UK oil industry in its female share of professional and managerial positions. However, the proportion of women in engineering in BP was well below the proportion of engineering graduates who are women (even taking into account that BP tends to recruit only graduates with first class honours or upper second honours degrees).

Staff turnover rate was greater for women than for men. After five years 83 per cent of men were still with the company compared to 65 per cent of women. Projecting those trends, half the men would still be working for BP after 24 years, but half the women would have left after nine years. The major reason for this tends to be marriage and pregnancy, but it should be emphasised that over 80 per cent of the women who leave are in the non-professional grades which have higher turnover rates than professional female workers. BP conformed to the statutory requirement to hold open for 29 weeks after confinement the job of any women who had been employed for two years or more, but offered no additional support such as creches part-time work, or re-entry schemes, to encourage its female employees to return to employment after maternity leave.

POSITIVE ACTION

Recently a growing number of organisations in the UK (including a number of multinationals) have introduced positive action programmes and equal opportunity policies, in order to provide women with the same job opportunities as men. These include such diverse institutions as the Wellcome Foundation, Thames Television, Sainsburys, Westland Helicopters, Rank Xerox, Abbey National, GEC, HM Treasury, the Greater London Council, IBM, the Civil Service, the National Westminster Bank, the Midland Bank, and the West Yorkshire Metropolitan County Council.

All the evidence so far suggests that positive action benefits both male and female employees in an organisation. Positive action programmes have been shown to assist in discovering and utilising hidden resources; improving efficiency and productivity; increasing morale, motivation and job satisfaction of both employees and management; and helping decrease staff turnover rates. Hence, for all these reasons, positive action can also prove *economically* beneficial for an organisation (Robarts and Ball, 1981; Wainwright, 1983). Positive action is not about discriminating against men but is about providing genuine equality of opportunity for men and women whatever their ages. Positive action involves detailed analysis of women's current position in the workforce and the aim is to identify the reasons for job segregation and the blocks to career progression.

The scope of the positive action research project at BP

Besides a general analysis of the position of women in BP as a whole, the project concentrated on the Engineering Department, consisting of Central Engineering (ENG), Business Technical Support (BTS) and Projects Department (PRJ); and the Department of Oil Trade and Supply. The two major departments were chosen to represent the two extremes of female professional employment in BP.

The three engineering departments operate within Group Engineering and Technical Centre. The Central Engineering Department provides a range of professional engineering and consultative services through specialists in specific disciplines; Business Technical Support offers a source of applied technology and experience in engineering and operations; and the Projects Department provides a project management service to the Group's businesses. More than 700 professional engineers work in these departments at any one time and some 450 are working in the London base. The Department of Oil Trade and Supply operates within BP Oil International, which is responsible for BP's oil supply, refining and marketing business worldwide. OTS is responsible for acquiring and transporting most of the oil refined and marketed by the BP group. With one or two exceptions, the Engineering Department has only been recruiting female engineers in the past four years. In 1983, at the time of the study, there were still only 12 female engineers compared to over 700 male engineers. In Trade and Supply, on the other hand, there were 25 female professionals compared to 114 male professionals, and women had occupied professional posts for a number of years. OTS had a reputation for employing a high percentage of female graduates compared to most other BP departments.

Stage 1 of this study investigated possible structural barriers to women's career development in recruitment policies, training, promotion procedures and so on. This involved meetings with employees responsible for recruitment policies; training practices; staff performance appraisal system; staff development committees including a 'High Flyer' scheme; committee and executive programme; residential assessment boards; job evaluation system; staff consultative committees; staff data system. In addition, relevant literature, manuals, brochures, interview forms, and specifically requested statistical data were examined.

Stage 2 investigated possible attitudinal barriers. A semi-structured interview was designed including questions relating to attitudes to, experiences of and opinions about the following issues:

(1) recruitment and interview procedures;
(2) training courses and job experience opportunities;
(3) job satisfaction and utilisation of skills;
(4) career intentions and prospects (including barriers);
(5) grading systems (and High Flyer scheme);
(6) promotion procedures such as assessment, job evaluation; non-traditional career paths, career counselling;
(7) attitudes of colleagues and subordinates;
(8) attitudes of supervisors and managers;
(9) provisions for maternity/paternity leave, creche, flexi-time,

part-time work, job sharing, career breaks, and refresher courses;

(10) positive action in BP.

On this basis interviews were carried out with 119 men and women employed in the engineering Department and the Department of Oil Trade and Supply.

The men interviewed in Engineering included 29 line managers, personnel officers and terminal managers; six branch managers; and 16 male engineers. All 12 of the female engineers were interviewed in addition to 20 female secretaries (including the secretarial co-ordinator) and eight female clerks. A number of formal interviews were carried out with women working at different oil sites. In the Department of Oil Trade and Supply, four male branch managers were interviewed; 18 female professionals; one female senior secretary and five female clerks and supply assistants.

With the exception of managers, all employees, both males and females, were asked exactly the same questions by the interviewers. Managers on the other hand, were not subjected to the same semi-structured interview format, but were questioned more about their general attitudes and opinions relating to BP policies and practices, and their female and male subordinates. It should be emphasised that confidentiality and anonymity were assured throughout the study.

In addition, dozens of informal interviews and discussions with other employees took place. They included an open lunch-time session to which secretaries from other departments were invited to discuss the job of being a secretary in BP. From the beginning the study also involved numerous contacts with the 'Women in BP' group. The group was formed in July 1982 with the general aim of helping women make the best use of their skills and talents and to encourage a much greater participation of women in as many areas as possible within the company. The group has an elected organising committee and receives moral and financial support from BP management. The group has organised numerous public meetings and lectures and has also collected statistics and information on career development needs of women working in BP.

RESULT OF STAGE 1 ANALYSIS OF THE ENGINEERING DEPARTMENT

In the Engineering Department 85.9 per cent of the employees were males; 76.3 per cent of women working in Engineering were concentrated in the non-professional secretarial and clerical grades, below grade 7, compared to only 0.8 per cent of men. Looking at the grade range 7 to 10 (including graduate trainees), there were only 23.8 per cent of the total female workforce in these grades compared to 52 per cent of the total male workforce. There were no women in grades higher than grade 10; 29.4 per cent of the male workforce were in grades 11 and 12, and 13.2 per cent occupied grades between 13 and 17.

There were, as mentioned, a total of 12 female engineers and 700 male engineers (450 based in London); that is, 1.7 per cent of engineers were women. The four women in grade 8 to 8.1 consisted of two chemical engineers, one civil engineer and one electrical and control engineer. Of the two women in grade 9, one was a civil engineer and one an oceanographer. The most senior woman in the Engineering Department was a grade 10 planning engineer. There were five trainee female graduate engineers; two of whom were chemical engineers; one an electrical and control engineer; one an instrument engineer and one a mechanical engineer. In contrast there were 22 male graduate trainee engineers. A new opportunity opened up for women when, late in 1983, the Engineering Department formed a new Management Information Division, and introduced a commercial apprenticeship scheme. The first person to be recruited on this scheme as a commercial apprentice was a woman who originally applied for a secretarial post in the Engineering Department and expressed a desire to switch eventually from secretarial work to commerce. As she had attained the Business Education Certificate I (BEC I) she was immediately chosen for an apprenticeship; she was then sponsored to study for the more advanced qualification, BEC II.

In addition the Planning and Cost Division introduced a commercial graduate entrance scheme which besides engineering, also seeks specialists in accounting, maths, computers and business studies. The first successful applicants, appointed late in 1983, were two women; one postgraduate chemical engineer and one from BP Corporate Planning with postgraduate qualifications in maths and operations research.

A number of senior personnel managers predicted that the number of female engineers in five years time will probably remain exactly the same at about a dozen, unless a positive action policy programme is carried out in BP. In the words of one manager: 'Positive recruitment is not enough. There is no point staffing the place with good quality women if the environment is discouraging; if they are good, they can move elsewhere without difficulty'.

BP produces a mass of recruitment literature giving prospective employees information about the various businesses and specialist departments. An examination of these booklets revealed that while the majority were careful not to include the words 'he' or 'she', there was no policy statement emphasising that all positions were open to both men and women. Moreover, the majority of photographs in these booklets were of men at work; where women were included they were pictured doing traditionally female desk-bound jobs such as typing, computing and laboratory work. There was no indication, for example, that BP employed any women engineers. Even so, a number of the dozen female engineers now working for BP, are actively encouraged by the Engineering Department to persuade more women to take up engineering and apply for jobs with BP. This involves giving talks at both schools and universities.

All BP employees who are involved in interviewing potential recruits at universities, will have attended a two-and-a-half-day BP Interviewer's course run by external psychologists. The vast majority of people who complete this training course are male. Besides being told that both sexes are to be treated equally, the course syllabus included no training concerning the differences between male and female interviewees especially in relation to the attitudes of interviewers. Interviewers are also given a copy of the 'BP Interviewer's Guide'. In the 1983 guide all potential recruits are referred to as 'he' although there is a qualifying statement at the beginning stating that reference to 'he', or 'his' or 'him' throughout the document means both male and female. The functional profile of the characteristics and qualities of suitable recruits for the Group Engineering Centre refers to 'Male or female candidates . . .' and emphasises mobility. Other than this, no reference was made concerning equality of opportunity throughout this Interviewer's Guide.

At the time of the study all graduate recruitment interviewers in the Engineering Department had been men due to the lack of fully-fledged female engineers. However, there were plans for one of the women engineers to interview potential recruits the following year (although, because of her discipline, she would be restricted to recruiting Civil Engineers); and both young female and male engineers had met the graduate interviewees in their pre-interview waiting rooms, and chatted with them.

RESULTS OF STAGE 1 ANALYSIS OF OIL TRADE AND SUPPLY

In the Department of Oil Trade and Supply (OTS), the majority of employees (69.3 per cent) in grades 4–12 were male, compared to 30.7 percent who were female; 58 per cent of women were in grades below 7.1 compared to 6.1 per cent of men. There were no women in grades above 12 while 15.7 per cent of men occupied grades 13 to 18. However, while the women in grades 4 to 7.1 tended on average to have worked in their jobs longer and to be older than their male counterparts, the opposite trend appeared to be the case for women in grades 8 to 12, compared to men in these grades. A similar trend was found in the Engineering Department.

There were a total of 18 female professionals (in grades 8–12) and 108 male professionals (in grade 8–18); that is, 14.3 per cent of professionals were women. However, the majority of women were concentrated in the lower professional grades 8–8.1 and there was only one woman at grade 12.

Interestingly, two professional women in OTS had returned after maternity leave to work part-time. (Since the completion of this study, one has returned to full-time employment.) One of these women was a grade 9 business analyst with the Systems Division and gave computer advice and advice about future planning. She was doing the same job as she had done before taking maternity leave and worked three days a week in the office. The other woman part-timer was the highest graded female in OTS (grade 12) and previously was a Supply Economics Coordinator. Since returning to work on a part-time basis, she had been given a newly created position dealing with Systems Liaison for OTS. Hence, she was no longer working in OTS but is still parented with the OTS Department (a quite common practice in OTS). She spent two days per week in the office and half a day working at home.

Table 11.2 presents a breakdown of the graduate intake of males and females in OTS between 1976 and 1983. The female graduate intake peaked at 45.5 per cent in 1980; that year also saw the largest numbers of female graduates — five out of a total of 11 graduate entrants. However, since then there has been a decrease in the number of females recruited and in 1983 only one of the ten OTS graduates was female, that is, 10 per cent of the total intake. (Three women were offered jobs, but two turned the offers down, so that 30 per cent of offers were to women.)

TABLE 11.2   *OTS graduate intake, 1976–83*

Year	Male	Offers Accepted Female	Female % of total	Total
1976	9	1	10	10
1977	9	2	18	11
1978	9	2	20	10
1979	6	3	33	9
1980	6	5	45	11
1981	10	2	17	12
1982	3	2	40	5
1983	9	1	10	10
Total	61	18	23	78

Predictions by personnel managers concerning the number of female professionals in OTS were similar to those in Engineering relating to female engineers. It was forecast that the number of OTS female professionals would probably remain about the same within the next five years.

The shortcomings in the training of interviewers and in recruitment literature discussed previously also applied to OTS graduate recruitment policies and practices. For example, in the 1983 'BP Group Graduate Opportunities' booklet (first edition) the section dealing with OTS had no photographs of women and both the case study examples are identified as being male graduates.

However, unlike the Engineering Department, graduates are recruited from all disciplines including languages, and commercial as well as technical subjects. This is the major reason for OTS having a tradition of high female graduate recruitment compared to most other BP departments. Graduates are also required to be numerate and to have good all-round communications skills.

RESULTS OF STAGE 2 ANALYSIS

It should be emphasised that as part of an action-orientated project, the interviews were not designed in order to present the findings using sophisticated statistical techniques. Rather the objective was to find out about women's and men's own personal experiences and attitudes in BP — both the similarities and the differences.

While the majority of male branch managers in engineering, and male engineers, maintained that there were equal opportunities in BP, the majority of all female groups interviewed, and the branch managers in OTS, thought this was not the case. In addition, many male and female interviewees mentioned that they did not think there were equal opportunities in BP for coloured and ethnic minorities. Generally all the female groups were in favour of the formation of the 'Women in BP Group', viewing it as an important support. Male managers and male engineers on the other hand were less convinced of the value of this group.

Women's experiences and attitudes

As a group secretaries were the most dissatisfied with their job opportunities. Many, especially the more highly qualified, wished to branch away from secretarial work, and dissatisfaction stemmed from not being treated properly by managers and professional employees; 'working for too many people'; and working mainly as copy typists.

The group who reported being most under pressure were the female engineers: less than half saw themselves staying with BP compared to three-quarters of the male engineers; and the reasons were based on dissatisfaction with problems and pressures at work, *not* because they planned to have a family in the future. Future career prospects were reported as being better in Oil Trade and Supply by both female clerks and female professionals compared to their counterparts in engineering; and female professionals in OTS foresaw fewer potential career barriers. However, for female engineers, barriers included restrictions concerning work in the Middle East; on sites; and offshore on rigs and boats. Prejudice from male engineers; men on sites; male managers; and clients were also problems. The female engineers also mentioned their high visibility which sometimes led to feelings of isolation, and performance pressures associated with being 'token women'. Nevertheless, although the female professionals in OTS reported less pressure, they too faced problems such as lack of mobility; restrictions on working in Japan and the Middle East; resistance from other men at work especially from male traders; and prejudiced attitudes towards women from a few of the male managers. Another concern was their future dilemma over whether to have a family given the lack of facilities in BP to accommodate the working mother. Finally, a major barrier for those professional women without a degree was their non-graduate status.

On the other hand, for all female secretaries and clerks interviewed, the major barriers highlighted as hampering future career prospects were somewhat different. They mentioned the lack of vacant job positions and job vacancy lists; the technical nature of the work hampering understanding and decreasing job satisfaction and work performance; and the difficulty and lack of opportunity, encouragement and training to break out of secretarial work and clerking into other jobs. Difficulties were also voiced about getting upgraded (especially now new information technology was being used by secretaries and clerks): in Engineering, over half the secretaries and clerks believed they deserved upgrading. In particular, female clerks maintained they were discriminated against compared to their male counterparts.

Almost all of the female secretaries and clerks in both Departments said they would welcome the opportunity to learn about other jobs and opportunities within the company. Secretaries and clerks were least satisfied with the assessment process. Overall criticisms concerning assessment from all interviewees included the secrecy of parts of the assessment reports; the fact that it is once a year rather than more frequently or on a more informal continuous basis; and the lack of objectivity.

A number of women from *all* the female interviewee groups voluntarily raised sexual harassment as a problem for them at work. In fact, for a few of these women it was a major problem with which they found difficulty in coping.

Men's experiences and attitudes

Male branch managers in Engineering were as a group most against the introduction of parental provisions for women and men, such as maternity and paternity leave; a BP crèche; part-time work and job sharing. Male branch managers in OTS and female OTS clerks were also against such provision. The majority of all the other interview groups (including male engineers) supported the maternity leave scheme (some believed it should be extended); and were in favour of BP introducing paternity leave; a crèche; and part-time work and job sharing. In particular, professional women in OTS were watching carefully how the two women who had returned after maternity leave, to work part-time, were being treated.

On the whole the attitudes expressed by male engineers on the employment of female engineers were favourable. Those engineers who most resented female engineers were those who saw them as a threat; as career blocks; and as being given preferential treatment. Interestingly, these men were picked out by their female engineering colleagues as causing them problems in the work environment. Nevertheless, the younger male engineers maintained that women engineers had a lot to offer to engineering and contributed to a more healthy working atmosphere. The male engineers did acknowledge that their female counterparts were faced with additional pressures and career barriers. They also pointed to the problems faced by male engineers in learning how to cope and adapt to working with female colleagues. A number of male engineers suggested they would benefit from appropriate training in order to tackle this problem.

However, male managers in Engineering, such as line managers, site managers and branch managers, were as a group the most prejudiced against women engineers. They generally claimed that in theory they had no objections to the employment of female engineers; in practice, almost all of them predicted potential problems and had misgivings. These included ideas that female engineers are not sufficiently mobile, especially if they marry; and are a poorer company investment as they are likely to leave to have children. They claimed there was danger and lack of facilities for women working offshore or in places such as the Middle East; and resistance to female engineers from male site managers, clients, consultants and contractors. A number of managers asserted that having women engineers as managers would cause too many problems. Some of them also believed there was a danger of being overprotective towards the female engineers.

In OTS the branch managers had far more enlightened attitudes towards female professionals and maintained that they had just as good career prospects as the men. Even so, they did feel that women in their department faced additional barriers compared to men.

A POSITIVE ACTION PROGRAMME FOR BP

Assessed cumulatively the results from this study indicated that unless a long-term positive action programme was implemented, the position of women in BP (both professional and non-professional) was unlikely to improve within the next five to ten years. Senior personnel in both the Departments of Oil Trade and Supply and of Engineering predicted that the number of professional women would in five years time remain unchanged. In fact, due to the heavy pressures being experienced by the few female engineers, the likelihood is that their turnover rate will be high and consequently there may be even fewer female engineers proportionally to males in 1988. This study has shown that there is a wealth of female talent (including secretaries) which is being underutilised, which in itself is an economic loss for the company. Prejudice and discrimination are hampering women's career development prospects and there is little company support enabling women to combine a career and a family. Consequently BP will continue to lose female employees unless it introduces better facilities such as crèches; part-time work; and job re-entry schemes.

A detailed programme of positive action was recommended to BP. Among the immediate steps BP was recommended to take were setting of targets for recruitment and appointment of women into professional and managerial positions; introducing new training courses for women, for instance, to enable secretaries and clerks to move into computing or take up commercial apprenticeships; introducing new training courses for men about equal opportunities; elimination of bias from all aspects of recruitment, and reappraisal of assessment procedures and internal appointment procedures. Restrictions on women's opportunities for working offshore should be eliminated as far as possible.

BP was recommended to consider increasing maternity leave; and introducing paternity leave and flexi-time. Part-time work and job sharing schemes for women returning after maternity leave should become official BP policy. In the longer term re-entry schemes should be introduced to allow women who have had children to return to BP after a break from paid employment.

Among other long term policies BP was recommended to re-assess the role of secretaries in the organisation; to develop a code of practice on how to deal with sexual harassment; and to begin a feasibility study into how the company could provide child-care facilities for its employees.

To implement the positive action programme BP was recommended to create a senior position in the Personnel Department of Equal Opportunities Programme Manager; to set up a Positive Action Committee including representatives from the Women in BP Group; and to formulate and distribute a BP Equal Opportunities Policy Statement.

BP responded positively by formulating and disseminating a policy statement on equal opportunities and giving responsibility for pro-vision of advice and guidance on equal opportunities to a member of the Personnel Department. Graduate recruitment literature has been redesigned and some training seminars on equal opportunities legis-lation have been run. Regular statistical reports will be prepared on numbers and levels of women and ethnic minority employees in BP in the UK. Further studies will be carried out on provision of training for women, especially training to meet the needs of non-graduate staff; and on the extent to which the adoption of more flexible working arrangements might contribute to the retention of women with young families and to ways of managing the 'career break'.

When BP were first approached about considering the implemen-tation of a positive action programme, concern was voiced by mem-bers of the company over the loss the company was experiencing due to highly valued women in senior positions leaving to have babies in their late 20s and early 30s and not returning after maternity leave. The financial losses in terms of recruiting and retraining replacements for these women were considerable. Certainly, it is to BP's credit that it not only consented to an outside consultant carrying out an Equal Opportunities Audit, but is now proceeding with a programme of action. It is of interest to note that the number of female engineers had increased by 1985 from 12 to 16!

REFERENCES

M. J. Davidson and C. L. Cooper, *The Problems Faced by Women Managers and What Can Be Done to Help Them* (Sheffield: Manpower Services Commission Report, 1983a).

M. J. Davidson and C. L. Cooper, *Stress and the Woman Manager* (Oxford: Martin Robertson, 1983b).

M. J. Davidson and C. L. Cooper (eds) *Working Women: An International Survey* (Chichester: John Wiley, 1984).

M. McCormack, 'Professional Women in the Oil Industry', *Women and Training News*, vol.4 (1981) no. 8.

S. Robarts and E. Ball, *Positive Action for Women* (London: NCCL, 1981).

D. Wainwright, *Through the Bureaucratic Maze — Managing an Equal Opportunities Programme* (London: Runnymede Trust, 1983).

Index

Africa
  Vanity Fair in, 93
  Plessey in, 184
agriculture, 46, 48–9, 148–50
Arbitration and Conciliation
  Advisory Service
  (ACAS), 201
Argentina, 85
Asia, 47, 48, 63, 95, 98
  Plessey in, 184
  Tootal in, 97
  Vanity Fair in, 93
Australia, 95, 149
  Plessey in, 184
  Tootal in, 97, 98, 100, 101
  Vanity Fair, 93
Belgium, 80
  Levi Strauss in, 91
  Blue Bell in, 92
  Vanity Fair in, 92
Brazil, 7, 85
  electronics industry in, 129–42
  French investment in, 132
  Vanity Fair in, 93
Britain, 6, 13, 20, 23, 28, 31–5, 56,
  80, 88, 122, 137, 147, 150–1, 174,
  184, 186, 195, 207–8
British investment in developing
  countries, 12, 19, 20, 84, 96–9,
  Brazil, 132
  Morocco, 95
  Philippines, 95, 96–8
  Tunisia, 95
British investment in non-European
  developed countries, 12, 19, 95,
  184
British investment in other
  European countries, 12, 19, 40,
  57, 61, 65, 87
Canada
  Vanity Fair in, 92
Cheap Labour, 3, 4, 8, 30, 103–4
  and US firms, 91–3
  in developing countries, 75–7,
  82–4, 95, 102, 114, 165, 167–8,
  174

  in Ireland, 49, 56
  in UK, 34–6, 100, 111, 118, 126
Chemical industry, 12, 14, 39,
  40–8, 57, 61, 63–6, 74, 87, 91,
  132
China, People's Republic of,
  and Tootal, 99
Civil Service, UK
  and positive action, 210
clothing industry, 3–4, 9, 14–16, 22,
  25, 31, 39, 47–53, 57, 80–8, 90
  Benetton, 102–3
  developing countries, 77
  Germany, 61, 64, 68–76
  and knitwear, 86
  London, 100, 102
  UK, 88
Comecon, see Eastern Europe
construction industry, 150, 169
Costa Rica, 174
Cyprus, 81, 86
Denmark, 80
developing countries, 165, 168
  and Germany, 63–4, 66, 73,
  76–7, 81–4, 87, 94, 144
  and Tootal, 99, 101
  European investment in, 114–15
  Levi Strauss in, 91
domestic responsibilities, 3, 6, 8,
  130–1, 137, 149–53, 156, 170,
  172, 193–4, 220–1
drink and tobacco industries, 46,
  61, 68, 70–1
Eastern Europe, 85, 86, 90, 103
  Comecon, 98
EEC, 4, 7, 8, 30, 41, 43, 51, 57,
  80, 85, 86, 87, 88, 89, 90, 103,
  104–5, 106, 114, 145
electronics and electrical industry,
  3, 4, 5, 7, 9, 13, 14, 15, 16, 19,
  25, 30, 31, 32, 33, 39
  in Brazil, 129, 130, 131, 132, 138,
  139
  in France, 130, 131–8, 139
  in Ireland, 40, 41, 44, 47, 48, 50,
  51, 52, 54, 55, 56, 57

in Scotland, 116, 121, 185, 186,
  189
in UK, 185
in Wales, 185
see also semiconductor industry
Engineering Employers Federation
  (UK), 183
equal opportunities
  and BP, 217–19
  legislation, 44
  and multinationals, 1, 106
equal Opportunities Commission
  (UK), 208
equal pay, 157
ethnic minorities, 100, 165–6, 170,
  172–3, 180
Europe, 4, 5, 7, 9, 12, 51, 57, 63,
  76, 78, 80–2, 86, 88, 91, 94–5,
  102–3, 106, 113–14, 165
  European periphery, 47, 90, 81,
    85–6, 90, 144–5, 165, 167, 169,
    174, 184
  investment in developing
    countries, 114–18, 127, 133,
    142
export of jobs, 4, 12, 20–1, 73–5,
  84–5, 96, 129, 140–2
Far East, 81, 85, 90, 100, 102, 103,
  112–18, 123
Federation of Textile and Allied
  Workers (France), 99
female employment, 9
  decline in, 4, 14–19, 69, 81
  instability of, 7, 38, 58, 111, 116,
    148
  localisation of, 6, 35
  structure of, 14–19, 44, 67–70
female intensity of employment,
  16, 18–19, 23–9, 50, 52, 74, 81,
  123, 129–30, 136, 168
female participation rates, 4, 6, 12,
  32, 43, 67, 148
Finland
  Vanity Fair in, 93
food processing industry, 12, 14–16,
  31, 39, 46, 48, 61, 70, 71, 132
France, 1, 17, 80, 83, 86, 88, 95,
  99, 133, 181
  Benetton in, 102–3

electronics industry in, 129–42
investment in Brazil, 132
investment in Germany, 167, 174
free trade zone, 5, 39, 95
German investment in developing
  countries, 63–6, 73–87, 132
German investment in
  non-European developed
  countries, 62, 63, 75
German investment in other
  European countries, 10, 51, 53,
  57, 63, 75, 86, 98, 148
Germany, Federal Republic of, 1,
  4, 7–8, 56, 60–88, 147, 165–6,
  174, 179, 181
Greater London Council
  and positive action, 210
Greece, 56
HM Treasury
  and positive action, 210
Hong Kong, 3, 81, 83, 84, 95
  Levi Strauss in, 91
  Tootal in, 99–100
Hungary
  Coats-Patons and, 85
  Levi Strauss in, 92
industrial action, 8, 157–8, 160
  factory occupations, 93, 176–7
  international co-operation in,
    196–7
  strikes, 95, 166, 176–7
Industrial Development Authority,
  Ireland, 39, 50–1, 57, 145, 154
industrial relations, 33, 35, 50, 56,
  92, 93, 102, 121–2, 133–5, 160,
  174–5, 186
Ireland, Northern, 27–8, 148
  Vanity Fair in, 93, 94, 105
  Tootal in, 98
Ireland, Republic of, 1, 5, 7, 27,
  38–57, 80, 88, 117, 144–62
Irish Federated Union of
  Employers, 49
iron and steel industry, 32, 61, 165,
  185
Italy, 51, 80, 88, 102–3, 118, 133,
  166, 176, 196, 202
Japan, 5, 7, 9, 31, 91, 95, 97, 167,
  217

Benetton in, 103
semi-conductor industry in, 113–14, 118
Vanity Fair in, 93
Japanese investment in developing countries, 92, 113–15, 132
Japanese investment in Europe, 5, 7, 31, 51, 53, 65, 88, 117
labour market segmentation, 67, 106
Latin America, 47, 85, 92, 184
Luxembourg, 80
Malaysia, 3, 5, 85
Tootal in, 97, 99
male employment
greater concern about, 30, 51, 111
Malta, 86
Blue Bell in, 92
Mexico, 3, 29, 31, 48
Levi Strauss in, 91
Middle East, 207, 217, 219
Morocco, 83, 86, 95, 98
motor vehicles, 14, 22, 46, 48, 61, 63–6, 64–5, 137
multinational corporations
accountability of, 9–10, 104–5, 126
and employees rights, 105–6, 134–5
and investment incentives, 27–30, 38–9, 41–2, 50–1, 91, 93, 117–18, 145
mobility of, 9–10, 165, 181, 204
National Union of Tailor and Garment Workers (UK)
and Vanity Fair, 93
Netherlands, 65, 80, 86, 105, 166
new international division of labour
definition of, 2
theories of, 3, 4, 7, 73
new technology, 7, 9, 32, 68, 76–8, 91, 94, 99, 101, 103, 118–20
New Zealand, 100, 149
nimble fingers, 2, 9, 113, 131
Norway, 207
occupational segregation, *see* sexual division of labour
occupations

engineers, 207–8, 213–14
management and professional, 215–16
operative (assembly work), 31–2, 55, 119, 120, 123–4
secretaries, 217–18
technicians, 119, 123–4
offshore processing, 2–3, 86–7, 94–5, 106, 114, 161, 165
oil industry, 206
in UK, 206, 207, 209
Pakistan, 85
pharmaceuticals, 39, 40, 41, 47, 57, 61, 160
Philippines, 5, 85, 95
Levi Strauss in, 91–2
Tootal in, 92, 96–8
plant closures, 46, 93, 148, 166–8, 174, 176, 183, 188
Portugal, 81, 86, 95
positive action, 10, 210, 219
Puerto Rico, 167
and Blue Bell, 92
and Ireland, 48
recruitment, 4, 33, 48–9, 120–1, 160, 209
regional policy, 27–30, 38–9, 50–1, 57, 91, 93, 117–18, 132, 145
and capital grants, 41
relocation of investment, 3, 19, 30–1, 39–40, 61–6, 77
restructuring of industry, 4, 27, 31–2, 34–5, 41, 51, 74, 165
retailing, 100
Scotland, 7, 8, 28, 30, 149, 186, 189, 194, 197
Benetton in, 102,
Plessey in, 183–205
semiconductor industry in, 115–26
Tootal in, 99
Vanity Fair in, 93, 105
Scottish Development Agency, 117, 125, 191
semi-conductor industry, 112–20
production process, 112, 113, 115–19
service industries, 13, 43, 52, 67, 68, 148, 160, 161

sexual division of labour, 2, 7, 8, 34, 35, 54–5, 57, 76, 130–1
  in electronics, 31, 113, 124–6, 138–46
  in garments, 91, 94, 120
  in oil industry, 206–8
  in TV tube production, 168–9
  in textiles, 145
sex differentials, 5, 6
  in aptitudes, 131
  in earnings, 44, 104
  in employment changes, 18–19, 31, 51
  in industrial action, 194
  in occupations, 70, 141
Silicon Glen, 118, 120
  see also Scotland
Silicon Valley, 113, 118, 123, 124
Singapore, 3, 48, 81, 82, 84
skills, 2, 113, 130–1, 136–7, 191
South Africa, Republic of, 149
  Plessey in, 184
  Tootal in, 98, 101
  Vanity Fair in, 93
South East Asia, 4, 5, 31, 48, 92, 132
  Levi Strauss in, 91
  Tootal in, 97, 99, 101, 102
South Korea, 81, 84
Spain, 56, 92, 93, 132, 133, 166, 167
Sri Lanka, 84
Switzerland, 65, 132
Taiwan, 3
textile and garment industry, 3–9, 13–16, 24, 39, 46, 49, 51, 57, 84–6
  artificial fibre production, 87–8, 91, 157
  Brazil, 132
  EEC, 80–3, 90, 104
  Germany, 65–77
  Ireland, 145, 148, 157, 161
  UK, 88–9, 98
Thailand, 82, 85
Third World, *see* developing countries
trade unions, 33, 44, 48–50, 55–6, 76, 92–5, 102, 104–5, 129, 134–5,

145–5, 153–5, 160–1, 167, 168, 170–8, 181–6, 191–202, 204
AUEW, 186, 198–9
Association of Professional Executive, Clerical and Computer Staff, 186
CFDT, 135
CGT, 135
Electrical, Telecommunications and Plumbing Union, 186
Federated Workers Union of Ireland, 56, 154
Federation of Textile and Allied Workers, 99
IG Metal, 176–7
International Textiles, Garment and Leather Workers Federation, 92, 103
Irish Transport and General Workers Union, 56, 154, 156, 160
National Union of Tailor and Garment Workers, 93
TASS, 186
training, 39, 126, 135, 141, 169
Tunisia, 83, 86, 95
Turkey, 8, 165
UK, 1, 5, 7, 12–13, 19–36, 51, 95, 133, 149, 184–5, 195, 206, 208–9, 221
  Benetton in, 103
  Blue Bell in, 92
  Courtaulds in, 95
  Levi Strauss in, 91
  Plessey in, 184–9, 197
  Tootal in, 96–102
  Vanity Fair in, 93
US investment in developing countries, 123, 132
US investment in Europe, 40, 42–6, 50–1, 53, 56–7, 61, 62, 65, 90–3, 104, 114–15, 117, 166–7
USA, 3, 5, 3, 40, 42–3, 46, 53, 56, 62–3, 82–3, 91–3, 96–7, 99, 112–14, 123, 132–3, 184
Vietnam
  Bidermann in, 94
Wales, 28, 30–5, 117
West Yorkshire Metropolitan

County Council
and positive action, 210
women's consciousness, 5, 8, 9, 95,
131, 133, 144–7, 161–2, 170–3,
179, 194, 217
women's organisation

in the community, 6, 158–9, 166,
178–81, 198
in peer groups, 155–9
in trade unions, 5, 93–4, 95, 104,
153–9, 174–6, 198–200
Yugoslavia, 86

Index of Companies

Abbey National,
and positive action, 210
Adam Opel, 61
Advanced Micro Devices, 114
AEG-Telefunken, 61, 166, 167,
169, 173, 174
Agache Willot, 91
AKZO, 46, 87
Allied Thread Company, *see*
Tootal, Philippines
Amdahl, 53
American Thread Company, *see*
Tootal
Apple, 53
Arcotronics, *see* Wedge Holdings
BR
Asahi Chemical Industry Company,
51, 88
Atari, 53
Baird Textiles, *see* William Baird
Ltd
BASF, 61
Bayer, 61, 88
Benetton, 102–3, 106
Bidermann, 90, 94
Blue Bell, 90, 91, 92–3
Bradmill Industries, 98, 101, 102
British Home Stores, 100
British Leyland, 185, 188
British Motor Company, *see* British
Leyland
British Petroleum (BP), 206–21
Burlington, 51, 91
Burr-Brown, 115, 117
Burroughs, 111
Courtauld, 80, 87, 91, 95

Coats Patons, 84–5, 91
C & A, 95, 100
Da Gama, 98, 101
Daimler Benz, 61
Debenhams, 95
Digital Equipment Corporation, 53,
117
Dollfus-Mieg, 91, 95, 99
Du Pont, 88
Enka, 87
Esso, 61
Fairchild, 114
Fiat, 46
Fieldcrest, 46, 51
Floating Point, 53
Ford Motor Company, 46, 61
Freudenberg and Co., 61, 91
Friedrich Krupp, 61
Fujitsu, 114
GEC, 210
General Electric, 53
General Instruments
Microelectronics, 117
Great Universal, 100
Hitachi, 33, 35
Hoechst, 61, 88
Honeywell, 111
Hughes Microelectronics, 115, 116,
189
IBM, 61, 184, 210
ICI, 88
Indy Electronics, 117
Intel, 114
Intercontinental Garments
Manufacturing Co., 95
Inverwear, 94

Lee Jeans, *see* Vanity Fair Corp.
Levi Strauss, 90, 92
  in Belgium, 91
  in France, 91
  in Hungary, 92
  in Philippines, 91–2, 96
  in Southeast Asia, 91
  in UK, 91
Littlewoods, 95
Mannesmann, 61
Marks and Spencer, 100–1
Matsushita, 114
Midland Bank
  and positive action, 210
Monsanto, 88
Montefibre, 88
Mostek, 53
Mothercare, 100
Motorola, 114, 115, 117
National Semiconductor, 115, 117
National Westminster Bank,
  and positive action, 210
NCR, 111
NEC Semiconductors, 115–17
Nestle, 61
Nino, 51, 91
Perkin-Elmer, 53
Philip Morris, 61
Philips, 61, 113, 166
Plessey, 184, 185
  Plessey Capacitors 183–205
Provost, 91
Rank Xerox,
  and positive action, 210
Raysil Gowns Ltd, *see* Tootal
RCA, 166, 167, 174
Reemtsma, 61
Rhone Poulenc, 88
Robert Bosch, 61
Sainsburys,
  and positive action, 210
Sanyo, 114
Scott Lithgow Shipyards, 121
Seindensticker Group, 87
Shell, 61
Shin Etsu Handotai, 117
Siemens, 61, 113

Slimma, *see* Tootal
SNIA, 46, 51
  Sniafibre, 88
Sprague Electrical, 189
Telegraph Condenser Company,
  185
Tesco, 100, 101
Texas Instruments, 113
Thames Television,
  and positive action, 210
Thompson Brant, 167, 174
Tootal, 91, 96–102, 105
  American Thread Company, 101
  in Philippines, 92, 96, 98
  Raysil Gowns Ltd, 100
  Slimma, 100, 101
  Tootal Lebel, 100
  Tootal Thread, 99
Tootal Lebel, *see* Tootal
Tootal Thread, *see* Tootal
Toshiba, 114
Toyobo,
  and Blue Bell, 92
Triumph International, 61, 75,
  84–5, 90–1, 96
Unilever, 61
Vanity Fair, 90, 91, 92–3
  and Lee Jeans, 93–4, 105, 187,
    191, 194
Varian Associates, 53
Videocolor, 165–79
Volkswagenwerk, 61
Wang, 53
Wedge International Holdings, 188,
  201
Wellcome Foundation,
  and positive action, 210
Wellman, 51
Westinghouse, 53
Westland Helicopters,
  and positive action, 210
William Baird Ltd
  Baird Textiles in Philippines, 95
Woolworth, 100
Wrangler, *see* Blue Bell
Zenith, 53